THE UNNATURAL LOTTERY

CHARACTER AND MORAL LUCK

CLAUDIA CARD

D0067708

TEMPLE UNIVERSITY PRESS

PHILADELPHIA

Temple University Press, Philadelphia 19122
Copyright © 1996 by Temple University.
All rights reserved
Published 1996
Printed in the United States of America

Text design by William Boehm

Library of Congress Cataloging-in-Publication Data
Card, Claudia.
    The unnatural lottery : character and moral luck / Claudia Card.
      p. cm.
    Includes bibliographical references and index.
    ISBN 1-56639-452-X (cloth : alk. paper) — ISBN 1-56639-453-8
(pbk. : alk. paper)
    1. Character.   2. Fortune.   3. Feminist theory.   4. Philosophy.
I. Title.
BJ1531.028   1996
170 — dc20   96-1316

THE
UNNATURAL
LOTTERY

To the memory of my father, Walter Munro Card (1911–1973),
and the futures of my nephews,
Jason Date Card
Ryan Kazuo Card
Matthew Miller Card
and
Eric Douglas Card

Contents

Much of the luck with which this book is occupied attaches to politically disadvantageous starting points or early positionings in life. Moral luck is luck that impacts either on character development or on one's ability to do morally good or right things in particular contexts. The positionings that interest me for their impact on moral character also interested Nietzsche in his genealogy of morality. His hypotheses were that deep-seated or pervasive bad luck produces *ressentiment,* a hateful, destructive envy of those better off, and that this attitude lies at the root of our concepts of moral goodness and evil.[1] Yet his evaluation of *ressentiment* was mixed, if not ambivalent. For he saw that it could also make us clever and that cleverness can be empowering.

On my view early bad luck is influential in developing many kinds of character, not just the kind that bothered Nietzsche, and I do not find hatred and envy at the root of moral concepts. The same external conditions can impact us differently as they combine with other variables, including our often arbitrary choices. My working hypothesis is that, ethically, there are many ways of being good and many kinds of character displaying different strengths and weaknesses. Yet I do not try to prove this abstractly. It is a hypothesis that guides my inquiries, which, if successful, may then support it. Although the hypothesis sounds empirical, it involves a response to the philosophical question whether "virtue is one," whether ethical goodness is the same in all of us. My view is not that certain virtues are more *appropriate* to certain people but that different combinations of circumstances in fact provide opportunities for, stimulate, nurture, or discourage the development of different virtues and vices, strengths and weaknesses of character.

More than two decades ago something that interested me in the topic of mercy, on which I published my first essay, was that its best rationales seemed to involve an appreciation of the fact that "there but for the grace of God go I" — in effect, an appreciation of moral luck (although the term had not been coined).[2] During the same period I published another essay defending a retributive view of liability to punishment.[3] The mercy that interested me presupposed a retributive understanding of punishment. My objective now, as then, is not to let us off the hook morally by showing that fate determines who we become. I am no fatalist. I find luck influential but not ordinarily determining. It narrows and expands our possibilities, often through the agency of others over whom we have no control and often through the medium of social institutions. It helps us appreciate and imagine possibilities, and it also causes difficulty with our doing so in some cases. When it removes all our possibilities for moral goodness, what we have is not moral luck but fate. My objective is to explore some virtues, some vices, and our senses of responsibility and integrity in ways that acknowledge luck as significant in what we rightly regard as our ethical character and our ethical choices. If the result is often humbling, it also can generate pride in what we have managed to make of ourselves and our opportunities under difficult circumstances that others' luck spared them.

Although personal reflections on why I am who I am often lie in the backgrounds of inquiries in this book, I am not moved by a sense that luck has been unusually cruel or kind to me. My sense of how it has treated others is at least as much a motivating concern. Much of the salient luck in my life has been in individuals I have known. I never won the lottery nor have I ever been materially wealthy, but I have had great friends. My parents left me little materially besides a few debts, although they left indelible marks on my character. My negative luck has been mostly in social environments; either the environment was bad or there was a lack of fit between the environment and me. Yet I have not felt the rigors of severe poverty, although I went through primary school with children who did. Nor have I been (to my knowledge) a direct target of racism, although members of my extended family were interned in concentration camps during World War II for no other reason than the national origin of their parents, and my partner's parents were barred from attending high school in Alabama in the 1930s because they were black. Nor have I directly experienced the social challenges of severe prolonged disability or illness, although my mother did. Nor have I had to recover from the ravages of alcoholism, although two of my childhood friends did and my father never recovered. Still, a glance at my life may be instructive in its very ordinariness.

I began school as a social misfit, an outgoing child, passionately loved and occasionally abused, in many ways precocious but whose parents' religious, political, and sexual values were at odds with those of the village community (Pardeeville, Wisconsin) in which we lived. I learned to appeal to laughter and developed a thick skin. From age five I was in love with girls and women but believed I could not do much about it and did not, for decades. My entertainment skills developed further, and I found solace for many years in piano lessons (within the economic reach of most villagers at fifty cents per half hour lesson), learning discipline in the process. Consistent with the English and German ethos of Pardeeville in the 1940s and 1950s, my parents believed in corporal punishment, administering it freely but with little consistency. My mother, who took decades to learn to say no to my father, said it constantly to my younger brother and me. We became imaginative liars, and our skin continued to thicken. When I was eight, my mother suffered a paralytic stroke, permanently damaging her right side. Her misfortune reprieved me from frequent physical punishments, although the verbal excoriation intensified and for the next decade I inherited household tasks from cleaning and ironing to marketing and meal preparation.

Thus I learned both rebellion and responsibility early. Responsibility won out when two more brothers were born. By creating imaginary worlds I learned to make life interesting for myself in the face of early hard work, as I had earlier relied on fantasy for self-healing from punishments. As I escaped between chores and scoldings into music and ideas, my intellectual skills outpaced my social ones. They still do.

One thing I consistently did right was to get As, a habit that eventually earned me college scholarships and graduate school fellowships. By twelve I was a fanatical student, and by thirteen, my nearsightedness was no longer concealable. Early unrecognized nearsightedness produced, I now believe, a certain physical insecurity, especially in the world of competitive team sports, where I thought I was a natural coward. Under then Wisconsin law my closest brother was permitted a paid job (a paper route) in high school while I, as a girl, was not, although more *work* was expected of me (at home). He learned to manage money. I learned to volunteer. Every child in Pardeeville (and for miles around) had free swimming lessons — a Village Board decision taken to minimize tragedies in our two lakes. After three years' military service, my brother spent college summers as a lifeguard. I discontinued life-saving classes to help with babies at home, where I learned baking, canning, wallpapering, the small daily economies, how to make do with little cash flow. My mother, who by then could write no other way (because of her stroke), taught me typing. Thanks to years of piano lessons, I learned the typewriter keyboard and a decent speed in four hours and spent college summers at typing jobs, save one on a student tour in Europe, a reward from extended family for prior home service. My brother did marine boot camp that summer, just long enough before Viet Nam that he is now alive (and sleeps well in Seattle).

In many ways, my character is a complex product of meeting and failing to meet the challenges of relative disempowerment in less-than-friendly environments. At that level, my story has parallels in the ordinary stories of many women, many people of color in the United States, many Jewish children raised in predominantly Christian environments, many lesbians and gay men, and many who have lived from an early age with disabilities or health impairments. As our stories enter the body of data on which philosophical ethics is theorized, perhaps the shape of ethical theories to come will reflect a greater appreciation of the roles of luck in moral development.

Beginning in the 1970s when I became "radicalized" by lesbianfeminism, I did what felt like starting all over. To create courses in feminist philosophy and lesbian culture, I had to set aside what I had been doing (work on punishment and theories of justice), do an enormous amount of interdisciplinary reading (especially histories I was not taught in school), and connect with new colleagues in many departments and institutions. I began attending new conferences, speaking to new audiences in ways I had never spoken before, experimenting with new teaching styles. For a long time it felt as though I was not able to draw in a deliberate or self-conscious way on my graduate training, nor on my years of untenured teaching and research. Mine was a struggle to become realistically subjective, to set aside my fantasy worlds and re-enter the real one to discover who I had become, how I connected with others, what my possibilities were.

When I began to publish again in the 1980s, it was "in a different voice," although not the one that Carol Gilligan wrote about in 1982.[4] I drew on my life-experiences, both in and out of the academy, which I had not done in my earlier work on justice and punishment. The chapters below integrate my earlier research and training with my more radical work and integrate my radical work with some of the work of philosophers who have not been so immersed — at least in their philosophical work — as I have been in radical causes.

Parts of many chapters in this volume have as predecessors lectures presented at conferences and universities from 1976 through 1994. The earliest such roots underlie parts of Chapters Six, Three, Seven, and Five, whose ancestors were heard by audiences, respectively, at Iowa State University, Dartmouth College, the Midwest Society of Women in Philosophy, and the University of Wisconsin Center System Philosophers' Association. Later ancestors of many chapters benefited from discussions with audiences at the Universities of Buenos Aires, Cincinnati, Kansas State, Minnesota, North Carolina-Chapel Hill, Northern Michigan, Oswego, San Diego, Syracuse, Virginia Commonwealth, and Wisconsin and at conventions of the Midwest Society of Women in Philosophy and the American Philosophical Association as well as a conference on gender and philosophy at the Esalen Institute. Early work was supported by a sabbatical semester in 1986 and two summers' research support from the University of Wisconsin Graduate School. A Vilas Associateship during 1989–91 helped substantially, for which I thank the William F. Vilas Trust and the Women's Studies Program at the University of Wisconsin.

For an atmosphere of cooperative inquiry I thank the many students who took my "Feminism and Sexual Politics" course where I first lectured on rape and sexuality in the 1970s and early 1980s, and many other students who have taken my courses and seminars since then in feminist ethics, advanced ethical theory, and classics in feminist theory. For organizing first-rate conferences on women and legal theory at the University of Wisconsin Law School in 1985 and 1986, which discussed antecedents of Chapters Three and Seven, I am grateful to Martha Fineman. For a superb conference on violence and terrorism in 1988 that led to much of the current shape of Chapter Five, I am grateful to Christopher Morris and R. G. Frey, and for an outstanding conference on racism and sexism at Georgia State University in 1991 that stimulated a forerunner of Chapter Eight, I am grateful to Linda Bell and David Blumenfeld. Enthusiastic support from Louis Werner (who died in 1977), Maudemarie Clark, and Amelie Rorty helped with early efforts toward Chapter Six. Temple University Press's former editor Jane Cullen has earned my permanent gratitude for her nurturance of this work through many years. To Victoria Davion, Marilyn Frye, Ruth Ginzberg, Maria Lugones, Richard Mohr, Joann Pritchett, and Marcus Singer I am grateful for long-term friendship and good advice of many kinds during the past decade.

The good luck that sustained the writing of this book includes many more friends, colleagues, and correspondents who offered comments on chapter drafts and much support, including Jeffner Allen, Annette Baier, Bat-Ami Bar On, Sandra Bartky, Lorna Benjamin, Susan Bordo, Bernard Boxill, Richard Brandt, Harry Brighouse, Joan Callahan, Norman Care, Chris Cuomo, Marcia Falk, Joel Feinberg, Owen Flanagan, Vivian Foss, Marilyn Friedman, Bernie Gert, David Goldberg, Bill Hay, Sarah Hoagland, Lester Hunt, Alison Jaggar, Sharon Keller, Noretta Koertge, Elaine Marks, Lynne McFall, Howard McGary, Nellie McKay, Michelle Moody-Adams, the late John Moulton, Alexander Nehamas, Nel Noddings, Martha Nussbaum, Lucius Outlaw, Chris Pierce, Ann Pooler, Josie Pradella, Annis Pratt, Joan Ringelheim, Ellen Rose, Jean Rumsey, Naomi Scheman, Fran Schrag, Vicky Spelman, Michael Stocker, Nancy Thomadsen, Laurence Thomas, Lynne Tirrell, Joyce Trebilcot, Elton Tylenda, Terry Winant, Iris Young, and Margarita Zamora.

For permission to draw on work published previously, I am grateful to MIT Press for materials used in Chapter Three from "Gender and Moral Luck" in *Identity, Character, and Morality: Essays in Moral Psychology*, ed. Owen Flanagan and Amelie Oksenberg Rorty (1990), to the *American Philosophical Quarterly* for materials used in Chapter Six from "Gratitude and Obligation," *APQ* vol. 25, no. 2 (Apr. 1988), to Cambridge University Press for materials used in Chapter Five from "Rape as a Terrorist Institution" in *Violence, Terrorism, and Justice,* ed. R. G. Frey and Christopher Morris (1991) (Reprinted with the permission of Cambridge University Press), and to Routledge, Chapman, and Hall for materials used in Chapter Seven from "Intimacy and Responsibility: What Lesbians Do," in *At the Boundaries of Law: Feminism and Legal Theory,* ed. Martha Albertson Fineman and Nancy Sweet Thomadsen (1991). Brief forerunners of Chapters One and Eight appeared in the *Journal of Social Philosophy* vol. 22, no. 1 (1991), and in *Overcoming Racism and Sexism,* ed. Linda Bell and David Blumenfeld (Lanham, Md.: Rowman and Littlefield, 1995), and a briefer ancestor of part of Chapter Four appeared in *Hypatia: A Journal of Feminist Philosophy* as a symposium piece on Nel Noddings's *Caring: A Feminine Approach to Ethics and Moral Education* (Berkeley: University of California Press, 1984).

THE
UNNATURAL
LOTTERY

LIFTING VEILS OF IGNORANCE

Philosophy, like art and religion, offers a kind of salvation. It can remove us from the stress of material life and give us the heart to go on. Yet philosophy is not done in a material vacuum. It involves an apprenticeship of study with time off from other labor and builds on prior generations' work, preserved in archives. European philosophy and its descendants have been for two and a half milennia the province of relatively leisured men who trace their intellectual heritage to free men of ancient Greece. Although Plato admitted a few women to his Academy, it has been for most of recorded history socially privileged men who were apprenticed as philosophers and whose work fills the archives.

Before the twentieth century the most significant transitions in the development of European philosophy were its movements between religious and secular homes, its coming under the dominance of Christianity for centuries, when much ancient philosophical work was preserved from destruction by Muslims and Jews, and then its breaking relatively free of religious dominance and protection in the early modern period. These transitions showed in the topics explored, who became apprenticed as philosophers, for which audiences they wrote, styles as well as contents of their critiques, and which points of view were represented in their writings.

In the twentieth and twenty-first centuries, the most significant transitions in the descendants of European philosophy may come from the increasing access to academic education of people with social histories of disempowerment: the working classes, Jews, people of color with histories of oppression in white societies, women of all classes and ethnic backgrounds, people with disabilities, people living openly lesbian or gay lives. Many from these groups do not always (or only) trace their intellectual heritages to men of ancient Greece. As with earlier transitions, the transition to this multifaceted pluralism can be expected to show in the kinds of topics to which philosophers attend, the audiences for whom we write, the styles as well as contents of our philosophical critiques, the points of view we represent.

Among the welcome differences such changes could make in philosophical ethics is an increased appreciation of the roles of luck in who we are and who we can become, in the good lives available to us and the evils we may be liable to embody. For, luck is often best appreciated by those who have known relatively *bad* luck and have been unable to escape steady comparison of their lot with those of others.

Moral Luck

Luck found a place in the philosophical conversations of ethics in the mid-1970s. Bernard Williams and Thomas Nagel's symposium "Moral Luck" (which introduced the term) attended to examples of individuals who took major risks with their lives, met with accidents, or suffered reversals of political fortune.[1] In the 1980s Martha Nussbaum explored connections between luck and ethics in Greek tragedy, and the coherence of the concept of moral luck was given yet further support in essays by Margaret Walker.[2] It was oftener challenged, however, in the journals, where the question whether moral luck is a coherent concept has been a subject of dispute.[3]

"Moral luck" refers to such facts as that how we become good or bad, how good or bad we become, and whether some of our choices turn out to have been justified are matters into which luck enters substantially. Some of these facts seem mundane. Yet controversies arise over what they imply. Chapter Two defends moral responsibility against the skepticisms of Williams and Nagel, with special attention to contexts of oppression and abuse. The idea of responsibility, especially of taking responsibility, is a continuing theme in ensuing chapters.

Williams calls the luck that enters into character development "*constitutive* moral luck" and that which enters into the justifiability of particular choices "*incident* moral luck." Disputes in the journals about the conceptual coherence of moral luck have fastened primarily on incident luck, the luck of particular choices, largely ignoring constitutive luck. Like the luck with which Martha Nussbaum and Margaret Walker have been primarily concerned, however, the luck with which this book is concerned is often constitutive luck, the luck of character development. I tend to find incident luck of interest for its impact on character.

In the history of philosophical ethics, the view that character development is significantly influenced by luck was appreciated more by Aristotle than by Immanuel Kant. For Aristotle, the good life was a happy one. This meant that it was, among other things, a fortunate life. Happiness is to be prized, not praised. But Aristotle's happy life was also a life that was lived in accord with virtues, for which we are praised. Aristotle acknowledged that happiness depends at least modestly on the cooperation of "externals," such things as good birth, good health, and good looks.[4] This observation could mean simply that living in accord with the virtues is not enough to make us happy, that our virtuous choices need to be supplemented with external goods. Alternatively, it could mean that in order to live a life in accord with the virtues, we need at least the modest cooperation of externals, things beyond our control. Both readings are plausible, and both are suggested by Aristotle's remarks. The view that acquisition of the virtues depends in part on externals, however, implies constitutive moral luck. For eventually, we come to externals over which we have no control, and over which we could not even conceivably have control, such as the circumstances of our birth and our early childhoods.

In modern philosophy, Kant's position has had greater influence than Aristotle's. The position of Kant — no aristocrat — has been especially attractive to democrats and egalitarians because it holds that good moral character, as a sense of duty, is accessible to everyone. Kant presents that accessibility as the ground of human dignity.[5] Persons, as rational beings, have an absolute value, he maintains, because we give ourselves a moral law from which we can determine our duties, and he held that we can all act as duty requires, come what may. On this view, our goodness (or badness) is entirely up to us. However unlucky we may be, *we* still determine whether we meet the challenges life offers us well or poorly.

Like Aristotle, Williams, Nagel, and Martha Nussbaum have taken as paradigms of moral luck lives that began from a combination of generally privileged social positions. The more usual cases, however, are lives with beginnings that are relatively disadvantaged along significant dimensions, such as having a socially disvalued gender, race, ethnicity, or class, or a socially stigmatized disability, illness, deformity, or disorder. Being socially disadvantaged along one or more such dimensions is not enough to make one disadvantaged on the whole, as disadvantages in one area may be compensated for by advantages in others. And often the nature of one's position may not be readily visible. Still, the dimensions of powerlessness take their toll. They impact the way we develop, as do our "closets" if we choose to "pass."

In this book, I take as my paradigms the luck of middle- and lower-class women who face violence and exploitation in misogynist and class-hierarchical societies, of lesbians who face continuing pressure to hide or self-destruct in societies hostile to same-sex intimate partnerships, of culturally christian white women who have ethnic and color-privilege in white christian and racist societies, and of adult survivors of childhood abuse. Many of the issues, however, have parallels or analogues in the cases of those socially disadvantaged or privileged in other ways.

Thus, I come closer to Kant's starting point than to Aristotle's, insofar as my paradigms are the ordinary lives of ordinary people, lives that are generally politically disadvantaged though sometimes also privileged in limited ways. Although I have been deeply affected by Kantian liberalism, I am skeptical of Kant's apparent assumption that the same basic character development is accessible to everyone. Even if his optimistic belief that everyone has opportunities to become good contains more truth than some would admit, I doubt that the opportunities are the same for everyone, that the level of difficulty is the same, and, consequently, that the goodness available to us is likely to take the same forms.

Circumstances of oppression can illustrate the point. Economically oppressive circumstances offer relatively little opportunity or encouragement to develop the virtue of liberality. Not only can oppression make certain virtues difficult to develop, but the question arises in view of the damaging nature of oppression whether those who are oppressed are moral agents at all. In feminist philosophy, this has complicated the question of how resistance by the oppressed is possible.[6] From where can the requisite strength of character and resourcefulness come? So let us turn briefly to the concept of oppression.

Oppression

More than a decade ago Marilyn Frye called attention to patterns suggested by the etymological roots of "oppression": pressing against—reducing, molding, immobilizing.[7] Footbinding exemplifies all three. Less dramatically, contemporary middle-class and even working-class ideals of femininity in the United States also reduce female development and mold it as they constrain female motility — matters explored by Iris Young's discussion of "throwing like a girl."[8] On a larger scale Marilyn Frye notes that oppressive social institutions catch us in double-binds so that no matter what we do, it is wrong and we are wrong. This situation systematically undermines the development of self-respect.[9]

In *Justice and the Politics of Difference* Iris Young carries the analysis of oppression further by examining five of its "faces": exploitation, marginalization, powerlessness, cultural imperialism, and violence, suggesting that different "faces" come to the fore in different historical instances of oppression.[10] If exploitation and cultural imperialism are salient faces of slavery, marginalization and violence are often salient in anti-Semitism and in antilesbian and antigay hostility. Power disadvantages take many forms, some more damaging than others, and the different forms may be interrelated in complex ways.

My awareness of oppression and how easily it can be hidden first took shape in regard to religion. During the 1960s when I taught philosophy of religion, I found that texts in that field often assumed that philosophy of religion was simply philosophy of Christianity. My research into Jewish history and religion revealed histories of oppression by Christians omitted not only from philosophy textbooks but from the entirety of my public education and from the educations of most of my students. In the processes of hiding and marginalizing, the textbooks and educational curricula were continuing the oppressive exclusionary histories that they failed to acknowledge.

By the mid-1970s I identified strongly with feminism in its radicalesbian, gynocentric incarnations. Many patterns salient in the oppressions of women and lesbians can be found in other dominated or oppressed groups as well, however. Consider, for example, Laurence Thomas's identification of patterns of evil in American slavery and the Nazi genocide.[11] Slavery and much of its subsequent legacy of racism illustrate oppression that has a salient face of exploitation. Anti-Semitism and the genocide for which it helped prepare the way illustrate oppression with the salient face of marginalization leading to concealment, eventually to elimination and obliteration. The exploitation and elimination (or marginalization) patterns exist in tension with each other, and there is overlap between oppressions characterized by each. The European slave trade, for example, killed millions in the process of exploitation and in order to exploit others, and marginalization is a significant aspect of racism in the United States today, although it is (tautologically) less visible to whites than is racist violence. Exploitation is also among the patterns of anti-Semitism — Nazi doctors experimented on Jewish prisoners and European Christians relied on Jewish moneylenders — although marginalization and worse have sometimes been more salient faces of Jewish oppression. Under slavery, genocide was subsidiary to exploitation and threatened to undermine it, whereas in the Nazi genocide, exploitation was subsidiary to concealment and elimination and could threaten to undermine them also. The two patterns can also blend into each other in that, as Thomas argues, a people exploited as slaves for seven generations may be utterly decimated as a people with their own culture, language, social institutions, and so forth. At this point, exploitation assumes the face of genocide.

The basic patterns of exploitation and elimination (or concealment) are also discernible in other forms of racism and in the oppressions of women, of lesbians and gay men, of workers, and of those who are disabled. Many women, for example, are exploited for heterosexual and domestic service as wives and as caretakers of the young, the old, the sick, the disabled of both sexes. Lesbians and gay men, on the other hand, have been hidden or killed. Prostitutes have been exploited *and* either killed or led to premature deaths. Industrial workers, exploited for productive labor in capitalist societies, have also been led to premature deaths. Those with mental disorders, on the other hand, have been hidden in attics, basements, and "total" institutions, and, as is too often the case with the physically disabled, their talents allowed to go to waste or to atrophy.[12]

Exploitation is double-edged. To be useful to others, we must be encouraged to develop qualities that *can* also be turned to our own purposes. If our exploitation requires us to make judgments, we may develop critical skills that interfere with the tendency to identify with oppressors. Without the capacity for judgment, our utility is curtailed. Exploitation thus sets limits to the "reduction" aspect of oppression and provides a wedge for resistance. Yet, even in the worst of imaginable circumstances, people have resisted.

It may seem a priori that living constantly under the imminent threat of death would utterly destroy one's moral agency, or at least one's scruples. During my undergraduate days it was commonplace to hear comparisons of Nazi concentration camps with Thomas Hobbes's state of nature in precisely this respect. And yet, Holocaust survivors' narratives reveal an enormous variety of responses to atrocities that exceeded Hobbes's worst nightmares. Simon Wiesenthal's memoir *The Sunflower*—with which I often begin my course in introductory ethics—narrates his encounters in a concentration camp where it never seems to occur to him to take anything but a moral approach to question after question about what to do and whether his choices were the right ones.[13] He did not find oppression an excuse, or even an occasion, for moral insensitivity.

Following the lead of Marxist philosophers who took up the perspectives of oppressed workers in the paid labor force, women in recent decades have created courses in feminist philosophy, attending to the narratives of women who have survived many forms of oppression. Feminists began reflecting philosophically on concepts previously ignored or treated flippantly, such as "gender," "lesbian," and "rape." In the 1980s feminist philosophy became more pluralistic, more attentive to the intersections of sex, race, and class, and more specific. In 1986 *Hypatia: A Journal of Feminist Philosophy* became an independent journal, offering special issues in such areas as feminist ethics, feminist epistemology, or feminist philosophy of science.[14] These developments and others like them are bringing the data of histories of oppression into the mainstream of contemporary philosophy.

Feminist Ethics and an Overview

Carol Gilligan's continuing articulation of the "different voice" of women, the best-known influence in the development of feminist ethics, has fostered and provoked a growing body of literature in and on "care ethics."[15] Care ethics emphasizes the importance of valuing and maintaining relationships of care and connection. Among the most troubling aspects of care ethics has been its potentiality to valorize one-sided caring relationships and abusive relationships and to neglect women's needs to learn self-defense and to set boundaries in the face of violence.[16] As with the voices of survivors of war atrocities, women's voices even in times of so-called peace present a variety of responses to the challenges of living under threats to life and limb. Judith Herman compares women who are vulnerable to domestic violence and rape with men in combat in terms of the traumas they suffer.[17] These and interrelated topics are discussed in Chapters Three through Seven.

Chapter Three takes up the question whether virtues are gender related, with special attention to the work of Carol Gilligan. Here I argue that although domestic contexts may call for different moral sensitivities than the contexts of markets and governments, we also need to consider whether the sensitivities women have developed in domestic contexts are also responses to oppressive conditions. If so, some of what we hear in women's voices may be right for those conditions but not for better ones. It is also possible, however, that some of the responses we hear are not good even in oppressive conditions. Listening to women's voices with what Theodore Reik called "a third ear" can sometimes reveal moral damage, such as a misplaced sense of gratitude, as well as moral insights.[18] A challenge for feminist moral philosophers has been to distinguish the insights from the damage.

Chapter Four discusses limits of care ethics, with special attention to the work of Nel Noddings, who finds justice a relatively unhelpful concept for ethics.[19] This chapter argues that in two major areas care without justice is inadequate to respond to the dangers of certain evils. One area is our relationships to strangers. The other is relationships of intimacy. This chapter also argues, however, that theories of justice need a greater variety of paradigmatic evils than the economic ones that have dominated theorizing about justice in recent decades. In so arguing, I draw on Nel Noddings's more recent work on women and evil.[20]

Chapter Five analyzes rape as a "protection racket" and terrorist institution that sets a context for the social construction of female desires to ingratiate ourselves with men. In this context the abuse of women in heterosexual relationships is condoned, and the position of women is conducive to the development of misplaced gratitude for a male "protection" that is often little more than a withholding of abuse.[21] This chapter also takes up briefly the feminist antipornography campaign as aimed at combatting rape terrorism and argues against recent attempts to defend pornography by appeal to the liberalism of John Stuart Mill.

Chapter Six, for which Chapter Five sets a background, examines the concept of gratitude and its associated sense of obligation, with special attention to the paradoxical idea of a "*debt* of gratitude." Gratitude is supposed to be for something given freely, and yet if it was given freely, how can it impose a debt? In unraveling this paradox, this chapter has an eye to distinguishing between well-placed and misplaced gratitude, and it has a longer-range objective of advancing the philosophy of friendship. One route to working out from under the protection racket has been lesbianfeminism. In a misogynist society, women's need for protection is real. The trick has been to get it without supporting our continuing need for it. Lesbianism presents itself to many as a live option here. The question whether being lesbian is a matter of luck or choice is a continuing topic of discussion, which I examine at length elsewhere.[22] I see it as having elements of both. Chapter Seven takes up an ethical aspect of that question under the heading of responsibility, returning to some of the themes of Chapter Two, and argues that for purposes of taking responsibility, being lesbian is better conceived as an erotic orientation than as a sexual one.

Achievements similar to those of feminist philosophy characterize recent developments by philosophers of color in the United States. Within the past fifteen years, philosophers of color have produced substantial bodies of inquiry attending to political issues of race and ethnicity and taking up issues in ethics, epistemology, and metaphysics from the perspectives of people of color.[23] The Society for Blacks in Philosophy was established in the early 1980s, and the American Philosophical Association publishes a major newsletter, "Philosophy and the Black Experience."[24] Like feminist philosophy, with which it overlaps, this body of work is expanding philosophical agendas with issues that previously received scant attention, such as connections of "race" with such concepts as "nation."[25] Slavery, an institution for decades cited by moral philosophers as a test case for utilitarian ethics, is finally beginning to receive the systematic and detailed ethical examination that it deserves as a topic of moral concern in itself.[26]

In the spirit of acknowledging both that white is a color and that it has been socially privileged in the United States, the final chapter in this volume reflects on the interrelated concepts of "race" and "ethnicity" from my perspective as a white woman with Anglo-Saxon protestant and Celtic roots. This chapter reflects on moral stances toward such categories, on their meanings, and on ways in which being inside socially constructed ethnic and color categories becomes part of our moral luck.

In the balance of this introduction, I comment on two features of my philosophical orientation that characterize this book and many other works in the recent, more pluralistic philosophical scene. They are *holism* and historical *particularism*. I turn first to particularism.

Historical Particularism

By "particularism" I understand approaches to philosophical issues that take explicitly as appropriate subjects of philosophical investigation, and as data for philosophical reflection, the experiences of and concepts articulated by *historically defined communities or groups,* rather than concepts or experiences that are presumed to be universal. Particularists may concentrate on a particular culture, for example, or a particular gender. Particularist projects do not pretend to be about the whole world, life, or even human nature in general, although they may turn out to have global significance. Nor do they pretend to be about some aspect of life, of the world, or of human nature that can be presumed even to *interest* everyone or to reflect everyone's experience (although, again, it is possible that they may).

"Particularism" so understood does not imply nominalism, the metaphysical view that only individuals (particulars) *exist*. Nominalists deny the reality of universals, such as justice or goodness, maintaining that although there are just acts and good things, justice and goodness are not also things in their own right. Historical particularists need take no stand on the reality or unreality of universals. Instead, as I understand it, historical particularism is a practical orientation in project definition and methodology. Practical — or methodological — particularism may be readily confused with nominalism. But a practical particularist need not be a nominalist. A methodological particularist can leave open metaphysical questions concerning the reality of universals, because the issue is over what is interesting and worthwhile, not over what exists.

The particularity of historically defined inquiries is not always obvious, however. In setting particularist projects, feminist philosophers often reflect on mundane distinctions that have not been part of the traditional philosophy curriculum — distinctions that mark gender, race, or social class, for example. Such reflection is easily seen as evincing an interest in *human nature*. For everyone is gendered and has ethnic roots, and everyone experiences the effects of social class. And it is true that some feminist philosophers *have* investigated gender as an aspect of human nature. Alison Jaggar does this in *Feminist Politics and Human Nature*, although she is also deeply concerned with differences in the significance of gender for women and for men.[27] Yet others have been more interested in reflecting on specifically female experience than on gender as a category that applies to everybody. Marilyn Frye and Sarah Hoagland, for example, reflect specifically on the experience of women and lesbians.[28] In reflecting on female experience, we are self-conscious of our perspectives as female, not just human, and of the fact that we are not giving equal time to the perspectives of men.

Recently, the prospect of carrying self-consciousness of our specificity to its theoretical limits has raised troubling questions about the subject matter and the perspectives of its theorizers.[29] If the realization that there are no generic humans is what underlies one's focus on women or one's self-identification as a woman, the realization that there are no generic women soon may lead to a more specific identification, say, as a white woman. But as there are no generic white women, either, we may specify further, perhaps as a middle-class white lesbian. No matter how specific we get, there are always differences to be noted among the members of our categories. Carrying the tendency toward specificity to its theoretical limit would seem to require that we simply point to particulars, without categorizing at all. But then, how could we even talk about what moved us to point in the first place?

The perplexities of the tendency toward specificity are exacerbated by the realization that the social categories that we find interesting to explore are not static. What the category "woman" contains is not the same as the contents of its ancestor category, *wifman*, which at one time unambiguously designated a wife.[30] What "African American" refers to is not the same in the 1990s as it would have been in the 1890s (had that been the term in vogue), prior to many immigrations from the West Indies. Heracleitus (536–470 B.C.E.) insisted that changeability, rather than permanence, was the salient fact of reality, dramatizing this insight by insisting that he never stepped into the same river twice. Similarly impressed by social change, some lesbians today are skeptical of the identity "lesbian."[31]

Not only the contents of our categories but also our vocabularies change. Within my lifetime, U.S. citizens of African American descent have classified themselves or have been classified as Negroes, colored people, blacks, Afro-Americans, and African Americans.[32] Woman-loving women have called themselves lesbians, female homosexuals,

Sapphists, amazons, dykes, queers, and outlaws. Even the same term often has different shades of meaning and suggests different values in different cultural contexts.

With identity terms, we can be *very particular indeed* about what we want to be called. Particularizing seems to have no end. And as the above discussions suggest, particularity—or specificity—has degrees. "Woman" is more particular, or specific, than "human" but less specific than "lesbian." It is only against a historical background of an alleged focus on "humans" that a focus on "women" could even be identified as "particularist."

There is a companion phenomenon of particularist audience. Feminist philosophy is often addressed specifically to women (although not necessarily to feminists) rather than to readers of undefined gender, even when the author's intention is that men should also have access to it. Growing bodies of feminist work are now often concerned with even more specific communities of women, as in the case of Joyce Trebilcot's *Dyke Ideas*.[33] Such philosophy does not speak directly to all philosophical readers, although any might take an interest in it. Its data are not the data of all our lives, but then, neither are the data of the philosophical traditions. Particularist authors may use the pronoun "we" in ways that do not include all readers, in a deliberate response to the convention of using "we" for relatively privileged white men and "they" for everyone else. Although the older uses of "we" continue to be appropriate in some contexts, in others it often alienates those of us who cannot identify with references to "our" servants or "our" wives.

Does a particularist use of "we" then perpetuate exclusions in the same way that *we* found objectionable when used by those dominant in past traditions? It need not do so. As I argue elsewhere, it would be disrespectful to create expectations of inclusion in readers, say, by purporting to speak of the human condition and then to use language in ways that in fact exclude many readers.[34] But if an author does not create false expectations of inclusion, a particularist focus need not be disrespectful. It can be salutary for some readers to have to realize that they do not belong to the potential audience at the center of that author's attention, that they are perhaps not even part of the audience in that author's head. The deliberate and explicit self-consciousness with which feminist philosophers often address women should not create false expectations of inclusion among male readers, even if some male readers find such expectations natural as the legacy of their history of having occupied center stage. At various points in this work, I use "we" to refer to women, to lesbians, to philosophers, and to descendants of Northern Europeans, relying on context to make as clear as is needed for purposes at hand the scope of the "we."

It is, of course, both possible and in general desirable to take an interest in the data of the lives of people unlike ourselves. Yet a special, philosophical loss accrues to those who are routinely on the outside looking in, those whose lives are either ignored or treated disrespectfully in philosophical arguments that invoke the data of daily life in testing and developing ideas. A widely shared conception of philosophy is as a Socratic project of coming to know ourselves. This is what many understand by Socratic philosophy, meaning not the specific texts of Plato's Socratic dialogues but rather the ideal suggested in some of the earlier ones (such as Plato's *Apology*) that philosophy is a kind of self-knowledge.[35] Insofar as philosophy is a Socratic project of coming to know ourselves, reflecting solely on the data of lives that are not much like ours does not readily develop our own capacities for philosophical wisdom. If we have access only to philosophy that is based on the data of other people's lives, the activity of philosophical inquiry is likely to be far less engaging than it should be. Worse, empathy with some dominant points of view is dangerous for some of us in that it can encourage us to identify with attitudes hostile to ourselves. When philosophers uncritically invoke data embodying hostile or disrespectful attitudes toward women, for example, women are probably better off alienated than empathetically involved.[36] At any rate, such philosophy does alienate many of us.

Particularism in philosophy offers the potentiality of making philosophy a vehicle of self-knowledge for groups with histories of philosophical disenfranchisement. A question, then, is whether that means that it can make philosophy a good thing for us. Historically, philosophy has been not only a vehicle of self-knowledge but also a vehicle of self-deception. Some of its vulnerabilities as a source of knowledge should give us moral pause. It has presented men as though they constituted the species and society as though it consisted of privileged men. In so doing, it omits the perspectives of workers whose labor has made possible the leisure that philosophical investigation requires. The voices of such laborers might have articulated points of view and aspirations at odds with those embraced by, or sometimes even attributed to them by, philosophers. Those who have lacked the leisure for philosophy might also have exposed evils unacknowledged by philosophers whose inquiries their labors made possible.

My view is that a *self-conscious* particularism — one that does not pretend to be universalist — is more likely to avoid solipsistic and narcissistic arrogance and that it is thereby less liable to certain self-deceptions. Yet to avoid arrogance, we need consciousness of more than self. It has been characteristic of feminist particularists to be conscious of self not in abstraction but in relation to others and to be critical of representations of ourselves by those with systematic power over us. Also, if philosophy is not a luxury — as Ruth Ginzberg has recently argued that it is not — and if we can manage to elicit and support it without creating and supporting a relatively leisured class, it may reflect a more representative kaleidoscope of human activities and values.[37]

A case of particularism in style is the practice, which I follow in this book as I have followed it in others, of referring to women by both their first and last names, even after the first reference, rather than simply using patronyms after the first reference.[38] This practice maintains a lively sense of gender. More important, it avoids identifying us by naming practices that have subordinated us by subsuming us under men. There is no analogous reason to follow the same practice for men's names.

I turn next to holism and then to the question of its relationship to particularism.

Methodological Holism

Many feminist philosophers resist attempts to understand individuals in abstraction from their relationships to others. We tend to contextualize ourselves in relationships of friendship, companionship, cohabitation, coworking, and the communities, systems, or "wholes" defined by these and by other significant relationships. What I here call "holism" might perhaps also be called "relationism." Human relationships — especially our earliest relationships to primary caretakers, in which we have no say whatsoever — are a major source of luck in our lives. But even later in life, we often have little to say about how others respond to us. With whom we have occasion to form relationships is a fact often delineated by factors beyond our control.

As with particularism, I adopt a *methodological* holism. It does not commit me to the metaphysical view that individuals exist, or are intelligible, only through their relations to others, although that is an interesting and plausible idea. Holism in my work is a practical orientation in project definition, a special concern with interconnections and the wholes they create or disrupt.

Holism in much feminist thought has both a negative face and a positive one. The negative face consists in rejecting or at least questioning hierarchical dualisms or dichotomies that have been central to centuries of Northern culture: mind/body, reason/feeling, culture/nature, civilization/wilderness, man/woman (often represented as "masculine/feminine"), man/nature, and so on. The positive face has consisted in searching out and exploring nonhierarchical interdependencies and looking also for possibilities of decentralization of control and for less preoccupation with control.[39]

Consider first holism's negative face. Each side of the mind/body, reason/feeling, culture/nature, and masculine/feminine dualisms has its adherents. Socially, however, the lion's share of advantages — power, privilege, and prestige — has accrued regularly to those who have been identified with mind, reason, culture, and masculinity. The general point of these dichotomies and other related dichotomies has been to affirm control structures. These can become oppressive structures of domination and subordination: mind over body, reason over feeling, culture over nature, masculine over feminine, man over woman. A devaluation of what is subordinated is often used to "justify" the domination. These values even turn up even in philosophy as a profession in the opposition of "hard philosophy" (logic, philosophy of science, philosophy of mathematics) to "soft philosophy" (value inquiry in the areas of ethics, aesthetics, philosophy of religion, social and political philosophy). Resistance to the implied "femininity" of "soft philosophy" is at least one factor underlying the spectacle of some philosophers' attempts to structure value inquiry through mathematical formulae.

Historically, hierarchical dichotomies have been used against women of many cultures, who have been identified with body, feeling, nature, and the feminine. They have been used also by white societies to identify men of color with the feminine and with body, feeling, and nature. The move to reject or at least question these hierarchical dichotomies marks an interesting overlap of social protest philosophies, such as anarchism, feminism, and antiracism, with the newly developing fields of philosophical ecology and environmental ethics. This overlap can be seen in the movements of social ecology and ecofeminism.[40]

A characteristic form of the rejection of hierarchical dichotomies leads us to the positive face of holism, which is also another major area of overlap between social protest philosophies and philosophical ecology. The strategy, in all these cases, has been, not to allow one side of the dichotomy to swallow the other, but instead to emphasize and explore interconnections and interdependencies of mind and body, reason and feeling, culture and nature in ways that undermine the negative valuations regularly attached to the body, feeling, nature, women and in ways that expose questionable political purposes served by domination and by control of the body, feeling, nature, women. When we look at interrelationships as constitutive of various systems, we are also encouraged to ask whether a particular system is a good thing and whether it is doing well.

Holism as such is not incompatible with hierarchies and dichotomies. Wholes and systems can certainly be defined by relations of dominance and subordinance. From a functional point of view, hierarchies often appear natural and desirable. Chains of authority, for example, increase production efficiency. Military operations are difficult to conceive of without chains of command. If however, we evaluate a community or interaction not solely in functional terms but also in terms of phenomenological relationships between members of the community or interaction and their responses to one another, dominance and subordination present a different aspect. Hierarchies that involve dominance and subordination encourage a preoccupation with forms of control that alienate individuals from each other. Such alienation tends to block the empathy and identification required for bonding. It interferes with appreciations that form the bases of mutual respect. When people (and other animals) are known by proper names, for example, instead of simply by their functions (as wives, slaves, servants, livestock), it is more difficult to think of them simply, or even primarily, as beings who are likely to get out of control or to think of them simply, or even primarily, as beings functioning at this or that level of efficiency.

The chapters that follow reflect on the ethical consequences for relationships of being positioned early in life on the disfavored end of hierarchical dichotomies and to some extent try to envision what we might be like in more egalitarian or nonoppressive relationships.

A Few Questions

A certain difficulty may present itself to thinkers who find both holism and particularism attractive: it may not be obvious that holism and particularism are compatible with each other. For a particular suggests a part, something that is less than the whole. If we have a particularist focus, how can we claim to be at the same time holistic? How can those of us who sometimes encourage boycotts, withdrawals, even revolutions, any of which can be highly disruptive of systems, consider ourselves holists?

The answer to this query requires us to draw some distinctions. A whole (a system, perhaps a community) does not have to be the whole of everything. It does not have to be the whole universe. Holism — at least, methodological holism — does not imply that the best way to view *everything* that exists is as belonging to or integrated into one gigantic system. Nor does holism imply that every system is a good thing. Particularist feminist philosophers have been concerned with such wholes as consciousness (considered as a unity of feeling and intellect), households, communities, lands (in Aldo Leopold's sense of the land as a community whose members are animals, plants, soils, and waters), multicultural societies. These wholes are also historical particulars. They are particular communities, identities, cultures developed in particular lands. A particular community, system, or relationship may be poorly constituted or well constituted, thriving or decadent. Withdrawing from a poorly constituted whole is often a first step toward constituting a better one.

These considerations suggest two further questions, one for particularism and another for holism. I elaborate above on the question for particularism: Is there any nonarbitrary point at which to stop particularizing? Carrying particularity to its theoretical limit seems to reduce us to inarticulate pointing. The question for holism is about hierarchies and dichotomies: Can we eliminate them without defeating our own ends as social critics? Some "dichotomies" are necessary to critical reflection, for example, the "dichotomies" of right and wrong and of good and bad.[41] Feminist holists will surely be the first to admit, or rather insist on, the importance of evaluation. Yet evaluating seems to rely on and support what may look, at first, like hierarchical dichotomies: the acceptable and the unacceptable, the justifiable and the unjustifiable, and so on.

In response to the first question, why should we stop at a focus on women (for example) when women also differ along many other dimensions, there is probably no good reason to carry methodological particularism to its theoretical limit. Particularism has a *historical* importance, which sets limits to its value and makes a variety of "stopping points" nonarbitrary. Particularism takes on importance against the background of histories in which particular groups of people have been marginalized or treated disrespectfully. Feminist particularists in fact demonstrate lively interest in ethnic and other differences besides the gender difference. Not every conceivable kind of difference among us is historically significant, however.

In response to the second question, whether we can dispense with hierarchies and dichotomies without defeating our own ends, not all ratings and rankings govern or are correlated with distributions of power. Holism, like particularism, is important against the background of histories in which marginalization and disrespect have been damaging, resulting in our underdevelopment or in internalized hostility to ourselves. These kinds of damage do not result merely from employing the distinctions of right and wrong or good and bad. The question whether we can eliminate hierarchical dichotomies without defeating our own ends as social critics is really the question whether we can get along without value hierarchies or normative hierarchies. This question, however, is grounded on a confusion. The distinctions between right and wrong, or between good and bad, do not define hierarchies in the relevant sense. They do not define a *dominance order* or a distribution of power. Judging that something is right or good, justifiable or unjustifiable, does not assign to it any power whatsoever.

Some Conclusions and Future Directions

The growing academic consciousness of histories of racism, sexism, and class oppression suggests that particularism and holism will find places in philosophy for a long time to come. For me, feminist particularism and holism have meant a departure from the kind of philosophy with which I began as an undergraduate when I abandoned the naive cultural relativism of my parents for Marcus Singer's *Generalization in Ethics* and, following in a similar vein as a graduate student, became immersed in John Rawls's magnificent theory of justice.[42] It has also been something of a move away from Kant and toward Aristotle and Nietzsche, although not all the way.

Constructing principles of justice in Rawls's theory involved *donning* veils of ignorance, pretending to a certain amnesia in which we were to forget who we were (which I was only too happy to do) and abstract from most of our knowledge of history (where I was already far less knowledgeable than I should have been). A danger of this enterprise is that even were the veil to screen out our knowledge of our histories, it would not thereby inhibit the actual influence of those histories. If anything, the influence of those histories may actually be aided by our very lack of awareness or attention to them. The most successful veils may leave us vulnerable to biases that we are ill-equipped to detect. That is not necessarily a reason to give up on striving for the ability to attain the universality that the theory seeks. Rawls's more recent limitation of his theory of justice to a political conception that does not embody a comprehensive philosophical outlook but is intended to gain the support of an overlapping consensus still emphasizes commonalities, although in a way that is deeply respectful of differences.[43] Yet even this more modest conception of universality needs to be supplemented by other, more particularist, endeavors, which, for many of us, are more pressing. In poorly integrated multicultural societies plagued by ethnocentric racism and androcentric sexism, many of us need to learn to identify and then *peel back* veils of ignorance that we may not have known were already in place, ignorance that can serve questionable political ends. Ethically, we have ignored too much. Our identities are not transparent to ourselves, not determinable a priori, Descartes notwithstanding. Coming to know who we are, historically speaking, can be a difficult labor.

The ideals articulated behind a Rawlsian veil of ignorance are framed on the assumption that once they are accepted, everyone will for the most part abide by them. They are principles for what Rawls calls a "well-ordered society," which is a just society in which everyone has an effective sense of justice, in important respects the same sense of justice, and knows this about everyone else.[44] It is not clear how such principles framed for this ideal society are to connect with ethical issues arising out of histories of evil in contexts that are nowhere near just. It might seem that we could frame principles of justice behind a veil of ignorance on other assumptions than the assumption of perfect compliance, say, on the assumption that they would apply in the context of a society structured by histories of deep injustice. After trying this experiment in thinking about criminal justice, which Rawls has acknowledged belongs for the most part to "partial compliance theory," I have come to doubt that very much can be done along these lines behind a thick veil of ignorance, although in Chapter Four I consider some plausible abstract suggestions for a theory of basic evils.[45] For the most part, however, we need to get into the particulars of histories of injustice, and these drag us back to the world on the other side of the veil, or perhaps, they put us behind much thinner veils. It is no accident that Rawlsian theorizers behind the thick veil of ignorance operate mostly on assumptions of strict rather than partial compliance or widespread noncompliance. In discussing "the law of peoples," Rawls does give some serious attention to the problem of noncompliance, treating the noncompliance of some peoples as a problem regarding the limits of tolerance by others.[46] Yet even here he does not get very far into the difficult questions about what justice might require where those limits are exceeded.

A society in which ideals of justice are grossly violated is the one in which we live (as Rawls also acknowledges). This continuing history occupies center stage in my concerns. If philosophy is to be wisdom in the conduct of my life, I need it to connect with this history and not simply to offer me a fantasy escape from it. For this, it is not enough to confront the inequities of the "natural lottery" from which we may inherit various physical and psychological assets and liabilities. It is important also to reflect on the *unnatural* lottery created by networks of unjust institutions and histories that bequeath to us further inequities in our starting positions and that violate principles that would have addressed, if not redressed, inequities of nature.

As a legacy from the days of William James when libraries catalogued philosophy together with psychology, the Harvard philosophy graduate program had for many years a psychology requirement. Perhaps the time has come for philosophy programs to institute a history requirement (although academic history is not free of bias, either). Much of the data of the histories that philosophy needs are only recently being archived, acknowledged as important, and made more generally visible in the academy: histories of daily working-class life, women's histories, histories of Jews in the Diaspora, histories of so-called Third World peoples, Native American histories, Asian American histories, African American histories — histories that have been researched, critically evaluated, and defined by historians who identify and empathize with the people whose stories they tell.[47]

RESPONSIBILITY
AND MORAL LUCK

One's history as an agent is a web in which anything
that is the product of the will is surrounded and held
up and partly formed by things that are not.
— Bernard Williams, *Moral Luck*

The problem arises . . . because the self which acts
and is the object of moral judgment is threatened
with dissolution by the absorption of its acts
and impulses into the class of events.
— Thomas Nagel, *Mortal Questions*

Scepticism about the freedom of morality from luck . . .
will leave us with *a* concept of morality, but one
less important, certainly, than ours is usually taken to
be; and that will not be ours, since one thing that
is particularly important about ours is how
important it is taken to be.
— Bernard Williams, *Moral Luck*

Should it unsettle our sense of responsibility to realize
that how morally good or bad we are is not immune
to luck? In this chapter I support the view that it
should not, that appreciating the impact of luck on
our lives can add depth to our understanding of responsibility and increase our sense of morality's importance. One thing
that makes character valuable is that it prepares us somewhat for contingencies. Fortunately, this does not require that it not have arisen
from contingencies itself.

By "luck" I understand, following Bernard Williams and Thomas Nagel, factors beyond the control of the affected agent, good or bad, but not necessarily matters of chance. One person's luck may be another's choice or even a result of social practice, predictable by those in possession of the relevant information. We call it *our* (good or bad) luck when *we* cannot predict it and it eludes our control. What makes luck *moral,* however, is its involvement with our choices (or failures to choose) to do what is morally right or wrong or with our having a moral character—virtues, vices, integrity. The nature of that involvement, and hence whether moral luck is real, has been a subject of dispute ever since Williams and Nagel introduced the concept.[1] A plea for excuses as capable of diminishing our responsibility surely seems to imply that who we are or what we do is moral or immoral only insofar as it is up to us. Thus "moral luck" has an oxymoronic ring. If something is a matter of luck, how can it also be moral?

The impact on me of realizing that our histories as agents are webs in which all that is a product of our wills is supported by things that are not is an *ethical* impact. It moves me toward humility and mercy, virtues that acknowledge the unfairness of life but also presuppose a morally structured context of interaction. In this chapter I explore that context, presenting responsibility as an achievement, not a given.

The Problem

The moral nature of the impact of moral luck comes through even in Williams's account of it. He acknowledges that "the limitation of the moral is itself something morally important."[2] Luck indicates a certain absence of justice in who we are and what we can do. We do not all have an equal chance to be good, and our goodness is less up to us than our religious and moral traditions would have us believe. On Nagel's account, luck renders moral responsibility ultimately incoherent by making nonsense of the idea that we are autonomous agents. He also finds that we cannot give it up but appears to regard that as a kind of irrationality with which we are presently stuck.[3]

The challenge is to show how the importance and point of responsibility can survive the realization that the quality of our character and our deeds is not entirely up to us as individuals. I agree with Martha Nussbaum that if our goodness is fragile, that makes it even more important.[4] As for the point of responsibility, it varies with one's perspective. Williams and Nagel tend to look down and back, from relatively privileged standpoints and toward the past, focusing on such things as praise, blame, regret, punishment, and reward — the last two, historically, prerogatives of the powerful exercised for social control. That standpoint, however, may presuppose another more basic, a standpoint of future-oriented agency. I propose to consider what emerges when we look forward and up, toward the future and from the standpoints of those struggling to put their lives together. From this perspective, we are likely to think more of taking responsibility than of attributing it. The point of taking responsibility is often to construct or to improve situations and relationships rather than to control, contain, or dominate.

Williams and Nagel illustrate moral luck with cases much discussed in subsequent literature, which give an intuitive sense of what they had in mind by moral luck. Williams offers us (1) (a fictionalized) Paul Gauguin who left his wife and children, despite genuine concern for them, to devote himself to painting, not yet able to tell whether he would do anything great; (2) Anna Karenina, who left her marriage, her social life, and the son she loved for a future with Vronsky, her lover, unable to foresee that the new relationship could not support the weight it had to carry; (3) a negligent lorry driver who hit a child who ran into the street; and (4) an equally negligent driver who hit no one (because no one ran into the street). To these Nagel adds (5) the concentration camp officer who "might have led a quiet and harmless life if the Nazis had never come to power in Germany" by contrast with (6) someone "who led a quiet and harmless life in Argentina" but "might have become an officer in a concentration camp if he had not left Germany for business reasons in 1930."[5]

Williams contrasts incident luck with constitutive luck. Incident luck enters into the way particular actions turn out. Constitutive luck enters into the development of character. For either we may be liable to praise or blame. But Williams finds that incident and constitutive luck problematize morality in two different ways. Incident luck undermines the idea that we can always determine before we act which of our choices are justifiable. Constitutive luck undermines the assumption of equality regarding our capacities for moral agency. Many years ago Williams explored the moral ideal of equality.[6] Since then he has focused more on results and justification.

My interest is primarily in constitutive luck — luck in character development. However, luck in justification is relevant insofar as character development depends on particular choices. Where Williams's and Nagel's examples are most convincing, the luck they illustrate is both incident and constitutive in that certain of the agents' justifications (or lacks thereof) depend on who they become consequent upon their choices. The cases motivating my inquiry, however, differ from theirs. I am interested, from the agent's forward-looking perspective, in the implications for taking responsibility for oneself of a history of bad moral luck, such as comes with a history of child abuse or a heritage of oppression. Taking responsibility here is likely to involve consciously developing an integrity that does not develop spontaneously. This, I argue, is not the same as developing autonomy. The idea is not to develop *boundaries* between ourselves and our environments, although some boundaries may be necessary as means. Rather, the idea is to develop such things as reliability and bases for self-esteem. For both, interpersonal relationships can be critical. Being overly concerned with boundaries may hinder the development of needed interpersonal relationships.

I begin from the idea, first brought home to me in reading John Dewey and later reinforced by studying Aristotle and Nietzsche, that we are born not responsible (or "free") but at most with potentialities for becoming so, realizable to a greater or lesser extent with luck and hard work.[7] How hard the work may be partly a function of social privilege, which is also luck, from the standpoint of those doing the work.

The remainder of this chapter has five main stages, followed by a conclusion. In the first I return to the two perspectives and distinguish several dimensions of responsibility. The section following that presents taking responsibility for oneself as developing integrity rather than autonomy. The next one looks at responsibility for consequences as governed by higher order principles that refer to basic moral norms central to moral integrity. Here I argue that, although Kant's *metaphysics* of morals is challenged by the idea of moral luck, Kant's principles of imputation, and similar higher-order principles, can be used to defend the reality of moral luck against skeptics. The fourth section develops the idea that human interaction in basic social institutions and in relationships with significant others is our major source of moral luck. The fifth takes up survivors' resistance to childhood abuse and to political oppression, suggesting an analogy between multiple personality and the fragmentation of oppressed communities. Resistance to oppression in both cases illustrates the importance as well as the reality of taking responsibility for ourselves in the face of bad moral luck. I center taking responsibility for ourselves as a basic case underlying our ability to take responsibility for other things in any but superficial ways.

Dimensions of Responsibility

The Two Perspectives

Writing nearly three decades ago in a book on responsibility, Herbert Fingarette said, "I am concerned especially with two essential dimensions of responsibility: One is that of acceptance, of commitment, care, and concern, and of the attendant elements of choice and of the creativity in choice; the other dimension is that of the 'forms of life,' initially socially given and ultimately socially realized, which constitute the form and content of responsibility."[8] The orientation I have in mind in the idea of taking responsibility is, like Fingarette's, basically forward-looking. My interest here is in his first dimension, that of acceptance, commitment, care, and concern. By contrast, most essays on responsibility in contemporary Anglo-American moral philosophy look backward. They are preoccupied with punishment and reward, praise or blame, excuses, mitigation, and so on. This is true, for example, of the entry in Paul Edwards's *Encyclopedia of Philosophy*.[9] Two notable exceptions are Joyce Trebilcot's essay on taking responsibility for sexuality and the first chapter of Martha Nussbaum's study of luck and ethics in Greek tragedy and philosophy.[10] Williams briefly takes up a forward-looking orientation in commenting on the inadvisability of what John Rawls has called "life-plans," or "rational plans of life.[11] Nagel, in *The View from Nowhere,* offers as a substitute for autonomy something that sounds like *taking* responsibility, in a forward-looking sense: trying "to live in a way that wouldn't have to be revised in light of anything more that could be known about us."[12] But for the most part, both Williams and Nagel seem concerned with attributions of responsibility for what has been done or has occurred rather than with takings on of responsibility, which can be for what has not yet occurred or has not yet been done.

The backward-looking orientation embodies a perspective of observation — what Williams calls "the view from there" as opposed to "the view from here." The "view from there" is characteristic of an administrator and, to some extent, of a teacher or therapist. It is basically a third-person perspective, although we can learn to take this perspective also on ourselves. The forward-looking orientation embodies a perspective of *agency,* focused on what is not yet completed or does not yet exist. The two perspectives often are associated with different kinds of judgments. Attributions of responsibility, made from the observation perspective, ground judgments of desert, whereas taking on responsibility from the perspective of agency may involve judgments of one's worthiness (or fitness) to do so and of the worthwhileness of doing so.

In arguing that moral responsibility may be ultimately unintelligible, Nagel contrasts an objective standpoint — "the view from nowhere" — with a subjective standpoint, "the view from here." This sounds something like the contrast between the perspective of observation and that of agency ("the view from there" as opposed to "the view from here"). Yet the two distinctions are not identical. The view "from nowhere" is depersonalized, whereas the view "from there" need not be. As Peter Strawson argues in his essay on resentment, ordinary interpersonal interaction is not depersonalized.[13] Nor need our third-person judgments of others be depersonalized. Nagel's "view from nowhere" is supposed to yield objectivity. However, the view "from there" (the perspective of observation) need be no more objective than the view "from here" (the perspective of agency), even though the language of object and subject can seem right to describe the two orientations. From "there," the agent whose responsibility is in question becomes an *object* of observation (although not necessarily depersonalized) and responsibility may be attributed. From "here," the agent whose responsibility is in question is the *subject* and responsibility may be undertaken. Again, of course, one can take an observation perspective on oneself, in addition to taking the perspective of agency, although it is difficult if not ordinarily impossible to maintain both at once. (As we will see, multiple personalities do just that.) What is important is that observation need not move us from a world of agency to a world of nonmoral natural events.

It may appear that the forward- and backward-looking orientations illustrate what Carol Gilligan calls perspectives of care and justice.[14] Autonomy is central to her "justice perspective," from which we praise, blame, punish, and reward, whereas interpersonal relationships (a major source of luck) are central to her "care perspective." To the extent that care requires forward-looking responsibility, the moral ambition of escaping luck may be less prevalent than Williams and Nagel have thought. Perhaps what needs transformation is a morality of autonomy—what Carol Gilligan calls a "justice orientation." There may be something to this idea, and yet this picture of the division between justice and care is too simple (a matter on which the next two chapters have more to say). For, responsibility with a forward-looking orientation is ambiguous between a care-taking sense and others, such as accountability and management, which can involve considerations of justice. I turn next to such ambiguities in the concept of responsibility.

Ambiguities of "Responsibility"

"Responsible" can describe an agent either as having certain capacities or as having certain virtues. It can mean either having the capacity for moral agency, which we presume of people, generally, or having integrity, including the virtues of conscientiousness and honesty. A responsible person in the second and nonredundant sense is reliable, has good judgment, gives matters due consideration, and the like. Such virtues make us worthy of taking on responsibilities. To have the capacity is merely to be able to do such things. Yet the distinction is not sharp. Being able, here, is also being good at, to some extent. Worthiness, in this context, suggests superior ability. We develop responsibility as a virtue by first *taking* responsibility in ways that outrun our apparent present worthiness to do so and then carrying through successfully. Luck is involved both in the motivation to take responsibility and in our ability to carry through. Where that seems unfair, we may be able to take the unfairness into account, morally, in some of our evaluations.

That our motivations and carryings through are embedded in factors beyond our control does not imply that there is no control after all. Even the embeddedness of my computer software in a world that outruns its controls does not imply that the software does not really control anything or that we are always arbitrary to pick out the software rather than environmental conditions as relevantly responsible. We are sometimes right to blame the program, although not morally, of course—because it lacks the sensitivities and abilities of a person. Computer programs can *be* responsible for a variety of things. But they cannot *take* responsibility. They cannot (yet) become responsible for more than they were designed for. (Mine cannot — as far as I know.)

So let us look at the idea of *taking* responsibility. In taking responsibility, we locate ourselves as morally relevant centers of agency. Different sorts of agency suggest different senses, or dimensions, of taking responsibility. The following seem worth distinguishing: (1) the administrative or managerial sense of responsibility — undertaking to size up and organize possibilities comprehensively, deciding which should be realized and how; (2) the accountability sense of responsibility — agreeing to answer or account for something, or finding that one should be answerable, and then doing so; (3) the care-taking sense of responsibility — committing oneself to stand behind something, to back it, support it, make it good (or make good on one's failure to do so), and following through; (4) the credit sense of responsibility — owning up to having been the (morally) relevant cause of something's happening or not happening, taking the credit (or blame) for it. Initially, I also distinguished an obligation sense of responsibility — accepting or taking on obligations and fulfilling them on one's own initiative. But that seems needlessly redundant in view of the first three senses, any of which might be redescribed in terms of obligations. There are different kinds of obligations worth distinguishing in relation to these different kinds of responsibilities — formal and impersonal obligations as opposed to informal and personal ones — which I take up in Chapter Six in discussing the paradoxical idea of a "debt" of gratitude.

Although the above four senses of responsibility are interrelated and overlapping, only the last, the "credit" sense, is basically backward-looking. The first three are basically forward-looking. Each begins with an undertaking. Each has a second stage, follow-through. These two stages give rise to another ambiguity of "responsible." The judgment that someone took responsibility can be withdrawn if the person fails to follow through. ("I took responsibility for raising you when I adopted you." "You did not; you were never there when I needed you." Both claims can be true.)

Further, all four senses of "taking responsibility," including the backward-looking credit sense, require some initiative from the agent (different in each case). This is the "taking" part. Agents are more responsible when they take responsibility in a sense that shows initiative than when they do not. Initiative-taking is contrasted with such alternatives as being ordered, told, or asked to do something, or having someone else suggest it, but not with such possibilities as having the idea suggested by a fortuitous combination of events that one observes. Such observations are not thought to undermine initiative but, rather, to be occasions for it.

Williams's and Nagel's skeptical views concerning moral responsibility appear to be based on consideration of the fourth sense (the credit sense). Justice in punishments and rewards invokes this credit sense. But retributive justice is only a small part of morality. A basic lack of justice in our ability to be moral may, in fact, often undermine the retributive justice of punishments and rewards. From the point of view of justice itself, perhaps we should often take such justice (that of punishments and rewards) with more than a grain of salt. I believe we often do and for just this kind of reason.

Instead of taking responsibility freely, we sometimes find ourselves with it. We may be given responsibility, assigned it, inherit it, and then accept or refuse it. Acceptance here may also exhibit a certain initiative and thus be referred to as taking responsibility, although it exhibits less initiative than free undertakings. Ethical norms govern all of these activities and practices. We refer to *that for which* we have responsibility as our *responsibilities,* sometimes as our *obligations.* In the forward-looking senses, when we take responsibility for something, there is no assumption that we produced it. We may embrace or even identify with what we admittedly did not bring about, such as our ethnic heritage, on which Chapter Eight has more to say.

The forward-looking senses of "taking responsibility" are more basic not because praise or blame are due only depending on whether we follow through on voluntary undertakings but because we presuppose at least a minimal capacity in others to take responsibility in the forward-looking sense when we praise or blame them. We assume that they can take responsibility for themselves and their actions, in a general way — that they can manage themselves (in some respects), for example, and can make good on (some of) their failures — or at least that they could at the time that they acted. When we are persuaded that someone is not capable of such things, we tend to withdraw praise or blame. When we think others have lost such capacities through their own foolishness, we may feel frustrated that there is no longer anyone to blame.

Autonomy and Integrity

Autonomy

Williams set the stage for exploring moral responsibility without the illusion of transcending luck. His attitude seems ambivalent between skepticism about the value of morality and curiosity about how appreciations of luck might transform it. Often, his skeptical side dominates. My interest is in supporting the value of morality without the illusions.

To explore responsibility without the illusion of transcending luck, the perspective of agency in interpersonal relationships is a good place to begin. In the Anna Karenina story the relevant luck has its source in such relationships. The Gauguin story also involves interpersonal relationships (Gauguin's relationships with his wife and children), but they are not the source of the luck that Williams discusses in considering whether Gauguin was in some sense justified in his choice to abandon his family (although that luck could be discussed, too).

Responsibility in relationships necessarily involves luck, because it is partly up to others how relationships go and what they bring out and develop in us. Choosing relationships is choosing risks. Significant relationships affect who we become. They affect our basic values, our sense of who we are, our commitments, even our abilities to live up to those commitments.

In affiliating with others, we give up some autonomy, in the sense of independence from other agents. But we do not necessarily thereby give up some moral integrity—although we can do that, too, depending on the character of our affiliates. In affiliating our boundaries relax. The subject of action is often a "we," fluid in duration and content. Agency tolerates fuzziness in boundaries. Yet we may retain certain basic commitments and values and thus our individual integrity. Affiliations that do compromise our integrity are subject to moral criticism. Some sorts of autonomy, then, are unnecessary for morality.

In resisting Carol Gilligan's proposal of two ethics, care and justice, which assigned autonomy to the justice ethic and initially assigned relationships to the care ethic, Thomas Hill found three kinds of autonomy that need not be compromised by relationships.[15] One is autonomy as impartiality in certain kinds of judgment. Another is autonomy as an area within which an agent can decide free of others' interferences. The third is autonomy as an agent's freedom from the internal division that comes of being subject to one's own blind impulses and unexamined prejudices. The third sounds more like integrity than autonomy. The clearest is the second, that of areas of decision-making, which defines a kind of independence from others. As Hill points out, none implies that we are truly ourselves only when acting impartially, that our moral principles are independent of contingencies, that they admit no exceptions, that they govern only our wills and not our feelings; nor does any imply "that self-sufficiency is better than dependence, or that the emotional detachment of a judge is better than the compassion of a lover."[16]

Nagel has tended to think of luck as "external contingencies." For autonomy in at least Hill's noninterference sense, the distinction between external and internal does seem important. Applied to "contingency," however, "external" is either redundant or misleading. It is redundant if we understand "contingency" as external (to the agent) by definition. If we do not, two problems arise. One is that interaction makes what is external to each agent unclear, although it does not necessarily make their responsibilities unclear. What another does to me is not always something that just happens to me as opposed to something I do. Others' behavior can respond to mine; I may provoke, invite, or otherwise elicit it. But their responses can still be my luck. This is because the distribution of responsibility in interaction is frequently governed by norms regarding initiation and response. I may be lucky that you come to visit me and also partly responsible for it, if I invited you. On the other hand, my misfortune in being assaulted may not be my responsibility, even though my carrying a wallet or being on the street unaccompanied was among the causal conditions. If I am within my rights, I am not ethically responsible for the assault. To attribute responsibility we often need to know whether an agent violated justified norms. If so, consequences may be imputable specifically to that agent, despite the involvement of others.

The other problem with the view of luck as an external contingency is that luck can be clearly internal, as in the Gauguin case. We cannot always foresee what will emerge from within. Gauguin could not know a priori whether he would find in himself the talent, originality, and perseverance of a great painter. The external/internal metaphor for luck is thus misleading. A more relevant distinction is between what is and what is not contingent to our moral agency, regardless whether it is internal or external to ourselves.

Integrity

Nagel's concern with externality reflects a concern about luck's threats to *autonomy*. Williams, however, has been more concerned about its threats to *integrity*. The difference may be brought out as follows. Nagel has focused on the fuzziness of boundaries between agents and their environments, treating other agents as part of the environment in the same way as material objects or events in nature. His skepticism regarding responsibility turns on an apparent arbitrariness, from an observer's point of view, of distinguishing at a given time what does or does not belong to an agent and thus between what was done by the agent and what was produced by external factors. Williams, on the other hand, focuses on changes and developments *within the agent,* presupposing a workable sense of the agent's boundaries at a given time. What Williams finds problematic is the agent's identity over time, as potentialities unfold and the agent's values mature and change. Such developments present interesting problems for determining and fulfilling responsibilities, although they are not the same as boundary problems. Integrity — literally, wholeness, completeness, undividedness — involves considerations of consistency, coherence, and commitment, whereas autonomy involves considerations of dependence and independence.

Williams's skepticism regarding the advisability of planning in advance for one's life as a whole turns on the vulnerability to luck of our very identity. Because who we become is not immune to luck, our knowledge from here of what will be in our interests in the future is limited. Such limitations can threaten one's moral integrity — as a parent, for example (as in the Gauguin case). Contingencies of our development inaccessible at the moment of critical choice threaten our integrity when they interfere with our carrying through on obligations and commitments.

In taking responsibility for ourselves, we do participate in constructing our identities and thus in constructing some of the conditions of our own integrity. On Lynne McFall's analysis, however, integrity (without qualification) is not simply a matter of internal consistency or even coherence.[17] It requires an identity to which certain basic moral values and commitments are central. It is thus consistency or coherence with an identity that includes a certain content. She points out that we cannot betray commitments central to our identities without feeling that we are not the persons we had thought we were. Such commitments can be to other people as well as to projects vulnerable to reverses of fortune.

Not all of the contingencies identified by Williams and Nagel threaten an agent's integrity. Those of the lorry drivers may not, for example. Here we have negligence rather than choice, and the accident may not play a central enough role in the unlucky driver's life. Nor is it necessarily moral integrity that is threatened or supported. Gauguin emerged with a self-defining commitment that he could stand behind and thus with a kind of integrity, although not integrity without qualification (in Lynne McFall's sense). He found that he could live with his guilt and go right on painting. But he may not have utterly lost his moral integrity, either, despite this spectacular lapse in his moral career. It is conceivable that his character even improved on the whole as his morale soared. Anna Karenina's choice, in contrast, was a disaster. She could find no way, by herself, to make it good. She gave up her son and a life of relative freedom for a relationship that she ultimately could not enjoy. Her integrity was so deeply undermined that she lost all sense of her worth and ended her life in a somewhat incoherent vengeful effort at stimulating Vronsky's grief.

To develop and maintain integrity, we need to discover, assess, and sometimes make changes in our values, traits, and capacities. Luck enters at several points. The Gauguin and Anna Karenina cases illustrate luck of opposite kinds in choices instrumental to the relevant discoveries. To determine whether it makes sense to hold an agent responsible, we need to know whether that agent's luck made the development or maintenance of integrity impossible or impossibly difficult. To assess the moral justifiability of one agent's holding another responsible, we may also want to know how the latter's luck compares with that of the former.

Since some of our most deeply ingrained values and traits begin in early unchosen relationships with significant others, we may have difficult work to find their roots, assess them realistically, and come up with a tolerably coherent set. Further, since our development can be highly unpredictable, it is likely to be a matter of luck if we do not find ourselves later in life committed to responsibilities that it made good sense to undertake only in terms of values we have since abandoned. Appreciating the sources of our values and traits, the shared nature of our responsibility for them, and the roles of luck in our having the particular chaotic aggregate that we have can lighten the project of getting to know ourselves, even introduce humor. In this way it can have some of the same consequences as taking morality less seriously. What is taken less seriously, however, may be not morality but more specifically, individual autonomy. Perhaps Williams should have concluded that appreciating moral luck makes us take autonomy less seriously, from a moral point of view.

Kant on Imputation

Williams and Nagel attribute to Kant the idea that morality is immune to luck, presumably on the basis of Kant's famous remark that a good will lacking power to accomplish its purposes still shines like a jewel by its own light ("in a mire of contingencies," as Margaret Walker puts it).[18] Kant's metaphysics of morals does include the idea of an agency that is not subject to empirical causality. There are many reasons to doubt the coherency of this view. But Kant also does, in effect, acknowledge a certain role of luck in determining our responsibilities, an important wedge for the insertion of moral luck, however inconsistent that may be with his other views. His brief remarks on responsibility — or, as he calls it, "imputation" — acknowledge luck in what can be imputed to us. And what can be imputed to us can have implications for obligations we then come to have, which we may or may not be able to fulfill. Anna Karenina, for example, had an obligation to protect her son from some of the worst consequences of her decision to leave her husband, and ultimately she was unable to fulfill that obligation.

Kant's principles of imputation are higher-order moral principles in that they presuppose and refer to more basic principles of right and wrong, which determine whether an action was "due" or not. At the end of the general Preface to his *Metaphysic of Morals,* Kant asserts:

> The good or bad effects of a due action, like the effects following from the omission of a meritorious action, cannot be imputed to the subject (*modus imputationis tollens*).
>
> The good effects of a meritorious action, like the bad effects of an unlawful action, can be imputed to the subject (*modus imputationis ponens*).[19]

Kant's principles are sketchy and incomplete. They do not say, for example, what others are justified in doing to those to whom consequences can be imputed or what new obligations one may incur as a result of such imputation. Yet what they sketch is part of what is needed in a theory of moral responsibility. There is an implicit acknowledgment of luck in our responsibilities insofar as the consequences to which Kant refers include those the agent neither foresaw nor intended. Although he uses the language of "can" and "cannot," he is not articulating mere logical possibilities. These principles are put forward as moral principles determining what can be *rightfully* imputed.

Imputation involves not only the assigning of credit or blame but also the determining of forward-looking responsibilities. If bad consequences of my behavior are imputable to me, I may thereby acquire the responsibility to compensate others for damages. Applied to Gauguin and Anna Karenina, Kant's imputation principle for "unlawful action" (in the moral sense of "law") makes each responsible for bad consequences of their choices, as they chose to violate obligations already undertaken.

And what of the bad consequences of a meritorious action? Or of undertaking a risky one that was not required? We can become responsible for consequences here as well, although Kant does not mention these cases. In his infamous essay, "On a Supposed Right to Tell Lies from Benevolent Motives," in which he defends telling the truth to a would-be murderer about the presence in your house of an innocent fugitive whom you had, presumably, undertaken to protect, Kant tacitly appeals to his imputation principle for "unlawful actions" (the principle that consequences can be imputed to an agent who acts wrongly). An imputation principle regarding the voluntary undertaking of risks not wrong in themselves would have served him better. For, consider what he says:

> If you have *by a lie* hindered a man who is even now planning a murder, you are legally responsible for all the consequences. . . . It is possible that whilst you have honestly answered Yes to the murderer's question, whether his intended victim is in the house, the latter may have gone out unobserved, and so not have come in the way of the murderer, . . . whereas, if you lied and said he was not in the house, and he

had really gone out (though unknown to you), so that the
murderer met him as he went, and executed his purpose on
him, then you might with justice be accused as the cause of
his death.[20]

Kant is not simply reporting here on positive law but is taking a position
on how the liar ought to be judged, as a matter of justice. That view
would accord with his second imputation principle *if* we were to con-
cede the wrongness of the lie (which probably most of us would not; it is
easier to defend the view that telling the truth here would be wrong).
Kant's conclusion about responsibility presupposes, rather than estab-
lishes, that the lie was wrong. Although that presupposition is not plausible as the case stands, Kant's conclusion about responsibility for the
consequences gains in plausibility if we suppose that the liar had the
option of remaining silent regarding the fugitive's whereabouts without, in effect, communicating an answer to the question. That is, suppose the lie were in itself not wrong but merely risky, that it was not
necessary to protect the fugitive, although there was a chance that it
would. If I lie in such a case, I assume a risk (against which I would have
been protected, morally, if my lie were morally required). If luck is
against me, I become responsible in this instance for another's death,
not just causally but morally, in that I may incur responsibilities to
survivors as a result.

Apparently taking off from Kant's infamous essay and increasing
along precisely those lines the plausibility of Kant's conclusions, Jean-
Paul Sartre gives us another example of moral luck. In his powerful
short story "The Wall" a political prisoner is about to be shot (at
the wall) for refusing to divulge the whereabouts of his collaborator,
Ramon Gris.[21] In a last-minute attempt to divert his executioners from
finding Gris, the prisoner invents a story that Gris is hiding in the
cemetery. Unbeknownst to him, Gris has in fact lost his asylum and
needing a new hiding place, has moved to the cemetery, with the result
that the authorities find him by following the prisoner's directions. The
prisoner is then freed as an informer (and thereby unwitting betrayer
of his cause) instead of dying a hero. "Traitor" is too strong a judgment. But was he *innocent* of Gris's death? I do not think so.

Yet another horror story of moral luck, illustrating the same principle, is Edith Wharton's *Ethan Frome,* in which a sled crash intended as a
double suicide instead maims both parties for life, spiritually as well as

physically.[22] If we grant that the suicide would not have been wrong in itself, this story portrays another moral risk. Unlike the lorry driver examples, it will not do here simply to conclude that the disaster's improbability justified its risk. The improbability of the disaster may have justified the conclusion that the risk was probably justifiable, which is another matter. That conclusion acknowledges moral luck. Ethan Frome seems to have acknowledged it. At any rate, in the story he accepts the responsibilities of caring for both his wife and his one-time beloved, although the temptation to suicide could easily be far greater after such an accident than before.

Such stories offer tough cases for critics unconvinced of the reality of incident moral luck. Critics point out that luck in Williams's lorry driver example determines whether anyone has evidence to blame the driver but not whether the driver is really culpable.[23] One critic, Henning Jensen, also points out that resulting damage not within the risk created by the faulty character of the agent's act *should* not subject the agent to censure.[24] Both points are well-taken for that kind of case. Yet, the driver, presumably, had an obligation to be on the road (we might take that as a metaphor for making a living), which inevitably involves some degree of risk, and thus something like Kant's first imputation principle comes into play, namely, the principle that absolves us from responsibility for the bad consequences of those of our actions that were morally "due" (required). As "The Wall" and *Ethan Frome* show, however, we cannot always avail ourselves of this kind of excuse from responsibility for consequences not entirely of our own making. Neither the prisoner nor Ethan Frome was obligated to act as he did.

By Kant's second imputation principle, both Gauguin and Anna Karenina incur responsibility for bad consequences of their choices by virtue of acting contrary to their obligations. Gauguin was luckier in that he was at least able to make something of himself, even though that did not compensate his family. Anna Karenina was deeply unlucky. She became an instrument of her own deterioration, even though, causally speaking, it was hardly all her doing. If her husband Alexey Alexandrovitch, her lover Vronsky, some of her former society friends, and sexist social norms were also responsible, that is a separate point. Her responsibility is determinable somewhat independently of others', in terms of the risks of her own choices.

The cases of Ethan Frome and Sartre's prisoner are importantly more like those of Gauguin and Anna Karenina than like that of the unlucky lorry driver, from a moral point of view. Like the driver, Ethan Frome and the prisoner chose in the absence of knowledge of the consequences. Yet, unlike the driver (and like Gauguin and Anna Karenina), they could not cite obligations in justification for proceeding as they did in the face of relevant unknowns.

The claim that good luck might *morally* justify such choices as those of Gauguin or Anna Karenina needs qualification. Whatever the further results, the fact is not altered that others have been wronged. Paradoxically, in consequence of such wrongs an agent's moral career and character may actually improve. A new relationship or environment may bring out better things in the agent even though prior obligations conflict with the choices initiating these changes. Thus we may find the choices of Gauguin and Anna Karenina assessable adequately, even in moral terms, only in retrospect. Whether others are wronged in the immediate situation is only part of a fuller moral assessment of the agent that also includes how the agent's character and moral career develop. There may be no simple way to do justice to the complexities of such an assessment, just as there is no simple way to do justice to the assessment of conduct that is morally wrong although motivated by admirable moral concerns.

In a perceptive critique of Nagel's essay on moral luck, Margaret Walker (then Coyne) makes good sense of the idea that major life choices may be open only to retrospective justification.

> The agent is not a self-sufficient rational will fully expressed in each episode of choice, but is a history of choices . . . for whom episodes are meaningful in terms of rather larger stretches. . . . We ought not to be surprised that . . . pivotal episodes which give sense to large segments are adequately judgeable [*sic*] only in retrospect.[25]

We can take on responsibilities long before we are in a position to know whether what we are doing is justifiable in terms of its relations to other parts of our lives. This suggests that what is at stake in moral justification may be not just an *action* but the *agent*. Some judgments of whether an agent is justified may resemble Aristotelian judgments of *eudaimonia* (commonly translated "happiness" — "happy" in the sense of "fortunate") about which Aristotle even wondered whether we needed to consider what happens after the agent has died.[26] An important point for present purposes is that when we have or take responsibility for something that turns out badly, that typically gives us further responsibilities. Since the process of responding to our previous choices (and failures to choose) can go on indefinitely, it may be impossible to say whether a person is "justified" until that person can no longer choose.

Although Kant admitted luck in the shape and complexity of our moral careers under his principles of imputation, and although he also recognized that gender and ethnicity introduce elements of luck into character development, he did not appreciate the implications of such admissions for his metaphysics of moral agency.[27] He presented striving for moral perfection as though a morally complete self were present each moment, flexing its will like an invisible muscle in a material vacuum.

Interpersonal Relationships as Sources of Moral Luck

Because of the ease of sliding from the perspective of agency, within which we often excuse agents on the basis of nonmoral events, to a perspective from which we see only a nonmoral world of events, Nagel found "moral responsibility" an ultimately incoherent concept. Yet at the same time he found it to be a concept that we cannot help using.[28] He has not sought to abandon it. Rather, his account invites attempts to show that moral responsibility is more than a superficial idea.

One such attempt is the essay by Margaret Walker, mentioned above, in which she analyzes the concept of luck in relation to agency, arguing that luck and agency actually involve each other. "These notions," she writes, "are full members of a cluster of mutually sustaining concepts — the agency-matrix — which sort, and so stand (or fall) together."[29] On her account, "For something to appear as good or bad luck to us requires that it be unforeseen or unpredicted (but it need not be of an unforeseeable or unpredictable kind in principle, or ultimately); and that there is some agent to whom it stands in a particular way, in two respects. It must not be imputable to the agent as the agent's immediate issue, and it must bear favorably or unfavorably on the plans, designs, intended outcomes and payoffs, or projects of that agent."[30] To this we might add that what is central to something's nature is not part of its luck, for it is not then contingent with respect to that thing.

This analysis brings out the relativity of something's status as a piece of luck. My luck may be your responsible (or irresponsible) behavior. As Nel Noddings observes, "how good *I* can be is partly a function of how *you*—the other—receive and respond to me."[31] In their abstract accounts, Williams and Nagel identify luck with contingencies both external and "natural" in a sense that contrasts with "moral." Of their examples, however, only the Gauguin case turns on nonmoral ("natural") contingencies—namely, the talent and determination requisite to greatness—and they are internal to the agent. They belong to Gauguin's capacities for agency, although not for moral agency (and thus remain contingencies with respect to his moral agency). The luck of Anna Karenina and of the German citizens, however, which also belong to the realm of agency, is not entirely "natural" in a sense that contrasts with "moral." This is because it consists largely of unforeseen interpersonal interactions, with consequences for who the interacting agents become. To the extent that who they are when they choose is thus problematic, it is also problematic whose luck is in question. Presumably, it is the luck of Anna Karenina or the German citizens, at a particular point in time, the luck that they have such futures. The negligent lorry driver's bad luck is also not "natural" in a sense that contrasts easily with "moral." Although clearly external, this luck consists in the act of another, namely, the child who ran out into the street.[32]

None of these contingencies leads us out of the realm of agency to the world of mere cause and effect. They lead us back to the worlds of other agents, who may be victims (or beneficiaries) of still others, and so on. The literature on child abuse is a good example of such histories.[33] Luck central to the plots of ancient Greek tragedies that are discussed by Martha Nussbaum also consists primarily in the actions of others. Hecuba's character, for example, degenerates in consequence of her discovery, after she has been enslaved and her daughter Polyxena sacrificed, of the murder of her youngest son by the man with whom he was left for safekeeping.[34] Recognizing moral luck does not require what Nagel calls "the view from nowhere." All we need is the "view from there." Focusing as Nagel does on relationships between acts and events is neither necessary nor sufficient for coming to terms with moral luck. It is insufficient because as long as agents are formed and modified through interaction with other agents, there is bound to be moral luck within the world of agency. And it is unnecessary if the most important sources of luck do tend to lie in human interaction and development.

Obvious major sources of constitutive moral luck are relationships with significant others (parents, lovers) and relationships structured by basic social institutions (educational, economic). The point of taking responsibility for institutions and relationships is often to resist evils, such as those of oppression and abuse. The point of taking responsibility for oneself is often to avoid complicity in such evils. In looking at how bad luck is sometimes met and even overcome in a highly self-conscious way perhaps we can see more clearly the development of responsible agency and why it matters.

Oppression and Childhood Abuse

Women's oppression and childhood abuse are intertwined historically. Both are morally damaging, and the damage of one can apparently lead to that of the other. Oppression makes some of our choices difficult, others tempting, attractive, easy. It sets up child abuse by defining wretched conditions of childcare, making targets for sexual abuse of those who are fragile — the feminine, who are taught to be childlike, and real children — and insulating caretakers from accountability. Although it is morally problematic for beneficiaries of oppression to hold its victims responsible for bad conduct, victims have responsibilities of their own to peers and descendants. Overcoming and resisting our own oppression require us to *take* responsibility for situations for which others could not reasonably hold us responsible (in the credit sense), despite our complicity. Thus activists often prefer the term "survivor" to "victim," to emphasize activity rather than passivity, while at the same time retaining a sense of appropriate attributions of responsibility in the backward-looking, credit-and-blame sense.[35]

Taking responsibility is often complicated for the oppressed by moral damage they have sustained. One's character and values can change dramatically in the process of liberation. Some changes are even constitutive of liberation. In becoming liberated we discover and create "truer" values, even "truer" selves. We may discover the value of honor, for example, and cease to identify with the perspectives of those who put us down. Such resistance can come only from within. Liberation cannot come simply from outside. But how is it possible for us as damaged agents to liberate ourselves from the damage? And how can we act for our futures, not knowing just whom we may liberate?

When I think about this, I find that it helps to apply to oppressed individuals strategies analogous to those that an oppressed group uses in developing responsible agency. What is needed, first of all, is a kind of internal unity, integrity. Oppression splinters us (both within ourselves, as individuals, and from each other, within a group) by putting us constantly into double binds. A damaged individual who has splintered into several personalities, identities, or personality or identity fragments may be importantly analogous to an oppressed group. Even those of us who have not splintered that far are likely to be sites of seriously warring inclinations, moods, likes, and dislikes elicited by the double-binds of oppressive institutions.

An oppressed group (such as a group of women or members of a minority religious or ethnic group) takes responsibility for resisting its oppression by addressing, first, its internal hostilities (hostilities of members of the group toward other members), substituting strong internal bonds and cooperative networks. This requires internal communication, discovery of shared experience, learning about the sources of internal hostilities and how they function to mold members of the group in the interests of outsiders and to keep them preoccupied with basic day-to-day survival. Establishing internal bonds requires members of the group to discover what is of value in themselves independently of service to outsiders. Resistance also requires coming up with internal resources and reserving them for internal use, severing intimate connections with a hostile environment, learning to say no to external would-be controllers and to take the consequences. By such means, a group moves toward becoming a community. Its members may get into position to resist their oppression, to refuse to be molded, reduced, and immobilized, or marginalized, disempowered, exploited, and so forth. Their need for autonomy in relation to a hostile environment is relative to their history of oppression. Such autonomy does not imply that they will not be affected by what is outside. Rather, they will be affected differently. They will develop their own protection systems against outside dangers wherever possible, for example, instead of relying on outside protection, an example discussed further in Chapter Five in connection with rape terrorism.

In the case of some adults who were severely abused as children, the analogy between an oppressed group and a morally damaged individual is striking. If some who dissociate into multiple identities or fragments do so as a way to cope with stresses of abuse, they can also be like oppressed groups of people in the internal — or "horizontal" — hostilities and tensions they manifest. Just as some members of oppressed communities are often dangerously hostile to others, some personality fragments can also be dangerously hostile to others. Such internal war is counterproductive with respect to resisting outside oppression, although it may be the best a young person (or members of a group) can do at a given time to counteract depression and survive to an age at which more creative strategies become possible.

As a result of the recovered memory debates, the topic of multiple personality and its relation to childhood abuse has become even more controversial than it already was.[36] It already was controversial among psychiatrists who disagreed with each other on the question whether or not multiple personality is induced by suggestion by therapists. Now it is controversial among a wider public who disagree with each other about the trustworthiness of memory claims made by personalities or fragments, regardless how those personalities or fragments originated. The third edition of the American Psychiatric Association's *Diagnostic and Statistical Manual of Mental Disorders* (DSM-III-R) states under "predisposing factors" to multiple personality that "several studies indicate that in nearly all cases, the disorder has been preceded by abuse (often sexual) or another form of severe emotional trauma in childhood."[37] The fourth edition more cautiously states that individuals with "dissociative identity disorder" ("multiple personality disorder" in the previous edition) *frequently report* "having experienced severe physical and sexual abuse, especially during childhood" and that "controversy surrounds the accuracy of such reports."[38] Both editions find the condition diagnosed three to nine times more frequently in adult females and find more personalities or identities in females than in males.[39] The hypothesis that a misogynist social environment is often implicated is both difficult to resist and difficult to prove.

Regarding the validity of recovered memories, I take seriously, for purposes of publicity or legal action, the need to corroborate reports of abuse. Why suppose that memories here — unlike everywhere else — are infallible? But also I find that in many discussions of such reports, the independent evidence looks strong.

In published "multobiographies," as Ian Hacking calls them, of those who have been identified, or have identified themselves, as multiple personalities, there are often narratives of childhood sexual abuse perpetrated by trusted caretakers.[40] Hacking is skeptical of a causal connection between abuse and dissociation even where there is no reasonable doubt of the reality of either abuse or dissociation. Unlike some skeptics, he does not doubt the reality of either widespread child abuse or the experience, independent of therapeutic suggestion, of multiple identities. Yet, if dissociation is a response in the sense of a creative solution to the stresses of abuse, it should not be surprising that studies do not reveal it to be simply a causal effect of abuse. For responses in this context are actions taken by agents who can see themselves as choosing from among various ways of responding. The search for a causal connection comes from what Strawson might call a depersonalized point of view. Understanding dissociation as a response comes from a personalized one.

It is plausible that multiple personality, like the hostile divisions among members of an oppressed group, may have different sources, one of which is childhood abuse. For present purposes, however, it matters less whether the abuse is real in just the ways that an agent reports it than that she has such memories. Such memories are themselves a source of stress. What matters even more is the damage to integrity that can come from dissociation and subsequent horizontal hostility. Reading multobiographies of women some of whose personalities or fragments recall childhood abuse and others of whose fragments seem to identify with the abuser calls to my mind the experience of feminist consciousness-raising in the 1970s. Many of us, who did not think of ourselves as dissociated (however alienated we might have been), found that we had learned to identify with perspectives that were not our own, perspectives opposed to our own best interests. In the process of rejecting these identifications, we were not always right about the particular abuses we thought we had suffered from individual men. Yet what was important was the true realization that most of us had suffered those kinds of abuses from men and from male-dominated institutions. Identifying with their perspectives on ourselves seemed to us, in retrospect, to have been a coping strategy. Our ability to describe in that way what we did also revealed to us that we had, as individuals, more than one perspective and that some of our perspectives conflicted with each other. Seeing such phenomena as responses to external abuse makes a certain sense of them. But they present practical moral problems for anyone who has such experience, regardless of their source. Whatever the source of dissociation, fragments that are at war with each other interfere with the possibility of effective resistance to real future dangers.

In multiple personality there appear to be several centers of consciousness (from two to more than a hundred) with varying degrees of mutual awareness and communication, in some cases, no communication or mutual awareness at all. Some appear to take a perspective of observation on the one "in charge of the body," who takes the perspective of agency and may have no awareness of other personalities or fragments of herself who are "watching." Amnesia (part of DSM-IV's diagnostic criteria for dissociative identity disorder) presents obvious problems for reliability. The often conflicting styles, temperaments, desires, and scruples of different identities can also present major problems for one's ability to function as a social agent.

DSM-IV presents dissociative identity disorder explicitly as an integrity problem: "Dissociative Identity Disorder reflects a failure to integrate various aspects of identity, memory, and consciousness." But whose integrity problem is it? On the answer to this question DSM-IV appears to be in agreement with the philosopher Stephen Braude in assuming, or positing, some underlying psychic agency who has the integrity problem.[41] The analogy of an oppressed group not yet a community suggests a potential agent, however, rather than an underlying actual agent. In either case, the practical task is to produce appropriately responsible agency.

In dysfunctional multiples, some personalities exploit the naivete of others, especially of the one usually identified in the literature as the host. When in trouble, they may withdraw, leaving a perplexed amnesiac to take the consequences. Morally, a multiple (or even a fragment) who exhibits such behavior lacks integrity. Instead of taking responsibility, the dysfunctional multiple backs off. Her values, as those of a fragmented being at war with herself, are mutually inconsistent. No one is sufficiently in charge for her to be reliable, although she may be clever and many of her fragments or personalities highly skilled at "passing," having learned how from an early age.

In the case of the woman known as Sybil (and in many others), the therapist took reintegration as a goal, understanding reintegration as achieved when there is one unified sense of identity with no serious amnesia.[42] In the case of Truddi Chase, however, narrated by several of her ninety-two personalities, the therapist deemed such reintegration impossible because the fragment who might have been identified as the "host" had she been available (the one from whom the first others had split) was reported by the others as having "died," that is, as having ceased to have direct access to the external world, to be in charge of the body, at an early age.[43] Instead of reintegration, her therapist proposed the goal of cooperation among the remaining personalities, which they eventually accepted.

Fragments of a dysfunctional multiple, like the individuals in an oppressed group, cannot take responsibility effectively alone. Whatever one does is likely to be undone by others. Some sort of integration is needed to interrelate differently and thereby cease complicity in one's own oppression or in maintaining one's own distress. This requires that individuals, or fragments, learn to listen to each other and respect each other's point of view, to bond with each other instead of doing each other in, to learn as much as possible about the history and sources of internal hostilities and relevant external exploitations.

Ordinary acquisition of integrity, like the integration of a multiple, also requires reconciling values, perceptions, and commitments. It requires internal bonding — being committed to care for ourselves as well as respecting ourselves, distinguishing between friendly and hostile points of view on ourselves and within ourselves, recognizing the differences between being valued for ourselves and being valued only for what we are to others.

For a survivor of abuse who experiences herself as multiple the acquisition of integrity can have a life or death importance. Tolstoy's *Anna Karenina* ended her life in part because she could not or would not accept responsibility for the life to which her choice led. Some multiples live in fear of being murdered by a personality or fragment whose values and commitments may be wildly disregarded by others. Some fragments with such murderous intentions, apparently, have the illusion that they will survive the murder. Even where the importance is not life or death, integrity is important to morale and to the possibility of self-esteem and pride. Having certain kinds of commitments and living up to them both define who we are and form a basis for valuing ourselves.

It may be objected that the analogy between the integrity of a group and that of an individual is unsound, because an adult is supposed to have one unified sense of identity, whereas a group is supposed to have recognizably different members, each with senses of their own identities as individuals and not just as parts of the group. Yet a group can also become an agent in its own right, as when it becomes a community. And it is difficult to clarify the assumption that normal adults are supposed to have just one unified sense of identity if that means anything more than that they are not supposed to have serious amnesia problems or be deeply torn apart by their conflicting inclinations and values. Communities are not supposed to have serious communication gaps, either, or be seriously torn apart by conflicting interest groups. Even without amnesia, as individuals we may easily have more than one set of personality traits and values, which we may not bother to integrate unless circumstances call for it. Different interactions and environments actualize different and sometimes dissonant sides of ourselves. Taking responsibility for oneself need not presuppose the goal of eliminating internal difference or divergence. The goal instead may be, as in the case of the Troops for Truddi Chase and in the case of pluralistic societies, cooperation or commitment to shared basic moral values, such as honesty and respect.

Conclusion

By looking at the contrived acquisition of responsibility (and at choices to abdicate responsibility) in response to bad moral luck, I mean to give substance to the idea that understanding moral luck can add depth to our understanding of moral responsibility. Potentialities for becoming responsible may be realized without much self-consciousness in a moderately favorable environment. Agents are then in a favorable position to enter into durable positive relationships and to resist threats of harm to themselves and their communities. Under such conditions, autonomy may be less important than friendly interdependencies.

What develops without much self-consciousness under moderately favorable conditions may be stunted or damaged by oppression or abuse. The development of responsible agency then may require the deliberate construction of friendly space and a monitoring of what is permitted inside. The need for such autonomy, unlike the need for integrity, is thus seen as specific rather than universal and as having as its background a hostile environment from which separation is necessary for healing and growth. Such autonomy may be a prerequisite to integrity.

Responsible agency is not defined simply by autonomy, however. Morally responsible agency includes the integrity of having basic moral commitments and sticking by them. Responsible agency does not necessarily dissolve with an appreciation of our interconnections with the environments that produce and sustain us. Rather, it dissolves when *internal* connections are broken or inadequately developed. Friendly external bonds can play an important role in establishing and maintaining good internal connections. It may be our luck to have to, or not to have to, work hard or self-consciously to develop and preserve such bonds.

Nor is the importance of morally responsible agency diminished by differences among us in the ease or difficulty of developing it. For the importance of morality does not rest simply on the extent to which it enables us to take credit for self-manufacture. Its importance lies, in part, in grounding the will to resist such things as abuse, exploitation, and oppression.

WOMEN'S VOICES
AND FEMALE CHARACTER

Pasts we inherit affect who we can become. As gendered beings in a society with a history of patriarchy, women and men inherit different pasts, and consequently different social expectations, lines of communication, opportunities, barriers. If these things influence character development, they make gender part of our moral luck. This chapter takes up female moral luck in misogynist society. I understand female character not as one type of character but as a family of character possibilities that are understandable in terms of one's social positioning as female.

The idea that virtues (and presumably faults) may be gender-related is suggested by Carol Gilligan's work on female moral development, although she does not frame her hypotheses in terms of virtues and vices. In her influential book *In a Different Voice* she reports hearing two different moralities in the voices of women and men. She describes them as an ethic of care (or response) in the case of many women and an ethic of justice (or rights) in the case of most men.[1] She does not hold that either gender, or either ethic, is superior to the other on the whole but only that each centers different values and concepts. This, in turn, suggests that each gender may have different characteristic virtues (and, presumably, faults). Although she finds the voices empirically correlated with women and men, she says these voices are "characterized not by gender but theme."[2] Yet the empirical correlations are interesting for ethics given that ethical theorists have been until recently almost exclusively relatively privileged men.

The correlation is not simple, however. In an essay published five years after *In a Different Voice,* Carol Gilligan refines her account of the voices' distribution. She notes that although nearly all interviewees could readily understand and enter into the spirit of both justice and care orientations, they could not enter into both *at the same time* and that most tended to have a focus on, or preference for, one or the other as the one that felt more natural, more like the "right" one. In a study of eighty "educationally advantaged North American adolescents and adults," she found that "two-thirds . . . focused their attention on one set of concerns, with focus defined as 75 percent or more of the considerations raised pertaining either to justice or to care," that men and women "were equally likely to demonstrate the focus phenomenon (two-thirds of both sexes fell into the outlying focus categories)" but also that "with one exception, all of the men who focused, focused on justice" while "the women divided, with roughly one third focusing on justice and one third on care."[3] In other words, apparently, the focus of half of the women who focused was on justice. Still, if representative, her findings would be significant in that were only North American educationally advantaged men studied, the care focus could be missed altogether.

The European educationally advantaged creators of much, if not most, modern ethical theory sound like the men in Carol Gilligan's studies.[4] She may be right to emphasize differences in theme more than gender if the gender correlation gains its significance from social and political histories. That it does so appears to be supported by Sandra Harding's finding that the voices of African men have more in common with Carol Gilligan's care ethics than with the justice ethics heard in the voices of European American men.[5] Joan Tronto concurs, noting that "a more telling finding [than the gender correlation] is that the differences Gilligan found between men and women may also describe the differences between working and middle class, white and ethnic minorities, and that a gender difference may not be prominent among other groups in the population besides the relatively privileged people who have constituted Gilligan's samples."[6] If we distinguish gender as a social construction from sex as a biological category, however, attending to the gender correlation of Carol Gilligan's voices within societies that have histories of misogyny may be a good way both to expose biases in ethical theory and at the same time to gain deeper understanding of what has gone ethically wrong in those histories.

The two moralities as Carol Gilligan heard them differ in how they represent the self, relationships, and moral dilemmas, in where they find the greatest dangers, and in how they resolve conflicts. The care voice speaks of conflicts of responsibilities where the justice voice speaks of conflicts of rights. The care voice resolves conflicts by the method of inclusion. The justice voice uses methods of fairness, such as balancing claims or taking turns. Care encourages contextual thinking, narrative style. Justice encourages categorical thinking, applications of abstract principles. The justice voice finds *aggression* the major source of hurt. The care voice finds it in *failures of response*. The care voice defines the self through weblike networks of relationship. The justice voice defines the self in terms of individual achievement, understanding relationships hierarchically. Studies of their fantasies seem to show women who speak with the voice of care seeking safety in affiliation but men who speak with the voice of justice finding it in independence.

On the question of how these two patterns are related to each other, Carol Gilligan's views have changed. Her early idea was that at maturity members of each sex came to appreciate truths available to the other all along and that the two perspectives were then integrated: women with a care perspective found that it is important to include themselves in the range of their care (and thus to insist on rights for women); men with a justice focus found that it is not enough to restrain their aggression but also important to extend themselves in caring ways. "Development of both sexes would therefore seem to entail an integration of rights and responsibilities through the discovery of the complementarity of these disparate views."[7] After further interviews, however, she seems to have dropped the complementarity idea, putting in its stead the idea that justice and care offer alternative gestalts, like the famous duck-rabbit. We can conceptualize morality either way, she finds, but not both ways at once, and each gestalt has a place for everything found in the other one, but a different place.[8]

In allowing interconnections between the concepts of justice and care, the new view seems a theoretical improvement. Yet the inability to take both perspectives at once remains troubling in that we may need sometimes to resolve conflicts between the claims of rights and those of personal attachment. How can we judge ethical conflicts between considerations of justice and care if we cannot hold them in mind without a priori subordinating considerations of one sort to those of the other?[9] As Marilyn Friedman argues in looking at cases, neither a priori ranking is plausible.[10] An inability to entertain both perspectives at once may suggest the presence of something other than justice and care — such as an oppressive relationship — skewing both perspectives.

Carol Gilligan's finding of gender-bias in her (late) colleague Lawrence Kohlberg's conception of human moral development is implicitly similarly critical of contemporary philosophical ethics. Kohlberg's stage analysis of moral development traces the growth of a sense of justice more or less as John Rawls understands the sense of justice.[11] The stage that Kohlberg long regarded as highest is an orientation to principles of justice and welfare governing relationships on a formal, impersonal basis. Like his predecessor Jean Piaget, he presented justice as evolving from and replacing an ethic of personal relations. Yet personal relationships are not left behind in the lives of most adults. Neither considered the form moral maturity might take in informal, personal relationships, such as those of Anna Karenina with her husband, their son, and with Count Vronsky. Nor has modern philosophical ethics paid serious attention, until very recent decades, to personal relationships and their dilemmas. If something like Carol Gilligan's hypothesis were true, we might expect a bias in ethical theory toward justice, rights, and abstract action-guiding principles, given the history of sexism. Such biases are in fact evident in the ideal contract and utilitarian ethical theories that have dominated modern European and American philosophy for more than two centuries. Yet these kinds of theories have not agreed with each other on the priority of justice, nor have they always been dominant.

An ethically more modest hypothesis — less exciting, perhaps less romantic — also found in Carol Gilligan's work but often not distinguished from the "justice and care" hypothesis, is that the responsibilities of the different kinds of relationships that have been the focus of the choices of women and men in sexist societies yield different ethical preoccupations, methods, priorities, even concepts. A focus on differences in context and relationship is characteristic of the writings on women and care by Annette Baier, Virginia Held, Sarah Hoagland, and Joan Tronto.[12] In patriarchies, more of the responsibilities of certain personal and informal relationships are assigned to women and more of those of formal and impersonal relationships defined by social institutions to men. Drawing on different senses of responsibility distinguished in the previous chapter, I propose in the final section of this chapter to substitute for the justice and care hypothesis a more modest hypothesis connecting different senses of responsibility with the different voices. Even if ideals of justice do have special connections with some kinds of responsibilities and ideals of care have special connections with others, framing the hypothesis in terms of responsibilities may encourage more questioning of the justice of background distributions of responsibilities and their impact on the development of caring dispositions.

A significant advantage of the more modest hypothesis is that it will put us in a better position to identify moral damage resulting from and perpetuating sex oppression. When people find it necessary to affiliate with "protectors," for example, their affirmations of those affiliations may have little to do with love, though the language of love be the language of their discourse. Women's care-taking is often unpaid or underpaid labor performed from a variety of motives. Even more likely to be mistaken for a caring virtue is women's misplaced gratitude to men who take less than full advantage of their power to abuse or who offer the privilege of service in exchange for "protection." Women have assumed care-taking responsibilities as a debt of gratitude for such "benefactions," a matter explored further in Chapter Six.

Misplaced gratitude is one kind of moral damage women have suffered. There are others. Feminist thinkers are understandably reluctant to address publicly women's reputation for lying, cunning, deceit, and manipulation. But, *are* these vices, one may ask, if they are needed for self-defense? They are surely not virtues, even if they are justified from the point of view of justice. Those who tell just the right lies to the right people on the right occasions may have a useful and needed skill. But it does not promote human good, even if it is needed for survival under oppressive conditions. Human good may be unrealizable under such conditions. Lying blocks the trust of friendship. Adrienne Rich, exploring the idea of honor among women, noted long ago how disruptive lying is of trust.[13] Even though you are confident that I will lie to you only when I am justified, if you believe I am often justified, how can you rely on me?

Thus we need to be sensitive to the possibility that members of a sexist society give voice to vices or survival strategies (for which there would be no systematic need in a good social environment) disguised by the honorific language of "justice" and "care," which enables them to pass for virtues. Histories of oppression make it important to hear between the spoken words, to listen with a "third ear." The privileged are liable to arrogance with its blindness to others' perspectives. The oppressed are liable to low self-esteem, ingratiation, affiliation with abusers (for example, so-called female masochism), as well as to a tendency to dissemble, fear of being conspicuous, and chameleonism — taking on the colors of our environment as protection against assault.

Histories of exploitation lead many women to identify with service, to find our value in our utility or ability to please. Moral damage among both privileged and oppressed tends to be unselfconscious, mutually reinforcing, and stubborn. When our identities are at stake, oppression is hard to face. Beneficiaries face guilt issues and are liable to defensiveness. The oppressed face damage to an already precarious self-esteem in admitting relative impotence.

It may also be our moral luck to develop special insights and sensitivities, even under oppressive institutions. Divisions of responsibility may divide opportunities for moral insight by distributing differently the decision-making experience that develops it. That, however, is partly an empirical hypothesis and cannot be evaluated by the methods of philosophy alone.

The remainder of this chapter has three parts. The first offers a review of past philosophical traditions concerning justice, care, and women. The second contrasts the kind of feminist critique represented by Carol Gilligan with that of Mary Wollstonecraft, who is utterly skeptical of the idea of "women's virtues." Here I argue that correcting systematic misperceptions of women by men, as Carol Gilligan's work does, is not enough to vindicate women's characters, nor, therefore, to lend much support to the "corrective hypothesis" that women's values and aspirations can deepen and correct defects in dominant views of ethical thinking. Drawing on senses of responsibility distinguished in the previous chapter, the third part explores a way of reconceiving the two perspectives that makes the "corrective hypothesis" more plausible.

Women, Justice, and Care: Philosophical Traditions

The thesis that women and men have different ethics is not without precedent. Charlotte Perkins Gilman (a feminist who preferred to be identified as a sociologist) argued in 1898 that domesticated women develop an ethic of altruism that eventually has a civilizing influence on men, who need it because they develop an ethic of egoism in the competitive world of the marketplace.[14] Nor is it only feminists who have put forward such ideas. Kant and Schopenhauer, each misogynist in his own way, maintained that women and men are good in different ways that resemble Carol Gilligan's care and justice orientations. In ancient philosophy, however, where friendship received more philosophical attention, care was less associated with gender, and connections between justice and care received more emphasis.

The concept of obligation turns up in Aristotle's ethics under the heading of friendship rather than in the book on justice, which is where one would expect today to find that concept. In the opening chapter of his first book on friendship he observes:

> When [we] are friends [we] have no need of justice, while when [we] are just [we] need friendship as well, and the truest form of justice is thought to be a friendly quality.[15]

Apparently referring to these remarks a few chapters later, he says:

> Friendship and justice seem, as we have said at the outset of our discussion, to be concerned with the same objects and exhibited between the same persons. For in every community there is thought to be some form of justice, and friendship too; at least men address as friends their fellow voyagers and fellow soldiers, and so too those associated with them in any other kind of community. And the extent of their association is the extent of their friendship, as it is the extent to which justice exists between them.[16]

Aristotle's modern translator, Sir David Ross, warns the reader that "Bks. 8 and 9, on friendship, do not form an essential part of a treatise on ethics, and certainly so full a treatment of it seems out of place; it is not improbable that these two were originally a separate treatise."[17] These two books offer the most sustained discussion of friendship in the history of philosophy prior to the twentieth century. One may wonder where Ross thought such a discussion did belong.

What does it mean to say that friends do not need justice although justice needs friendship? On this view friendship is fundamental, underlying even justice. This is plausible if "friendship" in this context means simply *goodwill*, a concept Aristotle discusses explicitly only in his books on friendship. If "justice" here refers to legal recourse, the claim that friends do not need it may be sound as an ideal, if not as a generalization. Friendship relies on trust, leaving much to discretion. Rules are often less useful here. This does not imply, however, that *fairness* is unimportant. On the contrary, one's responsiveness where enforcement is not forthcoming is a greater test of one's fairness than where there is possible recourse to sanctions. Without a well-developed sense of fairness, friendship is thin and legal recourse may be needed.

Aristotle's view appears to have been that good friendship requires a fine-tuned sense of reciprocity. Regarding "unequal friendships" (among which he includes husband and wife), he thought complementarity might compensate for an impossibility of reciprocity in kind. However unsatisfactory that solution, he was at least aware of a problem here. In her early work Carol Gilligan observed that at mid-life men come to see the value of intimacy, whereas women tend to have seen it all along. This suggests a serious reciprocity problem when one considers the implications for the quality of heterosexual intimacy prior to mid-life or for the judgment of those who valued it.

Modern European ethical traditions have been far more ready than ancient ones to separate justice and care. Notoriously, Sigmund Freud criticized women's sense of justice as deficient.[18] As Carol Gilligan observes, the same behavior underlying this common criticism of women by men is often cited in modern times under different descriptions as evidence of women's "special goodness" — caring, sensitivity, responsiveness to others' needs, appreciation of the concrete particular.[19] Both the criticism and the praise are part of a dominant tradition in modern Northern moral philosophy.

Kant and Schopenhauer, for example, found virtues gender-related, with assessments of this purported fact differing less than one might expect, given their differing conceptions of morality. "The very thought of seeing women administer justice raises a laugh," says Schopenhauer, in his "prize" essay, *On the Basis of Morality*. "They are far less capable than men of understanding and sticking to universal principles," although "they surpass men in the virtues of *philanthropy* and *lovingkindness* [*Menschenliebe*], for the origin of this is . . . intuitive."[20] On women and principles, he followed Kant, who had exclaimed, "I hardly believe the fair sex is capable of principles," speculating that instead "Providence has put in their breast kind and benevolent sensations, a fine feeling for propriety, and a complaisant soul."[21] Within the terms of Kant's own moral theory, the implication was that women's virtues are not moral. This appears to have been his ideal for women, not something he saw as a problem.

Schopenhauer's views on women, rather than Kant's, have become notorious, thanks to Schopenhauer's vitriolic essay, "On Women," which mocks sexist ideals of female beauty: "Only the male intellect, clouded by the sexual impulse, could call the undersized, narrow-shouldered, broad-hipped, and short-legged sex the fair sex."[22] Although he believed character was inborn, we can read Schopenhauer's attacks on women today as an indictment of femininity rather than of women, if we distinguish between gender concepts (femininity and masculinity) as social constructions and sex concepts (femaleness and maleness) as biological categories. Nothing comparable can save the relevant views of Kant.

At the age of forty, Kant took up the topic of women in a work seldom read by moral philosophers and in a chapter announcing itself as on "the interrelations of the sexes." "Women will avoid the wicked not because it is unright, but because it is ugly," he observes, after remarking that "the virtue of a woman is a *beautiful virtue*" and "that of the male sex should be a *noble virtue*."[23] Traits identified here as women's virtues were identified in the previous chapter of the same work as merely "adoptive virtues" and contrasted there with genuine virtues. "Adoptive virtues" are not based on principle, although they can lead to (outwardly) right actions. Kant's view was that one with "adoptive virtues," such as sympathy and complaisance, is goodhearted, but that only one who is virtuous on principle "is a righteous person."[24] Kant's ideals for women are those we might expect for domestic pets. His "adoptive virtues" sound like developments of what he eventually called, in his work on religion, "predispositions to animality" by contrast with "predispositions to humanity."[25]

Kant's theoretical value distinctions should have enabled him to offer an unprecedented critique of sexism, one unavailable to John Stuart Mill, who later attempted such a thing within the more limited conceptual framework of utilitarian ethics. In his *Groundwork* Kant distinguishes relative value, or "price" — in Mill's terms, "utility" — from absolute value, or "dignity," a concept for which Mill's ethics had no very coherent place (which, fortunately, did not stop him from appealing to it in argument). What has a price can have substituted for it something of equivalent value. What has dignity has no price, no equivalent.[26] Only morality and humanity insofar as it is capable of morality have dignity, according to Kant. He presents as the very essence of immorality treating persons as though they have merely a relative value. Kant might have used this idea to expose the immorality of conventional valuations of women instead of endorsing those valuations. Instead he comes close to the view that women have price whereas men have dignity.

Because Kant does not reduce beauty to utility, his view of women may not be quite that crass.[27] Yet beauty is not an absolute ("unconditioned") value, according to Kant. At least, that its value is not absolute is implied by the view of the *Groundwork* that only morality and humanity insofar as capable of morality are absolutely good. Kant understood beauty to be a disinterested value. But there is no incompatibility between taking an interest in beauty and the enjoyment of beauty being disinterested in the sense that it does not consist in the satisfaction of (prior) interests. If, as his discussion suggests, Kant really took female value to lie in women's capacity to satisfy men's interests in beauty, he did fall into the position that — in his own unsurpassable terminology — women have price rather than dignity. Late in life when Kant returned to the topic of women in his *Anthropology*, he was no longer commenting on women's beauty but, rather, on our usefulness in curbing men's sexual impulses, for which purposes Providence had endowed us with sharp tongues and manipulative skills.[28]

Schopenhauer assessed female character by a different conception of morality from that of Kant. He found Kant's "adoptive virtues" to be genuinely ethical, holding that compassion is the motive that gives moral worth to actions, that it underlies both justice and what he called *Menschenliebe* (which E.F.J. Payne translates as "philanthropy").[29] Of these two virtues, justice and *Menschenliebe*, he found justice the more important. Thus in finding that women have more *Menschenliebe* and that men have more justice, he found women morally inferior. His view that either of these traits is a virtue is paradoxical, however, given his profoundly hostile attitude toward humanity. The greatest paradox of Schopenhauer's ethics is that he valued so highly compassion for beings whom he found contemptible.

Had Schopenhauer not rejected the Kantian concept of absolute value, he might have avoided that paradox. He might have held, in disagreement with Kant, that one of the things that gives humanity absolute value is the capacity to care, or certain forms of it, that this is what makes humans worthy of sympathy and compassion, as Kant had held that the capacity for a certain sort of respect is what makes us worthy of receiving that respect.

Something like this criticism that a wiser Schopenhauer might have made of Kant's theory of moral character is suggested by Carol Gilligan's attempt to vindicate the moral development of women in the face of the Kantian moral theory that is presupposed in the Kohlbergian literature on moral development.[30] Not love of humanity, however, but the capacity for affiliation is what Carol Gilligan claims to hear in women's "different voice." Something in what she hears seems ethically important and sound. "Women," she notes, "try to change the rules in order to preserve relationships" while "men, in abiding by these rules, depict relationships as easily replaced."[31] The sense of relationships as not replaceable recalls Kant's insistence that what has dignity cannot have an equivalent put in its place. However, relationships are valued in Carol Gilligan's care ethics as particulars, not as instances of general kinds, and through them, individuals seem to be valued also in their particularity rather than for what they have in common with human beings generally.

To sustain the view that the capacity for love is part of moral character, we need an understanding of this capacity that is comparable in sophistication to Kant's understanding of the capacity to act on principle. Just as not every passionate attachment to principle is valuable, neither is every passionate attachment to people. Kant appreciated this point in regard to principles. In a little-known passage from the same work in which he discusses women's "beautiful virtue," he says:

> Among men there are but few who behave according to principles — which is extremely good, as it can so easily happen that one errs in these principles, and then the resulting disadvantage extends all the further, the more universal the principle and the more resolute the person who has set it before himself.[32]

This danger did not deter Kant from the search for attachments to principle that are valuable in themselves, a search that led him to his famous Categorical Imperative: Act only on that maxim through which you can at the same time will that it should become a universal law.[33] Perhaps we should not be deterred either from searching for interpersonal attachments that are valuable in themselves. Virginia Held has argued recently that one of the things that distinguishes the relations of parents to children is that the value of the relationship tends to lie at least partly within the relationship itself rather than in some ulterior object to be achieved.[34] And yet, as the next section indicates, the obstacles to finding absolute values in women's voices in patriarchal society are formidable.

The most powerful criticism of care ethics in modern philosophy comes from Nietzsche, who targeted the ethics of Christian charity as a "slave morality."[35] The Gospels of the Christian New Testament present the disagreement between Jesus and the Pharisees over the value of the law as though it were a conflict between love and justice. Yet, Nietzsche heard this "love" as a fantasy of the weak who are unable to exact the justice they would rather have if they could get it. "Love" also becomes a euphemism here for such things as service to others and meddling diversions from one's own misery. In an age when Harriet Taylor and John Stuart Mill had argued, following Mary Wollstonecraft, that the character defects of powerless uneducated women were likely to corrupt the characters of their husbands and sons, Nietzsche saw "slave values" in democratic society as generally corrupting those who would be better off valuing power and autonomy.[36] On his view, justice originates in the ethics of those who value power and autonomy, whereas the ethics exalting sympathy, pity, and "love" has its source in a sour grapes movement by the impotent rabble.

I find Nietzsche's critique of morality more interesting than many of his positive ethical views. His accounts of both justice and friendship leave much to be desired, as he failed to appreciate such elements as reciprocity and attachment, which seem more essential to justice and friendship, respectively, than the power he exalted. However, we should take seriously in relation to women's voices in patriarchal society questions analogous to the critical questions he raised about Christian care ethics.

Women and Affiliation: Some Problems

I think of the views of Kant and Schopenhauer, and others like them from the academic canon, as "the patriarchal view." Feminists have criticized the patriarchal view from different angles. Like Carol Gilligan, some defend female character as "different but also valuable," arguing that the theories by which we appear deficient are faulty. I think of this as "the rosy view," because it makes everyone look good. Other critics, like Mary Wollstonecraft, reject so-called female goodness as a euphemism for vices in women that make it easier for men to control us.[37] In 1792 in *A Vindication of the Rights of Woman,* she argued that women in sexist society become morally deformed, neither loving nor just. Contrary to what the title of that work suggests, it was not really about rights but about female character. The intention, apparently, was to defend the education of women and girls to prepare us for equal rights with men. Noticing similarities between the vices of women and those of relatively powerless men in military service, she disagreed with her contemporaries Jean Jacques Rousseau and Kant on the gender-relatedness of virtues. Her view was that *duties* might vary but *virtues* are the same for everyone. She ridiculed the idea that men who were accountable to no one and women who were powerless, abused, and uneducated each have special kinds of goodness. I think of Mary Wollstonecraft's view as "the skeptical view." As she understood it, the problem with female and male character, as they are most readily distinguished in a sexist society, is not that they are incomplete or simply "different" but that they are warped from the start.

However mutually incompatible they appear, the protests of Carol Gilligan and Mary Wollstonecraft both seem right. Although I have wanted to find more truth in the rosy view, it seems to me utterly critical not to deny the truths of the skeptical view. And yet that view sounds something like the Kohlbergian position that Carol Gilligan has criticized and against which she has wished to defend the voice of care.

As with Nietzsche, I find Carol Gilligan's critique more persuasive than some of her positive hypotheses about the two voices. She exposes important misperceptions of women in her disagreements with Kohlberg, Freud, and others regarding what she calls the justice perspective, which she finds inadequate as a picture of human moral development. First, according to Kohlberg's moral stages, women can easily appear more concerned with approval and more conventional than men when what we are actually doing is exhibiting a concern for maintaining relationships. In maintaining relationships, we respect points of view different from our own and attempt to empathize with them. This does not imply that we agree with those views. In the interests of social harmony, we often do not *express* disagreement. Second, Freud found women to have "weak ego-boundaries," poor self-definition, problems with separation and autonomy, and a weaker sense of justice, at least "legal sense." He concluded that women are deficient in moral reasoning. Carol Gilligan turns the tables on him, suggesting that, on the contrary, men may have a problem with connection and, further, that this problem may be responsible for violence in men's fantasies about intimacy.[38] Finally, in response to the claim that women's sense of justice is deficient, Carol Gilligan points out that often women resolve conflicts by other methods than ranking or balancing claims. We may use the method of inclusion, for example, which she illustrates with the story of two four-year olds overheard at play.

> The girl said: "Let's play next-door neighbors," "I want to play pirates," the boy replied. "Okay," said the girl, "then you can be the pirate that lives next door."[39]

Carol Gilligan's sympathetic and insightful readings of women's responses are not totally inconsistent with the skeptical view, however. With a weaker power position and institutionalized dependence on men for protection against male assault and for employment, promotion, and validation, women are given reasons to seek "approval," usually male approval. Such approval is granted for obedience to conventions requiring affiliations with men, respect for their views, empathy with them, and so forth. There is no need to suppose that women value approval or conventionality for its own sake (or that we confuse "right" with "conventional" or "approved"), nor that we value these relationships in themselves. Many women learn early to be prudent. Many are convinced that this exchange is what heterosexual love is about, since, after all, convention requires women to affiliate with masculine protectors out of "love." How many such attachments are the product of what Adrienne Rich calls "compulsory heterosexuality," the result of orientations molded at an age when our powers of assessment are morally undeveloped?[40]

Similar problems exist for the issues of self-definition and autonomy. Given women's inferior political position together with the lifelong message that a woman "alone" is "asking for it," we should not be surprised that "studies show" women seeking to create and maintain affiliations. Not just any affiliation does the trick, however. Many women are terrified of lesbian connections and disdainful of interracial ones. But we learn early that identifying ourselves in relation to men (of the same class and race or ethnicity) as sister, mother, wife, or lover can reduce threats of assault. It does not follow that we do not know well where our boundaries end and those of men begin. We learn our places early. Yet we pay a price in obligations assumed by so "defining" our-selves (a matter taken up further in Chapter Six on the obligations of gratitude). In modern ethics reciprocity is associated primarily with justice, and yet, failure of reciprocity is a major cause of the break-up of friendships among political peers (that is, those whose power over one another is more or less balanced). Relationships in which wom-en's choices are circumscribed by social coercion are not good can-didates for representing women's values fairly or well, for they leave open the question what women would say in a more egalitarian social environment.

On the basis of fantasy studies, Carol Gilligan suggests that violence in men's fantasies is rooted in their fear of intimacy.[41] This merits fur-ther comment. She reports that in studies where subjects constructed stories in response to pictures, women tended to find safety in intimacy and danger in isolation whereas men tended to find danger in intimacy and safety in independence. Yet the examples of intimacy that she cites are heterosexual. We should be skeptical about the conclusion that women find safety here. Perhaps they find less danger than in imagined alternatives. The conclusion about men's fears may clarify why, if it is amplified and made more specific. The weblike relationships women construct are informal, even personal, but not always intimate. Like the nets women supplied in response to a picture of trapeze artists, wom-en's relationships with women are often for safety and protection — networks of connections, not sexual unions. These networks are not the relationships that men in the study seemed to fear. They seemed to fear sexual, or potentially sexual, heterosexual intimacy. Both sexes' fantasies are compatible with both sexes' fearing heterosexual inti-macy, each for different reasons. Women have reason to fear both isola-tion and intimacy, although we are taught to fear isolation even more. Networks are often cushions against the violence of intimate relation-ships. Where men do not construct such networks, perhaps they do not have a similar need. When they fear heterosexual intimacy, they usually have the power to avoid it.

If we are to examine fantasies for clues to our senses of danger, what about women's rape fantasies? Women are reluctant to articulate these fantasies and not always because they reinforce stereotypes of female masochism. Rape fantasies are not only of attack by rapists but also of attack on rapists, killing rapists, maiming them, and so forth. Intimacy has not cured the violence in women's lives. It has given the violent greater access to their victims. Rape is one of the most underreported crimes in large part because it is committed more readily by acquaintances and intimates than by strangers.[42] Domestic battery is a major issue in misogynist environments. Men's fears of rejection and entrapment by women in this context are not misplaced. Men's fantasy violence may betray their appreciation of implications of misogyny if what they fear is women's historically well-grounded fears of men, which predictably issue in the tangle of women clinging to men for protection and acceptability while at the same time withdrawing sexually, engaging in manipulation, daily resentful hostilities, and eventually fantasies of widowhood.

Women's failure to value separation and autonomy is a genuine problem. But the problem is political, not simply psychological. Women are systematically penalized for not being available on demand to children, relatives, spouses, lovers. A good example of women's moral luck may be that as a result of our political inability to end bad relationships, we have not learned to discriminate well between good ones and bad ones but have learned instead to assume responsibility for maintaining whatever relationships "fate" seems to throw our way. The great danger, as well as the great strength, of the method of inclusion is its presumption that there should be a way to satisfy everyone.

Inclusion brings us again to the sense of justice. Justice is not only a matter of ranking, taking turns, or balancing claims but also of recognizing deserts, which often elicit sympathy or antipathy. Sometimes everyone does deserve to be included. Although inclusion is an alternative to balancing claims, it is not necessarily an alternative to justice. The difference principle, in Rawls's theory of justice as fairness, could favor inclusion over competition or taking turns. This principle directs that basic social institutions be so arranged that those least advantaged are as well off as possible.[43] If a more inclusive solution were more to the advantage of those least well-off, the difference principle would favor it. If methods of inclusion are among the methods of justice, however, women's reputation for a weak sense of justice may be undeserved in proportion to the accuracy of Carol Gilligan's observations. Where inclusion is unjust, it is unclear what can be said to recommend it.

The truth that women's moral responses are often misread does not yet sustain the view that women's responses embody virtues or values that can deepen and correct dominant ethics. Often our reasonings reveal survival strategies or even vices. Still, the corrective potentialities of the data of women's lives, if not women's voices, may be genuine. To show how, I turn next to a look at those data as giving us a domain of basic informal and personal relationships.

Two Kinds of Responsibilities and Two Kinds of Relationships

In her earlier writings Carol Gilligan spoke of "an ethic of care" as "an ethic of responsibility," understanding responsibility as a capacity for responsiveness. The Kohlbergian tradition that she criticized accepted the Rawlsian view that the business of justice is to distribute rights. Hence, she also spoke of the "justice perspective" as a "rights perspective." However, two different views are conflated by these equations. One view is that women develop a care focus and men a justice focus. The other view is that women develop a responsibility focus and men a rights focus. Something like the "responsibility and rights" thesis may be more promising than the "justice and care" thesis, if we rephrase it as a thesis about two kinds of responsibilities correlated with two kinds of relationships, only one of which tends to center on rights. It may also be true that ideals of justice have a special applicability to the kinds of responsibilities and relationships that tend to center on rights and that ideals of care have a special applicability to relationships that do not center on rights. But if we do not begin from the assumption that the ideals of justice and care already structure each focus, we may be better positioned to ask ethical questions about what we hear in each case, about what ideals should be considered applicable.

The substitution of a "different kinds of responsibilities" hypothesis (or a "different kinds of relationships" hypothesis) for the "justice and care" hypothesis seems compatible with a direction that Carol Gilligan's own thought has taken. In essays written after *In a Different Voice*, she has emphasized power and attachment as yielding two ways of defining relationships and two ways of defining responsibilities. Although she retains the language of justice and care, she no longer contrasts rights with responsibilities or presents only care as having a relationship focus. Rather, she hears the two voices as occupied with different relationships and different responsibilities.

When we speak of relationships without qualification in a social context, often we mean personal relationships, informal affiliations. Suppose that instead of a "care focus" we were to speak of a focus on *informal and personal* relationships (or on the informal and personal aspects of relationships). And suppose that instead of a "justice focus" or "focus on rights" we were to speak of a focus on *formal or impersonal* relationships (or on the formal or impersonal aspects of relationships). Each kind of relationship gives rise to different kinds of responsibilities. That we can hear a "different moral voice" in a focus on the informal and personal—certainly different from the one that has dominated so much of modern ethical theory—is plausible even if it is not always the voice of "care" and even if the voice from which it diverges is not always that of "justice." We also need room to consider, ethically, whether certain kinds of relationships ought to be formalized and whether others may have become too formal.

The voice of informal and personal relationships, as noted at the beginning of this chapter, has not been very vocal in modern ethical theory. Paradigmatic ethical problems for most of modern ethical theory have been the problems created by distributions of power, not those presented by affiliation and attachment. Contractarian, utilitarian, and even intuitionist ethics all tend to reflect administrative practical wisdom and a focus on control that is formal and impersonal. Ideal observers and veils of ignorance give versions of the perspective of an administrator (who may be a member of a board rather than a lone administrator). This point of view is epitomized by John Rawls's theory of justice, the on-going fascination with the prisoners' dilemma, and consequentialist paradoxes concerning nuclear deterrence.

The data of modern ethical theory come mostly from the lives of those who focus their attention primarily on public worlds of law and commerce, as do the basic concepts: right (or duty, from law—the world of rights) and good (or interest, from commerce—the world of goods). Yet these same lives are also embedded in personal and informal relationships, without which the worlds of law and commerce could become relatively meaningless. Philosophers dissatisfied with the dominance of impersonal and formal relationships in the data of ethical theory have begun in the last few decades to turn their attention to friendship, which belongs to the area of personal relationships and informal practices—sexual intimacy, kinship, and a variety of networks.[44] As Annette Baier has observed, historically men have been able to take for granted a background of such informal and personal relationships with women for the reproduction of populations, women have had less choice than men about participating in these relationships, and men have had material stakes in not scrutinizing such relationships morally.[45] But, then, it should be added that women have also had material stakes, different ones, in not scrutinizing such relationships too closely. Responsibility in administration is a matter of supervision and management, accountability and answerability, primarily the first two of the four senses of responsibility that I distinguish in Chapter Two. That is not at all what Carol Gilligan meant in attributing originally to women an "ethic of responsibility." What she had in mind was, instead, responsiveness to needs, the idea of taking responsibility in the sense of looking after someone — which I distinguish in Chapter Two as the third sense, the care-taking sense of "taking responsibility" (to which I return in Chapter Seven). Here, the focus is on well-being, rather than on control. When the focus is on well-being, responsiveness comes to the fore. The administrative point of view is not noted for its responsiveness to needs.

According to Rawls, "justice is the first virtue of social institutions, as truth is of systems of thought," and justice is specifiable by principles defined from his thoroughly impersonal "original position" (for proposing principles of justice) with its "veil of ignorance" (of particular facts).[46] The primary subject of social justice, he finds, is "the basic structure of society," which consists of major social institutions that "distribute fundamental rights and duties and determine the division of advantages from social cooperation." Included in the basic structure are "the political constitution and the principal economic and social arrangements" as well as "legal protection of freedom of thought and liberty of conscience, competitive markets, private property in the means of production, and the monogamous family."[47]

As Susan Moller Okin has pointed out, Rawls seems ambivalent about whether the family is to be understood as part of the basic structure of society, which he understands as public, or whether it is a nonpublic association, to which principles of justice for the basic structure do not apply.[48] She argues convincingly that principles of justice for the basic structure of society ought to be applied to the family and that families are rightly regarded as belonging to that basic structure. Although I agree with both positions, I want to raise a different question: Is justice the *first* virtue of the family? The claim that justice is the first virtue of institutions sounds less controversial when made of markets and governments than when made of families. Even more generally, one could ask: Does the *basic* structure of society consist entirely or even primarily of institutions that govern the distribution of rights to the advantages of social cooperation? Such an account of the basic structure renders invisible the background of informal and personal relationships which, as noted by Annette Baier, sustain such things as markets and governments.

Susan Moller Okin is right that the family is, historically, part of the basic structure of society as we know it. I say "as we know it" so as not to beg the question whether an ideal society would include the family in its basic structure. The considerations that led Rawls to identify formal institutions as basic to society should lead us also (or perhaps instead) to identify as socially basic certain informal and personal relationships, such as those of lovers and the relationships between children and their early caretakers. These relationships have had the kind of first-rate importance that Rawls in *A Theory of Justice* attributes to institutions that he identifies as belonging to the basic structure of society even though the relationships we have with our "significant others" are in many, perhaps most, ways not suitable subjects of impersonal administrative control and their point is not only, or even especially, to distribute the advantages of social cooperation. Perhaps this accounts for some of Rawls's ambivalence about the status of family.[49] Some of its aspects are formal, regulated by law. Yet it is not obvious that these are the most important aspects. In any case, family relationships have tended to possess three critical features that Rawls cites as characteristic of basic institutions of society. First, they have been important to our "starting places" in life. Second, they have been critical to the development and maintenance of our senses of self-esteem and self-respect.[50] And third, they give rise to special responsibilities.

Consider, first, the idea of "starting places" in life. Rawls notes that people born into different social positions have different expectations because basic social institutions work together in such a way as to favor certain starting points over others, and he also notes that these inequalities, which tend to be deep, are not justifiable by appeal to merit or desert.[51] This is surely true. Yet it is not only in economic terms that starting points have profound effects. Personal relationships with early caretakers are an emotional starting point. Those who do badly as caretakers, even though they violate no rights, may do life-long harm. We have no more choice over these emotional starting points than over the class or economic position of our caretakers. The perspectives of children and the caretakers of children is not just a "rights perspective," although it is certainly a "responsibility perspective."

Consider, second, the effect of basic informal and personal relationships on self-esteem and self-respect. The social basis of self-respect in a just society, according to Rawls, is a certain publicly affirmed distribution of basic rights and liberties. However, self-respect and self-esteem also have roots in primary personal relationships, in the sense we develop of ourselves in such relationships as beings who are capable of faithfulness, understanding, warmth, empathy — in short, as having the qualities we should want in a personal affiliate, not only the qualities we should want in a "fellow citizen."[52] Our sense of these things may be fragile, if our initial affiliations were impoverished. Even with a good start, our sense of ourselves as having these qualities can be undermined later in abusive primary relationships and in an emotionally misogynist social context.[53] If the connection with self-esteem is among the definitive conditions of the ethical importance of justice in institutions, it might equally be considered among the definitive conditions of the ethical importance of the responsibilities of basic informal, personal relationships.

Finally, like the relationships defined by basic rights, informal personal relationships give rise to special responsibilities. However, these responsibilities are not closely correlated with rights. Others cannot usually bring claims against us if we fail. The differences between these two sorts of responsibility, or "obligations," as we often call both, are explored in detail in Chapter Six in connection with the paradoxical idea of a debt of gratitude. Kant attempted to capture some of these informal responsibilities with his concept of "imperfect duties" (which he later called "ethical duties" by contrast with "juridical duties").[54]

A promising idea that I find in the hypothesis that women's voices can deepen and correct modern ethical theory is that they may direct our attention to informal and personal relationships that raise issues not fruitfully recast as issues in the ethics of control. Acknowledging that informal, personal relationships are as basic as any in our lives does not imply that women have more or better knowledge of the ethics of such relationships, although we may. What women more clearly have had is more than our share of the responsibility for maintaining these relationships and less than a fair share of the responsibilities of participating in and defining formal institutions.

With these ideas in mind, I return briefly to Carol Gilligan's discovery that although her interviewees could readily enter into either the "care" or the "justice" perspective, they could not entertain both perspectives simultaneously. That phenomenon suggests that something other than justice and care is at work in each gestalt, perhaps the perspectives of dominance and subordinance, perspectives that would surely be difficult if not impossible to entertain simultaneously. A world in which oppression and its legacies are widespread is a world in which most people learn the perspectives of domination and subordination. Perhaps most of us would tend to find one of these perspectives somewhat more "natural" than the other, at least in certain situations, and it would be understandable why one could not adopt both perspectives simultaneously, as one cannot *be* both dominant and subordinate in the same relationship at the same time.

Now, however, there appears to be another possible explanation for the difficulty of holding both perspectives simultaneously. If in one perspective we attend to formal and impersonal relationships (or aspects of relationships) whereas in the other we attend to informal and personal ones, we would need to perform different acts of mental abstraction, or focus, for each. It may be difficult, or even impossible, to attend in detail to what each perspective reveals, or to maintain simultaneously a lively intuitive feeling for each. However, it also seems important that we be able to balance against each other the claims of morality from each perspective. Although the claims of impersonality may be peripheral to a focus on the personal aspects of a relationship, that may not settle definitively their moral importance in a particular case. We may need to be able to take a higher order perspective in which we can balance such things in a larger picture than either yields by itself.

Jung Chang's book *Wild Swans: Three Daughters of China*, a family saga and personal memoir of growing up in Mao's China, illustrates how the two perspectives might work together in individual lives.[55] In this memoir, the highly principled stances of Jung Chang's father come repeatedly into conflict with his personal responsibilities to his family, responsibilities that are prioritized by her mother, with whom Jung Chang appears, initially, more sympathetic. Her father refuses again and again to use his connections as a government official to obtain such basics as medical care for members of his family on the ground that members of other families are just as important and because he aspires to remain above the corruption in officials that he sees as responsible for so much injustice in China's past. Jung Chang's mother, in contrast, is forever responding to the needs of individuals (not only members of her own family). Yet, as the story unfolds, each parent comes gradually to appreciate the other's point of view and to see how each has a stake in the other's point of view. Each grows in consequence with the result that he becomes not only more caring but also more just and she not only more just but also more caring.

CARING, JUSTICE, AND EVILS

I n one sense caring is more basic to human life than justice: We can survive without justice more easily than we can survive without caring. However, this is part of the human tragedy because, in another sense, justice is more basic: Life can be worth living despite the absence of caring from most people in the world, perhaps even from most of the people we know, but in a densely populated high-tech world, life is not likely to be worth living without justice from a great many people, including many whom we will never know.

The view that caring is the fundamental moral attitude and that justice is not a very important moral idea has been espoused in different ways by the philosopher of education Nel Noddings and by the lesbian philosopher Sarah Hoagland.[1] In cultures dominated by Christianity, a certain strain of popular thinking also embraces this view. Sarah Hoagland's skepticism regarding the value of justice is based on the views that justice, duty, and obligation presuppose social antagonism and that because they develop ethics as social control in contexts of social antagonism they are not promising concepts for lesbian ethics. Nel Noddings's work, addressed to a wider audience, seems to take its inspiration, in part, from a distaste for the distancing of an ethic of principle. Neither cites religion as a ground of their views. I discuss Sarah Hoagland's position elsewhere.[2] Here I take up Nel Noddings's groundbreaking and influential work on caring, and as representative of thinking about justice, I continue with the work of John Rawls.[3] They share a concern with resisting evils, often the same evils. Each more or less ignores the other's point of view.

My primary concern regarding a care ethic is its inability to address major evils if it does not accord justice a serious place.[4] Yet I also worry that a justice ethic will not be well-positioned to identify major evils if its theorizers fail to draw on the experience of the oppressed. One appeal of care ethics has been its ability to enlist moral agents in identifying with the experiences of the oppressed, as in our society caregivers are often women or people of color with histories of oppression, and those for whom we care standardly include children, the aged, and the ill, all highly vulnerable to oppression. This ability needs to be integrated with the values of justice.

Evil is an ambiguous concept. In the singular it often refers to motives or character traits. That is not a sense with which I will be especially concerned. In the plural, it often refers to what is suffered or endured. The evils I have in mind in this chapter are suffered, endured, risked, and so forth. Thus I often refer to "evils" in the plural. Ultimately, however, I do not want to abstract from human agency. My concern with evils is from the points of view of those who suffer from what others do (or fail to do). It is in this sense that Laurence Thomas identifies American slavery and the Holocaust "vessels of evil."[5]

Consider everyday evils of two kinds: (1) evils that strangers inflict on strangers and (2) evils that intimates inflict on intimates. Each tends to raise different problems. Issues of racism and sexism can illustrate some of these differences. On one hand, resting all of ethics on caring threatens to exclude as ethically insignificant our relationships with most people in the world because we do not know them and we never will. Regarding as ethically insignificant our relationships with people remote from us is a major constituent of racism and xenophobia.

On the other hand, resting all of ethics on caring also seems in danger of valorizing abusive intimate or personal relationships, callous and cruel ones as well as abusive ones that sheerly exploit our capacity to take another's point of view. Care ethics threatens to exacerbate the positions of women and other caregivers in a sexist or otherwise oppressive society. But many abusive relationships are more cruel than exploitative. Evil treatment is not simply a matter of misuse or abuse in the sense of wrongful exploitation. Some evils involve practices or behaviors that have no legitimate uses whatever.[6]

Nel Noddings's "feminine approach to ethics" is something like Carol Gilligan's "care perspective." However, Nel Noddings's approach is more philosophical, elucidating norms and concepts, whereas Carol Gilligan's is more psychological, oriented to empirical studies. In her view that a care ethic is superior to an ethic of principle Nel Noddings goes further than Carol Gilligan, who has been more interested in rehabilitating care as a worthy subject of academic inquiry than in criticizing justice. On the gestalt hypothesis, Carol Gilligan's care ethics has places for the concerns of justice, although not the central places of the justice perspective. Thus, in Carol Gilligan's care ethics, justice is subsidiary, which brings that perspective or voice close to Nel Noddings's care ethics. A main philosophical difference between them is that Carol Gilligan is pluralistic and Nel Noddings monistic with respect to viable forms that ethics can take.[7]

As Virginia Held and others have pointed out, mother-child relationships and family living present ethically interesting paradigms in that at their best, these relationships are neither entirely contractual nor entirely voluntary and yet they clearly impose moral responsibilities.[8] Chapter Three expresses caution about how we listen to the voices of women in coercive contexts. By relationships that are not voluntary, I do not have in mind in this chapter coercive ones. Many relationships are neither voluntary nor coerced. We did not choose them, but neither did anyone else, nor need they be the product of socially coercive institutions. Relationships to parents, for example, are not forced but yet are ordinarily nonvoluntary in that we did not choose them. Although we can choose to sever relations with a parent, often that would not be reasonable. Analogous things might be said of some of our relationships to neighbors who arrive after we did. Where a close relationship is not entirely voluntary but is a source of fortune, good or bad, it is a likely source of moral luck. Our character evolutions are influenced by interpersonal relationships, especially with significant others. Thus, in tracing implications of ethical interdependence for individual character, Nel Noddings notes that "how good *I* can be is partly a function of how *you*-the other—receive and respond to me" and that "our own ethicality is not entirely 'up to us'" because "like Winston in *Nineteen Eighty-Four,* we are fragile; we depend upon each other even for our own goodness."[9] In this I find that she is right. Parts of the tale of Anna Karenina also illustrate the point. Nel Noddings's insight seems often overlooked by those whose focus has been on justice in formal relationships.

One may recall, however, that what Rawls calls the basic structure of society into which we were born is not something that we chose (although we can make choices that will affect it for the next generation) and that a major motivation of his theory of justice has been his appreciation of the involuntariness of our basic starting points in life, which have a great effect on the rest of our lives. Following Jean-Jacques Rousseau, Rawls seems to see inequalities of fortune in the "natural lottery" as something like a natural injustice (although he says they are not really injustices), to be redressed, to some extent, by social justice. At any rate, social justice on his view is to regulate the ways in which and the extent to which we are allowed to profit from such fortune. Thus, justice is not distinguishable from care simply by the voluntariness or lack thereof of the relationships in question. It seems in fact to be Rawls's intention to take account in a central way of nonvoluntary aspects of our situations.

Two differences are worth noting, however. First, in Rawls's theory, one's starting place in society and the luck it involves are primarily economically conceived. One's luck in being born into a certain family is acknowledged in the theory basically as one's luck in being born into a certain economic class. This ignores one's luck in being born to abusive parents, who may be, after all, economically well-endowed. As Susan Moller Okin argues, attention to parent-child relationships has the potentiality to expand the conception of "starting points" even for a theory of justice.[10] In particular, it has the potential to expand it beyond the economic conception that has dominated not only Rawls's theory but most contemporary philosophical theorizing about justice.

Second, and perhaps more important for purposes of this chapter, in Rawls's theory, as in Rousseau's thinking about the social contract, the point of attending to nonvoluntary relationships, such as the family, as starting points seems often to be to make up for something bad about them in relation to various ulterior ends that one may come to have.[11] The point does not seem to be to improve their intrinsic value. Yet, as Virginia Held notes, an important aspect of such nonvoluntary relationships as mother-child and other family relationships is that much of their value is intrinsic to the relationship rather than subservient to ulterior ends. Her interest, and that of such theorists as Nel Noddings, is often in evaluating and improving the ethical quality of such relationships considered in themselves. In this regard, care ethics has seemed to them, as to many feminist philosophers, to hold special promise.

Much sophisticated philosophical work has been done on the concept of justice during the past half century. The superficial justice of even-handed application of rules (regardless of their content) has been distinguished from a deeper justice manifested by rules that treat persons as equals and as possessors of a certain dignity. To appreciate persons as equals, the capacity for taking up their perspectives seems requisite, a capacity also agreed to be a significant element in caring.

Citing Rousseau, Rawls presents the sense of justice as building on capacities for love and trust.[12]

Philosophically sophisticated work is only recently begun on the concept of care. Of the philosophical work being done here, Nel Noddings's is among the most sustained, detailed and well-illustrated with a wide range of examples.[13] In *Caring: A Feminine Approach to Ethics and Moral Education* she offers a phenomenological exploration of caring and being cared for. As she observes, "care" has many meanings, not the least of which is "a burdened mental state, one of anxiety, fear, or solicitude about something or someone."[14] One virtue of her analysis is that it explains how burdensomeness can become a liability of caring. In common parlance, meanings of "care" range from "being concerned about" ("interested in," even "minding") to affectionate emotional bonding. "Do you care whether . . . ?" simply asks whether you attach any importance to something. "Care" in a sense meaningfully distinguished from "justice" is more specific. To possess the virtue of justice is, of course, to care (be concerned) about such things as equality and fairness, and thereby, about persons. What, then, is distinctive about care as a virtue? In the search for a response to this question, Nel Noddings's work is especially helpful.

On her analysis, activating the disposition to care requires real encounters with individuals. It is personal, and in this respect, contrasts with justice, which is paradigmatically impersonal. Nel Noddings presents one's ethical responsibility to care as the responsibility to meet those whom one encounters as "one-caring" — at least, to meet some of them that way (the question which ones eventually turns out to be an unanswered problem). The attitude of one-caring has at least three basic elements.[15] The first, which she emphasizes most, is *motivational engrossment*— "displacement" —in another, whereby we take up another's perspective. Second, there is a regard for, or *inclination toward*, the other; one-caring is "present to" the other. This seems less a matter of attachment than of availability, being there for another. It sounds like what Sarah Hoagland calls "attending."[16] And third, there is an action component, a disposition to certain activities, such as protection or maintenance. Nel Noddings emphasizes this element least.[17]

To have a ready way of referring to this conception of caring and distinguishing it from more abstract ones, I call it the *encounter* sense of caring. Not all encounters are caring. But the conception of caring most naturally distinguished from justice does involve a relationship to a particular other. The concept of relation as a particular connection is basic to Nel Noddings's idea of caring. As she puts it in her second book, *Women and Evil,* "A relation, in the perspective I adopted in *Caring* and will maintain here, is any pairing or connection of individuals characterized by some affective awareness in each," and "It is an encounter or series of encounters in which the involved parties feel something toward each other."[18]

Because the action component, which suggests care *taking* or care *giving* is the one least emphasized by Nel Noddings—because her interest lies primarily in the emotional, attitudinal elements—caring, on her account, is not primarily a matter of providing services or meeting material needs.[19] A care ethic built on this conception of caring might thus seem relatively invulnerable to being used to valorize oppression, perhaps invulnerable to Nietzsche's critique of Christian care ethics as a "slave morality." However, that is not clear. The first two elements—the inclination toward and motivational engrossment—are often important to meeting emotional needs and open the carer to profound exploitation, manipulation, and oppression. An ethic of care in the encounter sense may be more problematic for women than for anyone else, given women's socialization to identify as providers of emotional support and women's historic roles in heterosexual relationships and families as the primary emotional glue holding things together.

In the history of modern philosophy, these emotional aspects of caring have received very different evaluations. A Kantian tradition questions whether what Kant called pathological caring (caring based on feeling) is a moral virtue at all, on the ground that the emotional responses involved do not proceed from choice. Another tradition found in David Hume and Arthur Schopenhauer treats justice as a derivative virtue, based on more fundamental virtues associated with care, such as sympathy and empathy. Nel Noddings reverses the Kantian position, questioning whether justice is a virtue. On her view justice is a poor substitute for caring. Schopenhauer, on the other hand, found justice more important than *Menschenliebe* (see Chapter Three) apparently only because of his low estimation of men's capacity for empathy, although he found compassion indirectly at work even in justice. Once we learned abstract principles of justice, he thought, compassion did not, fortunately, have to be activated in individual cases. This distancing from the sense of what Seyla Benhabib calls "the concrete other" is precisely what troubles Nel Noddings.[20]

My worry about care ethics is not that caring does not proceed from choice. Often, I believe, it does or could, and even where it does not, it need not be forced. Nor is my concern simply that for whom we care is often a matter of luck. That fact can raise questions of justice, but it may also be important to care for many to whom luck has attached us. My concerns are with the bases of choices we can make about whether to care or continue to care, for whom to care, and how to treat those for whom we do not care, including those for whom we have chosen, rightly enough, not to care.

The remaining sections of this chapter consider in more detail why a care ethic without an important place for justice is ill-equipped to address evils of our relationships with strangers and with intimates and then considers how well a Rawlsian conception of justice is equipped to do so. In concluding, I propose building into a theory of justice an explicit acknowledgment of the basic evils that often seem to motivate care ethics, evils characteristic of oppression.

Our Relations with Strangers

Resisting evil, understood as refusing to participate in it, is a project that concerns Nel Noddings deeply. In *Women and Evil* she favors the idea that "evil is overcome not by a violent overthrow but rather by a steady refusal to participate in it."[21] It is clear from her discussions of death, illness, poverty, war, terrorism, and torture that she is profoundly concerned with resisting evil, avoiding it, and where it is unavoidable, mitigating its effects.[22] Looking at evil phenomenologically and through the experiences of women, she finds that the basic things we fear (in old age as in infancy) are *pain, separation, and helplessness*.[23] She attempts an account of such evils as torture and war in those terms. I return to that below. For the present, it will be enough if we can agree on some such examples of evil.

Consider our ethical relations with most people in the world, who are strangers to us and always will be. In the sense of "caring" delineated above, it is entirely reasonable to take the position (as Nel Noddings does) that no one should try to care for everyone. That prompts two further questions. First, what ethical notions *are* relevant to our relationships with strangers, persons whose lives we may significantly affect through our actions (or inactions) although we will never know them as individuals because we will never encounter them? Second, out of the billions of people in the world for all of whom we cannot possibly care (in the encounter sense), which ones should not be strangers to us? In other words, for whom should we care?

Consider the question what ethical concepts apply to our relations with strangers. Where we have no responsibility to care for others in the encounter sense, we still have responsibilities to refrain from doing them harm — to be careful, in a sense that does not require encounters with those for whose sakes we ought to take care. Technology extends our actions' effects far beyond the range of our encounters. Through environmental carelessness or use of nuclear weaponry, we can affect drastically, fatally, people we would never know as individuals.

Nel Noddings has agreed that being careful in this way is important.[24] And yet, being careful in relation to the welfare of others unknown to us is not caring in the encounter sense. It may draw on some of the same capacities, such as our ability to enter imaginatively into perspectives different from our own. But it does not require the psychological interaction with specific others that Nel Noddings specifies as what she means by "connection." Here is a place where justice is helpful in that it directs us to be heedful of the effects of our deeds on everyone impartially, not just on those for whom we happen to care. This is no small concession, when we consider how many more people may be affected by our sense of impartial concern than can possibly be affected by our ability to care in the encounter sense.

Keeping the focus on the individual, however, Nel Noddings attempts to anticipate this kind of objection with respect to some strangers and to devise a method by which our concerns can extend beyond the range of our immediate neighbors without simply adhering to a rule. By means of what she calls "chains" of connection, she holds that we can be prepared to care for others currently outside our circles of connection — such outsiders, for example, as our children's partners-to-be.[25] "Chains" are defined as "personal or formal relationships." "Personal or formal relationships," however, are not defined, and the "chains" offered as examples suggest differing interpretations. One example is the intimate partner of one's child, for whom one may be prepared to care because of one's child for whom one already cares. This example suggests that a "chain" has as a connecting link an individual whom one has encountered who has in turn encountered still others whom one has not (yet) encountered.[26] This makes sense of the metaphor of a "chain" in that the individuals known to us link us to others. Their caring is thus linked to our caring. Yet, to restrict ethics to such connections in a nuclear age would be preposterous. Such chains do not extend the range of caring far enough.

Another example offered to illustrate "chains of connection" is a teacher's future students who are simply potential placeholders in a formal relationship of teacher-student.[27] This example extends interpersonal connections further, but it does not make sense of the chain metaphor. On this model, a teacher is connected to potential students, but, by what? What is the "chain"? What are its "links?" Present students need not know future ones (in most cases will not). My present students may be connected chainwise with future students through me, but it is my basis for caring about those not currently my students that is in question. What links a teacher with future students appears to be the job (teaching), which is institutionally defined. But that introduces abstractions and departs from the idea of a phenomenological encounter. If the teacher-student relationship need only be institutionally defined, there need be no personal encounter between teacher and student even in actual teacher-student relationships, and in fact, students are often fairly anonymous to teachers.[28]

Still, if the basic idea is that an indefinite number of others who are presently strangers might enter into a relationship with me that I currently have to others, perhaps we have an answer to the question about ethical relationships between strangers for a care ethic: Those who are presently strangers are potentially not strangers. But it is not clear what that is supposed to imply.

Either the potentiality for real encounters will be realized or it will not. What are our responsibilities if those potentialities are not realized, as they never will be with regard to most people in the world? What is the significance of our preparedness to care for them? Does the existence of a potential relationship mean that potentially we have ethical responsibilities to those who are at present strangers? Or does it mean that because of that potentiality, we have such responsibilities now?

If the existence of a potential relationship that will never be realized implies that we have ethical responsibilities toward those strangers now, then, again, it appears that caring for them does not require an encounter. Nel Noddings and sympathetic interpreters suggest that we are to imagine an encounter, "attempt to visualize concrete subjects" and in doing so "consider real persons" about whom we already care.[29] However, if an imagined encounter can substitute for a real one, we do not have the kind of connection that involves mutual psychological awareness. The element of motivational displacement, then, does not connect with the particularities of actual individuals. We have, instead, an abstraction based on the particularities of other individuals we have known or the abstraction of an analogy: Be prepared to do unto strangers as you would do unto those for whom you (already) care. But this is a principle, perhaps a variant of the Golden Rule, which sounds like a way to express the fundamental principle of formal justice that if it is right for one person to be treated in a certain way, then it is likewise right for any (relevantly) similar person in (relevantly) similar circumstances to be treated in the same way.[30] Yet, an important motivation for an ethic of care in the encounter sense was to avoid the abstractness of principle and connect concretely with others. In the case of our relationships to permanent strangers, whatever ethical responsibilities we have appear still to be defined by abstract potentialities, even speculations. But if they can be acceptably defined by such abstractions as these, then why not by other abstractions such as those of other rules and principles?

Further, if we have responsibilities now toward those who are only potentially related to us, how are those responsibilities related to the ones we have toward those for whom we currently and unambiguously do care in the encounter sense? Are our responsibilities to potential "cared-fors" less important just because the relationships are only potential? Yet those strangers are actual people and the effects we had on them would be real, even if our encounters with them remain potential. From the point of view of justice, whether such potentialities were actualized often seems an irrelevant contingency. Suppose I teach a large lecture class in which I know only some students individually, as I am able to recall only some of their faces or only some ask questions or come up after lecture or come to my office. Yet all pay tuition and my responsibility is to teach them all. Some responsibilities (in addition to being careful not to harm them) I have equally toward those I never come to know individually, such as the responsibility to make myself heard even by those in the back of the classroom.

On the other hand, if a potential relationship implies only that potentially we have ethical responsibilities to strangers, are we free to take steps that would insure the unrealizability of that potentiality? Is that or is it not ruled out by the idea of being prepared to care? With respect to potential responsibilities, the issue of abortion comes naturally to mind. But an embryo or fetus is a potential person, not an actual stranger. Perhaps the embryo or fetus is not a stranger, however potential its personality, although in the sense of "relationship" that Nel Noddings has defined, it could be argued that no one yet can have relationships with it (because no one has yet encountered it).[31] The abortion issue is more complicated than the stranger issue in that it seems to present two kinds of potentialities: a potential relationship with a potential person. My concern here is simpler: If we have only potential ethical responsibilities to actual people who are strangers to us, that would seem to imply that we are, strictly speaking, free now to prevent the actualization of such potentialities, subject only to whatever restrictions might be imposed by our responsibilities to those whom we have encountered. There is room here, logically, for a distinction between responsibilities *to* strangers and responsibilities *regarding* strangers. However, if the point of such a distinction were to make responsibilities *regarding* strangers dependent on responsibilities *to* those for whom we care, again it seems to reduce ethics to an unacceptably parochial affair.

Another question regarding "chains of connection" is which relationships linking us to strangers count as ethically significant. "Formal relationships" suggests kinds of relationship, as opposed to particular relationships. But then, which kinds? What is the source of the "form"? Nel Noddings's examples suggest institutionally defined relationships, such as marriages and relationships defined by educational institutions. However, as in the case of teaching, such relationships need not include phenomenological connections, that is, individual personal encounters. Further, if "formal relationships" were institutionally defined, we would need justice to evaluate the relevant institutions. Some institutions arbitrarily exclude entire groups of people. If our formal relationships to others were only those defined by such institutions, it would follow that we had no formal relationships to people who were excluded and therefore no ethical relationships to them, either, unless we were connected by personal relationships. But that is not plausible. Yet, if "formal relationships" are not institutionally defined, how are they defined? What is the "form"?

Nel Noddings notes that her "ethic of caring locates morality primarily in the pre-act consciousness of the one-caring."[32] It thus seems the opposite extreme from act-utilitarianism, which takes consequences to be everything. If the idea of "chains" of connection between our present circles and potential cared-fors fails to extend our ethical concerns to strangers whose lives we can impact significantly, it seems unable to encompass responsibilities regarding possibilities of destroying or ruining the lives of billions of real people in other parts of the world toward whom the pre-act consciousness of one-caring may not be a live possibility for those who possess such destructive powers. Yet the existence of such real possibilities has produced major moral crises in the twentieth century. The restriction of caring to potential cared-fors whom one is somewhat more likely to encounter might explain why Japanese rather than German cities experienced nuclear destruction from the United States in 1945. But such an explanation sounds xenophobic or racist. Analogous observations hold with respect to (other) environmental crises.

In considering the cases of bus drivers, airline pilots, and air traffic controllers, each of whom may actually encounter few of those whom they affect, Nel Noddings says, "In such enterprises I behave responsibly toward others through proficient practice of my craft."[33] This response may take care of my responsibility to make myself heard in lecture even by those sitting in the back of the room. It will not do, however, as a general response if the responsibilities in question are conceived simply as defined by the "craft" or the job, if the job is taken as a given and not itself treated as subject to ethical evaluation. The Nazi doctors also proficiently practiced their crafts, which was, ethically, part of the problem rather than its solution.[34]

To be concerned to avoid participating in war, ecological destruction, and other cultural evils, we need not care in the encounter sense about potential victims. We need not be there for them in a way that evokes their conscious recognition of our conscious states or our conscious recognition of theirs.

Nel Noddings characterizes her "feminine approach" to morality as that of "one attached," by contrast with a "masculine approach" which is "detached."[35] This is a source of problems in regard to strangers. By definition, strangers are those to whom we are not attached in the intended sense, and yet our choices can impact heavily on their wellbeing. "Too often," she notes, "principles function to separate us from one another." As we will see, in her later work, she regards separation a basic evil. And yet, if by "separation" is meant "absence of connection" where a connection is understood as involving an encounter, we do not need principles to separate us. Everyone is already separated from most people on earth and inevitably so given how many we are and the limits of our personal resources. Since we can seriously affect far more people than we can encounter personally, we need an ethic that applies to our relations with people with whom we are connected only by relations of cause and effect as well as to our relations with those with whom we are connected by personal and potential encounters. Phenomenological encounter is not the only ethically significant connection. Because we intrude on each other's lives in many ways, we need to consider many kinds of connections and the conditions under which they can be good or bad. We also need to take seriously questions about establishing connections that are at present too rare, such as intercultural connections, especially where a history of injustice underlies the connections that fate appears to throw our way or render highly improbable.

With regard to the claim that principles too often function to separate us, it is also worth noting that there is a sense in which principles need not abstract from special connections with particular others. Whether they do depends on the content of the principle. The principles that it is good to honor parents, to value familial ties and relationships with intimates, and to be grateful to benefactors presuppose and apply to special connections with particular others. What some have found objectionable about acting on principle may have more to do with the content of certain principles than with the idea of abstraction.[36] The problem may be the blindfolded woman with scales and sword, the idea of justice and its impartiality. Social justice, insofar as it involves the idea of equality, is definable to a great extent independently of the motivations and consciousness of particular agents. This presents problems for any ethic that is defined solely in terms of the motivations or conscious states of agents.

Part of the point of justice, as Rawls has observed, is to make possible cooperative relationships among large numbers of people and among people who are not personally attached to one another but who nevertheless stand to gain mutually by working out shared arrangements for such things as the use, maintenance, production, and protection of resources. Justice applies to interactions among those who have a stake in securing certain common advantages by mutual cooperation. The need for cooperation among people who are not bound to each other by ties of affection is especially important in a society plagued by racism, ethnocentrism, and xenophobia. In a poorly integrated multi-cultural society dominated by phobic stereotypes, opportunities for interracial caring relationships are not what they should be. In such a context, if one's ethical repertoire is exhausted by caring in the encounter sense, what remains to operate with respect to many of the interracial consequences of one's conduct? Normally, this is one place for justice and respect for others. As Nina Simone put it in "Mississippi goddam," the point is not whether you "live next to me" but whether you support "my equality."[37]

A responsibility that seems prior to caring in the encounter sense is the responsibility not to perpetuate unjust practices that block opportunities for encounters that foster caring. Such practices are a major evil confronting many of us daily. One may argue, as Nel Noddings does, that it is sometimes justifiable to fear the proximate stranger and to limit our encounters with others for the sake of the caring relationships we already have. However, that concern invites the question how we came to have the caring relationships we already have. The concern to limit our encounters needs to be balanced by a responsibility to create opportunities for caring relationships where such opportunities do not spontaneously present themselves, owing to past injustices. Creating such opportunities is not the same as trying to initiate caring under existing conditions. It can be presumptuous to try to initiate caring relationships with those from whose oppression one has benefited. Nina Simone's "You don't have to live next to me . . . " may be an understatement of "I'd rather you didn't — I'd rather have political equality." In a pluralistic society with a history of racism, respect can be more basic than caring in that it is a precondition of the welcomeness of certain kinds of caring relationships.

Personal Relationships and Problems of Abuse

If a care ethic threatens to *ex*clude too much by ignoring our responsibilities to strangers, it also threatens to *in*clude too much by valorizing relationships better dissolved. Elevating caring into an ethical ideal threatens to valorize the maintenance by carers of relationships from which a carer would do better to withdraw at least in the sense of ceasing to be "present to" the other and available for emotional support. The care ethic also threatens to valorize unwanted intrusions generally into the lives of others, which is a common kind of occasion of the demand for justice. Issues of injustice often involve wrongful boundary crossing rather than failures of connection.[38] This is true, for example, of theft, assaults, battery, and rape. Although one might argue that when such offenses are committed against strangers, the very absence of connection can make the commission of the offense easier (at least, psychologically), no such argument is available regarding such offenses committed against intimates.

As I write this, the local newspaper is carrying a headline story on domestic abuse, quoting the district attorney as saying that in the past year, "fully one-fourth of all arrests were for domestic crimes" in the city in which I live.[39] And yet domestic abuse is still considered a highly underreported crime. Partner battery is one kind of abusive relationship in which the parties know each other. It has a special importance in a society that makes it often impossible for the abused to escape and that supports, facilitates, and even enforces abusers' continued access to victims and often penalizes survivors who fight back when they have no help.

Not all bad relationships are evil or even abusive. In many ordinary exploitative intimate peer relationships, one partner accepts but fails to reciprocate the other's caring, without the excuses of infancy, very old age, or disability, and yet the nonreciprocating partner may not be overtly hostile or prevent the other from withdrawing. In relationships that I consider clearly abusive, there is not only a lack of reciprocity in caring but also the presence of hostile control and often violence or credible threats of violence. These are evils.

Abusive partners are not continuously abusive. They can also be charming and share spontaneously their aspirations and valuations with partners whom they also abuse, and they may be charming not only when they are trying to make up after an assault. On Lenore Walker's cycle theory of domestic violence, such spontaneous responsiveness is part of the "hook" that she suspects helps keep battered partners trying to make the relationship work instead of trying to leave.[40] It is also confusing to battered partners, who cannot see batterers as nothing but batterers.

Referring to a famous burning bed case, Nel Noddings has argued that if we must exclude from our caring someone for whom we have cared, we thereby act under a "diminished ethical ideal."[41] By this, she does not mean that leaving is never the best option; she finds that, regrettably, sometimes it is. The best one can do here may not be very good. This kind of judgment is important to recognize. In the previous chapter I argue that although lying may be a justifiable and even life-saving skill under oppressive institutions, it is not conducive to human good. Such judgments embody acknowledgments of moral luck. It can be one's moral luck to be able in some circumstances to act at best under a "diminished ethical ideal." But it is also important to note some of the things that such a judgment does not imply and to consider more specifically when such a judgment does and does not apply to cases of withdrawing care.

Having to cut off someone you have loved is prima facie nothing to celebrate. There are different possible reasons why. Having loved the person in the first place may reflect poorly on one's ability to judge character. But then it is having loved the person, not leaving, that is occasion for regret. There it would not be plausible to say that in leaving one acted under a diminished ethical ideal. On the contrary, it sounds as though one's ideals expanded. Alternatively, one might regret the way that the relationship developed. The death of the relationship could be something to grieve if it showed initial promise. Yet even here, what are diminished may be simply our possibilities for continued growth in a relationship rather than ideals guiding our choices.

A more natural way to interpret the idea of acting under a diminished ethical ideal makes use of the idea of "moral remainders." Where there is ethical cause for regret, we have what Bernard Williams calls a "moral remainder" in the sense that even after we have done the best we can, there are things that will never be made right.[42] Some ethical conflicts—some hostage cases, for example—cannot be resolved without wronging someone (say, inflicting or permitting the infliction of undeserved harm that does not benefit the victim) even when those conflicts are resolved in the best way possible under the circumstances. In such situations, our ethical possibilities are diminished in relation to what they would be ideally. Here, the very ideals under which we act are compromised, usually as a result of the previous bad choices of others.

Simply withdrawing from an abusive relationship need not involve such a remainder. Just as failing to reciprocate caring is not necessarily abusive, ceasing to care for abusers does not necessarily wrong them. Even killing in self-defense need not wrong one's assailant. Burning bed cases, however, raise the question whether killing an abuser who is not at that moment engaged in an assault can count as justifiable self-defense. Here, the violence necessary for escape is arguably made necessary not only by the assailant's behavior but also by the failures of others who could have intervened helpfully but did not. Killing as a way out may thus seem at once excessive from the point of view of what the assailant deserves (in some cases, although not in others) but also required from the point of view of the victim and what circumstances make necessary to preserve her life. Logically, both could be right. In such a case the best the victim may be able to do is to act under a diminished ethical ideal.

This does not imply, however, that she is not growing ethically in the process. In ending the relationship, she may feel as though she is cutting off a part of herself. And yet she may be growing ethically in overcoming a sexist training to put others' needs consistently ahead of her own and to doubt her own judgment. Here, the complexity of the ideals involved may defy encapsulation in simple judgments. The increased richness of her ideals seems what enables her to recognize and refuse to accept bad relationships, freeing herself up for better ones. Yet, the means available to her for acting on that recognition may require acting under other ideals that are diminished.

Burning bed cases are not a problem only for care ethics. They are also a problem for justice. They illustrate situations that are aggravated by the injustices of others, defining a set of options for victims none of which may be thoroughly just to everyone affected. This is an area where morality may require the institution of practices designed to reduce the likelihood that such situations will arise. Without privacy conventions that support widespread toleration of domestic abuse, there would be fewer occasions for burning beds.

Where the best one can do as an individual is to identify the least unjust option, acting under a "diminished ethical ideal" is an appropriate way to describe the case. Still, many cases exhibit no such complexities. Many ethical conflicts are resolvable without remainder. One can often leave a bad relationship without harming others or without exposing them to worse harm than they deserve. Where there are no "moral remainders" in the sense that no one is wronged, I find no plausible rationale for the idea that leaving is acting under a "diminished ethical ideal."

Getting stuck in the "pre-act" consciousness of the attitude of one-caring can be ethically disastrous. It can confuse observers with respect to the question who is abusing whom, leaving us with the impression simply of conflict. Abusers often complain when frustrated that *they* are abused, since they are not getting what they want. Also, caring, even when we do not do much, can have the consequence of supporting people in projects of which we may explicitly disapprove, insofar as our emotional support makes it easier for them to do as they will. It can be difficult to decide when we can no longer support a friend or kin whose projects we find immoral. Many readers have disagreed with Nel Noddings's apparent intuitions about how to respond to one's racist aunt Phoebe, who has done one many kindnesses over the years, or to inquiries about one's mobster neighbor with whom one has had friendly relations.[43] There may be moral remainders whatever one does in such cases, although many of us would give more weight to protecting the innocent than to maintaining the personal connection, however disappointed we might be to lose the connection. Whether it is lost is a function not only of our choices and of the "pre-act" consciousness of our caring attitudes but also of theirs.

The case of abusive relationships suggests a significant moral gap in the encounter sense of caring. In its zeal to avoid an excessive individualism that does not give relationships their due, Nel Noddings's account does not explicitly include the idea of valuing individuals (including oneself) for themselves. Motivational displacement is not the same thing. We can enter into the perspectives of others, whether we value them or not, out of sheer necessity for survival, the necessity to anticipate others' needs in order to be a good servant or slave, for example.[44] Women learn well how to do this with men; slaves learn to do it with masters. To be ethical we need to preserve in ourselves, as well as value in others, a certain spiritual integrity as choosers who can accept or reject a relationship. Otherwise, we risk becoming tools, exploitable for evil projects that others devise. With a capacity for "motivational displacement" — receiving others into oneself — but lacking integrity one is in danger of dissolving into a variety of personalities, changing one's colors (values) like a chameleon in changing environments. Women know this danger intimately, and likewise those whose personal safety has regularly depended upon how well they were able to "receive others into themselves."

A more abstract way to put the point is in terms of the higher order nature of the capacities exercised in caring. Thus Max Scheler argues that what he calls "fellow feeling" cannot be a fundamental moral value. "The ethics of sympathy," he maintains, "does not attribute moral value primarily to the *being* and attitudes of persons as *such*" but "seeks to derive it from the attitude of the *spectator*" and in so doing "invariably *pre*-supposes what it is attempting to deduce" because "the sharing of another's pleasure can only be moral when the latter *is itself moral,* and warranted by the value-situation which evokes it."[45] The concept "spectator" may be too passive for the present context. "Attender" may come closer. But the point remains, even if we substitute "engrossment" for "sympathy." Being engrossed in and present to others cannot be a fundamental value. But the experiences capable of engrossing us and capturing our attention may exhibit values that are fundamental. In the next and final section, I take up some experiences that may be considered basic evils and propose that a theory of justice would do well to take them explicitly into account.

Evils and Justice

Does justice address the evils of racism and sexism better than an ethic of care in the encounter sense? Justice offers the advantages of impartiality and universal concern. But is it too unfeeling and abstract to be helpful, as Nel Noddings and others have complained?

Rawls presents justice first of all as a virtue of institutions, concerned with how their rules distribute the benefits and burdens of social cooperation. Thus his principles of justice presuppose value judgments about what is distributed. Accordingly, he includes as background a theory of "primary goods" to measure the value of the benefits and burdens of social cooperation. In *A Theory of Justice* he describes primary goods as what anyone can be presumed to value, regardless what else they might want.[46] In *Political Liberalism* the account is made more specific, and less intuitive, as those goods necessary to develop and exercise our moral powers for a sense of justice and for a conception of the good.[47] But in both works the list of primary goods is basically the same: "rights and liberties, opportunities and powers, income and wealth" and "a sense of one's own worth."[48] He proposed in *A Theory of Justice* that we think of these goods as instrumental, with one exception, namely, the "sense of one's own worth" (also referred to as "self-respect" and as "self-esteem").

But what about things that should be "distributed" to no one? Things that no one should have to suffer, no matter what anyone else wants? And what about what everyone can be presumed to want to avoid, no matter what else they may want? Both ideas suggest the concept of evil. Yet they are distinct ideas. Suppose we call what everyone can be presumed to want to avoid (no matter what else they want) *basic evils*. They are thus analogous to primary goods. Still, I think they are worth distinguishing from the more general idea of basic goods, for reasons that I will indicate shortly. If basic evils are what everyone can be presumed to want to avoid, let us then think of *evil treatment* as what no one should have to suffer, no matter what anyone else wants. I propose, below, a way to use the idea of basic evils to define evil treatment. For now, let us say that an institution, practice, or behavior is evil when it authorizes or consists in administering evil treatment. What makes oppression and many forms of racism and sexism evil and not just bad treatment is that they treat people in ways that no one should be treated, no matter what it does for anyone else.

To enable us to identify evil treatment, principles of justice may need as part of their background a theory of basic evils. We might think of it as a complication of the theory of primary goods, perhaps renaming them primary values. No doubt Rawls means his primary goods and the idea of a social minimum to do this job. But they do not yet seem well-designed to enable us to distinguish between evil treatment and injustices that are comparatively less serious.

The reason appears to be that Rawls presents his theory of justice as an ideal theory, meaning that its principles are constructed on the assumption that most people will abide by them most of the time, that the society in which they are to take effect is "nearly just," more or less "well-ordered" in the sense that its members have effective senses of justice and know this about each other. He does not regard criminal justice as part of ideal theory but finds that it belongs to nonideal theory, which would be designed on assumptions of the only partial compliance or noncompliance of members of the society in which it was to take effect. In a well-ordered society, or one that was nearly just, there would be no serious need to guard against the evils of misogyny and race hatred — such things as rape, the sexual abuse of children, domestic battery, or lynching. Attending to deep injustice, rather than simply to the ideal case, focuses us first on evils, on what it is most important to avoid, rectify, and prevent.

Here is where the work of Nel Noddings and Iris Young may be helpful. In *Women and Evil* Nel Noddings presents as basic evils pain, separation, and helplessness. She came to this view by examining women's experiences, looking for what we most fear. These three basic evils provide her framework for examining war, torture, terrorism, poverty, illness, and death — all matters with which justice should be concerned. With certain modifications, I find her view of basic evils plausible and important. When used in defining the idea of evil treatment, it goes a long way toward explaining the status as evils of what Iris Young identifies as "the five faces of oppression": marginalization, powerlessness, exploitation, violence, and cultural imperialism.[49] The concepts of basic evils and evil treatment also are important to punishment theory, as we need to be concerned that in trying to prevent evil treatment, we do not engage in it ourselves.

However, I want to modify Nel Noddings's basic evils a bit in view of difficulties mentioned above in discussing care. Scheler's critique of an ethic of sympathy would also apply to a conception of evil as pain, separation, and helplessness, if those concepts were not made more specific. For like sympathy, separation and helplessness are relational concepts and their values connected with the values of their relata. When pain is a higher order mental state, having as its object a belief that may or may not justify a painful awareness, its value depends on that belief. Nel Noddings's view is not that separation, pain, and helplessness are necessarily evils. Rather, her view is that they are prima facie evils in the sense that they always need to be justified.[50] Yet even this may be false.

The value of separation, for example, is not always a function of circumstances. Whether a particular separation is even prima facie bad depends on who is separating from whom or from what, not just on circumstances. Further, if separation is meant as the opposite of connection, it may be too specific in that it presupposes prior connections. However, human isolation — being unconnected with others, socially outcast — is prima facie an evil. Thus, the first modification I would make is to substitute "isolation" for "separation," understanding isolation as a matter of degree. The isolation of a human being from others, or refusing to alleviate such a condition however it may have come about, is something that always needs justification. An institution that inflicts or refuses to alleviate severe isolation without justification is rightly considered evil. These are examples of evil treatment.

Similarly with helplessness. To be helpless is to lack needed help for some action or activity. The disvalue of the helplessness depends in part on the value of the action or activity in relation to which one is disabled, not just on circumstances. Without such organizations as the SS, Adolf Hitler would have been helpless to carry out his ambitions, which would have been good. Under no circumstances would help for such a project be good and thus the value of Hitler's (hypothesized) helplessness would not be a function of his circumstances but, rather, of his project. However, impotence, the inability to act, is prima facie an evil. My second modification, then, substitutes "impotence" for "helplessness," again understanding impotence as having degrees. What distinguishes degrees of impotence from the relativity of helplessness is that it is a more general condition; impotence is disablement for all sorts of things. As with isolation, rendering someone impotent or refusing to alleviate impotence however it may have come about, always needs justification. An institution that inflicts or refuses to alleviate it without justification is thereby evil. These are also examples of evil treatment.

Pain is perhaps the most plausible candidate for a basic evil. Yet even the prima facie disvalue of pain depends on what hurts. Nel Noddings includes psychological as well as physical pain. Some psychological pain, such as depression, generalized anxiety, or nameless terror may be "lower order" in that it does not presuppose other more specific psychological states as its object. Usually, however, psychological pain suggests such higher order sufferings as grief, embarrassment, shame, guilt, and the like. These experiences are higher order in that they have as their object another psychological state, such as a consciously held belief.[51] Whether higher order psychological pain is even prima facie bad depends partly on this object. Suppose, for example, that my pain is guilt and its object is a truly reprehensible deed. Such pain is prima facie good.[52] Yet prolonged or severe physical (or lower order psychological) pain is prima facie an evil. My third modification, then, is to specify severe or unrelieved physical (or lower order psychological) pain as a basic evil, understanding again that there are degrees. Inflicting or refusing to alleviate such severe pain always needs justification. An institution that does so without justification is thereby evil. These are further examples of evil treatment. In each case, I understand justification in such a way as to allow that the inability to alleviate basic evils serves as a justification for not doing so.

These are not the only basic evils, but they are a good beginning. Being deprived of, or prevented from developing, Rawls's final primary good, self-respect, is also a good candidate for a basic evil. One may rightly lose a certain amount of self-respect upon appreciating the immorality of one's own conduct. However, that kind of loss can also be part of the basis for a renewed self-respect. As I cannot conceive of a justification for depriving persons of basic self-respect, I am inclined to say without qualification that an institution that does so is evil.

The first element of a definition of punishment is usually the idea of inflicting evil on an offender. Pain, isolation, and impotence have been inflicted on offenders as punishment, restraint, or both. If punishment is justified, however, it must not be itself evil treatment. It is difficult to justify complete isolation, impotence, or severe pain even as punishments. Yet lesser degrees of these evils are routine in discipline of children and in penal systems that rely on imprisonment and for discipline within prisons, on solitary confinement and refusal to supervise personnel who beat inmates. Appreciating the suffering of these things as basic evils should make the justifiability of punishment more controversial than it has been. Refusal to supervise inmates who rape other inmates is an evil that may seriously compromise the self-respect of victims, about which the next chapter has more to say. To whatever extent systems of punishment compromise the basic self-respect of those punished, they are evil and should be changed or abolished.

Basic evils are major ingredients in social oppression as Iris Young analyzes it: Marginalization isolates groups and individuals; powerlessness is impotence; violence paradigmatically is painful. Rawls's theory of justice is superb at explaining the evil of exploitation as a face of oppression. What Iris Young calls cultural imperialism sounds like it includes an assault on the development of self-respect. What makes oppression evil is that the human behavior responsible for the infliction of or refusal to alleviate these basic evils is so grossly unjustified. There is often even no pretense of justification. Isolation, impotence, pain, and assaults on self-respect are also central to the oppression of individuals in intimate partner battery and child abuse. Batterers not only hit, and incest perpetrators not only rape. Both also isolate their victims. The violence of domestic assault and rape not only injures physically but also commonly results in the impotence of posttraumatic stress. The suddenness of violence takes its victims off guard during episodes and keeps them in a state of constant fear between episodes. The result is victims, or survivors, who lack confidence in themselves as moral persons.

Iris Young suggests that we begin with domination and oppression as our paradigms of injustice.[53] Whereas Rawls focuses on the ideal case, she focuses on some of the worst. Yet if justice is, in Rawls's words, "the first virtue of social institutions, as truth is of systems of thought," a theory of justice should enable us to identify oppression and say what is wrong with it.[54] Rawls's theory was formulated with at least one extremely oppressive historical phenomenon in mind: hereditary slavery. Most seem to agree that his theory explains better than alternative views, such as utilitarianism, what is wrong with slavery. Slavery is unjust economic exploitation, and that is certainly part of what is wrong with it. Its inequalities violate Rawls's difference principle, in that they are not to the greatest benefit of those least advantaged (slaves). Yet that understates the case against slavery almost as much as pointing out its inefficiency. As Rawls also notes, the "offices" of hereditary slavery — positions defined by the rules — are not open to everyone under conditions of fair competition. (Slaves had no opportunity to be masters.) This also understates what is wrong. From the perspectives of its victims, what is primarily wrong with slavery is that it is oppressive: violent, disempowering, marginalizing, genocidal, an instrument of domination that destroys human potential and human culture on a phenomenal scale, often wantonly. Its violation of Rawls's first principle of justice, that "each person has an equal claim to a fully adequate scheme of basic rights and liberties, which scheme is compatible with the same scheme for all," comes closer to what is fundamentally wrong.[55] Yet even that is highly abstract. Filling it out in terms of primary goods yields yet another understatement: Slaves lack the basics that everyone can be presumed to want whatever else they might want. That is true, but it seems more to the point to say that they suffer evil treatment.

In *Political Liberalism* Rawls presents the primary goods as citizens' needs, mentions that his list may be expanded, and explicitly mentions the possibility of including freedom from physical pain.[56] Failure to satisfy a need suggests evil more readily than does failure to provide goods. Rawls's intention appears to be that basic liberties, supplemented by a social minimum below which no one would be permitted to fall, would free us from evils such as bodily assault and poverty. This reminds me of the utilitarian's faith that injustice will not turn out to be useful in the end. Perhaps so. But banking on it makes me nervous.

In answer to the question posed at the beginning of this section, whether justice ethics is better positioned than care ethics to respond to the evils of racism and sexism, I conclude that there is hope here if a just society is understood as one in which oppression is not tolerated and oppression is understood in terms of basic evils. One need not encounter those who are liable to suffer basic evils in order to be concerned to design social institutions so as to avoid, prevent, alleviate them, and so forth.

Schopenhauer and more recently Virginia Held and others have held that justice is *a moral minimum* and that a fuller ethical view would go beyond justice to include caring. Something like this also seems to have been Kant's view in that his perfect duties, which take precedence, sound like duties of justice, and some of his imperfect duties, which allow the agent a certain latitude and discretion, sound like responsibilities of moral caring. Schopenhauer and Nel Noddings, however, also seem to regard justice as a substitute for caring in many contexts where caring would be ideal but is unrealistic to expect. I suspect that something like the opposite of these ideas may be true. The demands of perfect justice may be so great that perhaps the best we can do in many contexts is to assume responsibilities of caring where we are able, although justice would be ideal. So far from providing a moral minimum, perfect justice seems to me to demand more than most of us are willing to contemplate seriously—which is all the more reason to focus on basic evils and on how to avoid, prevent, and remedy evil treatment.

RAPE TERRORISM

n an essay entitled "Why Terrorism Is Morally Problematic" Bat-Ami Bar On argues that terrorism forms the terrorized, that it "produces people who are psychologically and morally diminished," and that "it is, therefore, cruel."[1] Part of women's moral luck in misogynist societies is to be formed — or seriously exposed to the risk of being formed — by rape terrorism. Where it does not corner us into acting under a "diminished ethical ideal," to use Nel Noddings's phrase, it seriously restricts our mobility and thereby our experience and development. A raised consciousness about rape as a terrorist political institution may enable us to move beyond understanding as our only options those defined by this institution and may motivate us to combine with each other to undermine it.

Rape is a set of interrelated terrorist institutions. The one that I discuss in this chapter is a protection racket whereby women are compelled to seek the protection of some men against others. Martial rape often does not fit this pattern, although it may belong to a different protection racket whereby some men are compelled, by means of terrorizing women to whom they are attached, to seek the protection of other men.[2] Gang rapes, such as those Peggy Sanday uncovered in her research on fraternity gang rape, may be part of a training for war, or perhaps a substitute for it.[3] The rape terrorism discussed in this chapter might be called "civilian rape" in that it is committed even during times of so-called peace. However, Harvard psychiatrist Judith Lewis Herman (who uses the term "civilian rape") maintains that the "shell shock" in World War I combat survivors was the same post-traumatic stress disorder as is experienced by female survivors of domestic violence. She concludes that women and children subject to civilian rape and domestic violence are in a war.[4] The term "domestic rape" is ambiguous in that it can suggest either "civilian rape" or the more specific area of family violence. Not surprisingly, there is no convenient term to describe the subset of practices discussed in this chapter. The point to note is that the patterns this chapter explores are not the only ones, although they are widespread. They seem to me very basic patterns in that other forms of institutionalized rape, such as rape in men's prisons and martial rape, can often be understood as variations on them.[5] Interestingly, women's prisons exhibit a different phenomenon with respect to same-sex relationships, an apparently friendlier one that sociologists have called "familying" whereby women who fall in love with other women adopt each other's friends as "mother," "father," sister," and so forth, complete with "incest" prohibitions.[6] I do not know whether this custom includes protectionism.

How Bad Is Rape?

A feminist critic in the United States once argued that "while rape is very bad indeed, the work that most women employed outside the home are compelled to do is more seriously harmful insofar as doing such work damages the most fundamental interests of the victim, what Joel Feinberg calls 'welfare interests,' whereas rape typically does not."[7] This judgment takes rape to be simply an individual act, ignoring its relationship to institutional rules and thereby its terrorist implications. Rape as an institution has severe consequences not only for women raped but also for women terrorized into compliance and even for their daughters. It underlies women's willingness to do whatever work men find suitable for women to do. So understood, rape does indeed damage women's fundamental interests, although information on it is less public than (other) information on working conditions in the paid labor force.

The term "terrorism" as used in the public media suggests a kind of political activity, usually with international significance, focused on the powers of states or other territorial governments.[8] The restriction to _territorial_ politics, however, ignores the terrorism of _sexual_ politics. Ethically, that exclusion is arbitrary and irresponsible. It maintains the invisibility of routine violence against women, underlying visible sexist stereotypes. Rape and family violence, overlapping terrorist institutions, form a backdrop to the daily lives of women in sexist societies.

The philosophical significance of recognizing rape as terrorism is twofold. On one hand, philosophical discussions of terrorism are enlarged by it and our understanding of terrorism's workings is deepened by including the data of terrorist sexual politics. For they exemplify profoundly institutionalized forms of terrorism that tend to be overlooked in media portrayals of the terrorist as a mad individual. At the same time, the meaning and significance of rape and domestic battery can be clarified in relation to women's oppression by appreciating their terrorist implications, and the meaning of feminine character in a misogynist society can be better appreciated by understanding the terrorist context out of which it develops.

My first aim here is to elucidate what it means to call rape institutionalized terrorism. I do not attempt to support empirical claims about the facts of rape. Crime reports are one source of statistics, and yet it is generally agreed that rape is highly underreported. There is no consensus on how highly underreported it is, or even on how it should be defined. The analysis in this chapter should, however, clarify the significance of such lacks of consensus. In any case, it is philosophically interesting that without disputing facts many do not yet apply the concept of "terrorism" to rape. Recognizing rape as institutionalized terrorism is yet another step in clarifying what is wrong with it and how bad it is in relation to other forms of violence and abuse.[9] It is also important that we learn to resist rape's terroristic potentialities, which attach to the institution regardless of whether they also attach to a particular rape.

The claim that rape is a terrorist institution involves two views that some may find surprising. One is that rape is an *institution*. The other is that it is a form of *terrorism*. I take up these ideas in that order. For it is important to understand rape as an institution in order to show how it works socially as a form of terrorism.

Rape as an Institution

To my knowledge, the earliest extended feminist discussion of rape as a practice is that of Susan Griffin in her 1971 essay in *Ramparts* magazine, "Rape: The All-American Crime," a classic used in training manuals for rape crisis centers from coast to coast.[10] She also refers in that essay to rape as terrorism. The same year a much shorter essay, "Rape: An Act of Terror," by Barbara Mehrhoff and Pamela Kearon, published in *Notes from the Third Year,* gave explicit recognition in detail to the terroristic aspects of rape.[11] Although these theorists do not make explicit use of the concept of an institution, the idea is implicitly there, in one case in the allusion to All-American sports (as sports exemplify institutions) and in the other, in the idea of an extra-legal social structure designed to place "woman qua woman" "outside the protection of the law."

Rape is an institution not in the sense that it names an organization, such as the SS, KGB, FBI, or CIA, but in the sense that war and punishment are institutions. It is a fairly elaborate practice, with many historical embodiments and variations. As the institution of war includes the practice of punishment, both can include practices of rape. Following John Rawls, I use the terms "practice" and "institution" more or less interchangeably here and mean by both a form of social activity structured by rules that define such things as roles, moves, positions, powers, and opportunities, thereby distributing responsibility for consequences.[12] The more established a practice is, the more natural it seems to refer to it as an institution.

Many participants in the institution of rape appear not to think of themselves as participating in an institution or practice, a matter to which I return. Rather, they encourage each other to think of their behavior as natural, at least self-originating, or, at its most complicated, as a response to provocation by women.

A practice can take root, become institutionalized, so firmly that it is not necessary for anyone to supervise the operation as a whole. Individual participants find that they have their own good reasons, or failing that, excuses, for what they do. Such institutions form the core subject matter of what Kate Millett called "sexual politics."[13] "Sexual politics" does not refer simply to the politics of the state (or any other territorial political body) with respect to sexual activity, although it includes that. Nor is it concerned only with sexual behavior. "Sexual politics" refers to social norms that create and define distributions of power among and between members of the sexes, considered as such. Historically, rape has been a major sexuo-political institution.

"Rape," like "punishment," is ambiguous. It can refer to a specific kind of act, abstracted from its institutional setting, often (not necessarily) violent and painful. The same term can also refer, however, to an institution governing that act, an institution defined by rules that establish roles and positions, distribute responsibilities and opportunities, and create or withdraw power.[14] In the institution of punishment, some rules prohibit behaviors and specify penalties for offenses. Others govern the processes of policing, arrest, detention, and trial. Only some participants in the institution of punishment actually administer penalties. One may be hard put to say how much responsibility a particular individual participant bears for the punishment, or release, of any accused individual. Yet communities supporting and benefiting from such institutions can be held responsible and can take responsibility for the institution and its operations. The same holds true for rape.

Although there is controversy over the goals of punishment, most grant that deterrence of would-be criminal offenders is a legitimate aim. Whatever the justifying goals of the institution as a whole, they need not correspond with the intentional aims of participants at every stage or in every role.[15] They need not, in particular, correspond with the aims of those who administer penalties. Often, more specific rules of the institution offer incentives (such as salaries) sufficient to motivate individuals. Ordinarily, one supposes, those who administer penalties do it for the money, although there is room also for sadism. Still, they participate in the practice to the extent that their behavior is guided and evaluated by its norms, even if they are not themselves motivated by the overall goals served by the practice, and even if the guiding and evaluating is largely done by others who have power over them.

Analogous observations apply to the institution of rape. Just as deterrence from crime is a major task of punishment, the subordination and subservience of women to men is a major task of rape. Just as with punishment, the threat is what does most of the work.[16] Not all who support or follow the rules carry out or even witness particular acts of rape. As with the infliction of punishment, many who support it would rather not have to witness it. Those who do commit rape may have private motives of their own, such as revenge on other men. As with those who abide by the law, not all who follow the rules of rape need have the long-range aims or consequences of the practice "in mind" as they do, although they often do have more specific rules in mind, even if most would not describe what they have in mind as "rules." In the case of punishment, it may be primarily judges and juries, formal and informal, backing the rules in particular cases, who have the large-scale purposes "in mind." Similarly, in the case of rape, it may be primarily judging observers who have more large-scale purposes in mind as they judge. For the most part, however, the rules become "second nature," like the rules of grammar, and those guided need not be aware of the rules as learned norms. There is also room for controversy about the extent to which female compliance with male desire is due to the threat of rape. As with the relationship between punishment and compliance with the law, there is more than one story to be told here.

An ostensible difference between punishment in modern democratic states and rape is that punishment as defined (if not as practiced) by modern democratic states, as a temporary or permanent withdrawal of certain rights, is meant to be humane, not terrorist. This has not always been true of state punishments. In a democracy punishment is supposed to play the role of a stabilizer, providing people with a mutual assurance of general obedience to their common laws, thus making it rational for individuals to comply. It is supposed to be what people might well propose be carried out against themselves, should they fail to live up to their commitments, as a gesture of good faith and in recognition of their common liability to temptation.[17] Rape is not. It is not a liability to which one might reasonably submit, fantasy notwithstanding. Some rapes are less brutal than others. Yet rape is not meant to be humane, regardless of how it is done.

Rape as Terrorism

Stereotypes of the terrorist as mad bomber or airplane hijacker present terrorism as *public*, often idiosyncratically motivated *rebellion*, and focused on the power of *state governments*. The terrorism of rape does not fit that model. It is not entirely public. It is not focused on the power of state governments. It is not ordinarily a form of rebellion. Much about rape is clandestine. Its concern is sexual politics, rather than territorial politics. Laws officially prohibit rape. Yet constant danger to women offers men a ready source of material services in exchange for "protection." Barbara Mehrhof and Pamela Kearon observed in 1971 that "rape laws are designed to protect males against the charge of rape."[18] Governments certainly have been better at protecting certain men from accusations of rape than at protecting most women from rape.

Critics of popular views of terrorism, such as Jonathan Glover (and earlier, Emma Goldman), have rightly challenged the idea that terrorism is perpetrated only by enemies of the state. Glover writes: " 'Our' cause is usually supported by the resistance, by the underground, or by freedom fighters, while 'their' cause is often supported by terrorists. The use of the word 'terrorism' is often so loose and so loaded that it is tempting to abandon it."[19] Recognizing the existence of state terrorism helps us to realize that terrorism is not always public. Historically, state terrorism has often been carried out by secret organizations and accompanied by public disavowals on the part of government bodies.

When terrorism is thought of as public, it may be tempting to admire terrorists somewhat for courage and honesty or alternatively to deplore their manifest lack of shame. Thus Annette Baier asks: "Does the fact that the killing is done openly, with an eye to publicity, make it better or worse than killings done quietly and with attempted secrecy? . . . The person we call a terrorist (as distinct from the assassin) typically does her violence in the public eye."[20] It may be neither courage nor lack of shame, however, so much as necessity dictated by the terrorists' goals that determines whether a particular instance of terrorism is public or private. Terrorists working in the public eye aim to terrorize a certain public. Showing that they do not fear punishment can be necessary to succeed in terrorizing a government or other powerful body. Terrorists who are already relatively powerful (such as an established state government) need not make that point. They may have more to fear from publicity. For publicity could reveal that those terrorized into compliance were not acting voluntarily.

Terrorism is distinguished less by its ends or by the character traits it manifests than by its process. It is a tactic used to gain control of situations, or to fix or shift a balance of power, public or private. Terrorism is a shortcut to power or authority, a resort of the relatively powerless or of those unable to justify their uses of power to a public.

If humane forms of deterrence threaten penalties to which one might reasonably be prepared to submit in the event of one's evident disobedience, terrorism often manipulates target populations into compliance with demands they should reject, if rational, under calmer conditions. Terror as a tactic is an alternative to persuasion and argument, which are slower and riskier, and to humane forms of deterrence, which are also riskier and often more expensive. The work of Emma Goldman and Jonathan Glover on state terrorism suggests that terrorism is distinguished from the formally defined public threat of legal punishment in modern states more by the nakedness of its appeal to the motive of terror than by the political status of its perpetrators.

Terrorism involves planned or systematic manipulation. Terror—
panicky and heightened fear—makes us vulnerable to manipulation.
We feel an urgent need to act before it is too late. Thus we are in a poor
position to reflect or get things in perspective. We are in a poor position
to be prudent or just. Our attention is riveted by the threat of disaster
and what we can do to prevent it. We are thus not so likely to pay
attention to the terrorizer's situation, options, motivations, or aims,
except as they define what we must do to avoid disaster. We feel our
options narrowed to the point of almost no control.[21] There is a danger
for the terrorist of going too far, of freezing us instead of merely terrorizing us, with the result that manipulation becomes impossible. Terrorists, like other torturers, develop sensitivities and skills to avoid this
consequence.

Like other terrorisms, rape has two targets, in this case "bad girls"
and "good girls," those expendable ("throw-aways") and those to
whom a message is sent by way of the treatment of the former.[22] Women
and girls to whom the message is sent may not directly confront men or
boys they perceive as rapists. Some may not often *feel* terrorized by rape.
It does not follow that they are not victims of terrorism. When terrorism
is successful, the second target population (to whom the message is
sent) need not experience continual terror. Women successfully terrorized, and others socialized by them, *comply* with men's demands. As
reward and inducement to continue, they are granted "protection"
that they may feel they have "earned." The feeling of "earned protection" gives a sense of control. Daughters of terrorized mothers may be
shielded for a long time by being "properly brought up."

Women whose encounters with violence are most immediate and
most traumatic are not always most liable to manipulation by fear of
violence. Survivor rage can overcome fear. Having faced the apparent
worst, some women become dedicated to *non*compliance. Like their
sisters who did not survive, such women and others who have been
tortured or mutilated may be useless to men except to send a message
to other women to try thereby to secure their services: This is what will
happen to you if you are not "good," if you fail to do as we say.

An allegedly obsolete meaning of "rape" is "to carry off forcibly," a
kind of theft. Rape has historically been treated by men as a crime of
theft against other men. That idea is not totally obsolete. Men still often
regard the rape of a woman as an offense against her guardian—the
theft of something (the woman's "honor") that has a monetary value, a

prestige value, or both. From the guardian's point of view, rape is a source of anger, indignation, resentment, even bitterness, but not of terror. It is only from the point of view of women (or of men treated as women) that rape is terrifying. Omnipresent fear of rape controls women's mobility. Rapes of prostitutes, lesbians, and other women with no male guardians — and so having nothing to "steal" — receive even less legal uptake than rapes of women who have male guardians. Yet the terror of rape is a fact of daily life for prostitutes, lesbians, and others who have no male guardians. These are among the expendables ("throw-aways") liable to being used to send a message to women more likely to be compliant.

The Protection Racket

Feminists aside, philosophers have said little about rape. This could be surprising, considering how much they have said about violence against men. Except for accusations invented by European Americans to "justify" lynchings of African Americans, rape has not been, until recent years, even an issue — that is, discussable.[23] Men have officially acknowledged that rape is wrong, but so obviously wrong that what was to discuss? Feminists have had to make an issue of rape.

Since Susan Griffin's essay on rape as the "all-American crime," it has become commonplace among feminists to regard rape as the linchpin of a male protection racket in misogynist societies.

> In the system of chivalry, men protect women against men. This is not unlike the protection relationship which [organized crime] established with small businesses in the early part of this century. Indeed, chivalry is an age-old protection racket which depends for its existence on rape.[24]

Rackets *create* danger in order to sell "protection." Historically, organized crime expanded its power base by securing service and payment through terrorist means, from bombings to individual torture and mutilation. Historically, also, rape and the threat of rape have secured women's services for men who have represented themselves as protectors while they terrorized other women or supported other men who did.

In an essay with the memorable title, "Coercion and Rape: The State as a Male Protection Racket," Susan Rae Peterson argues that rape is a state-sponsored institution.[25] Rape is a "Rawlsian kind of 'practice,' " she says, a "form of activity specified by a system of rules which define offices, rules, moves, penalties, defences, and so on, and which give the activity its structure."[26] If a state fails to protect women against rape but succeeds in protecting at least certain classes of men against rape charges, she argues, it supports a "racket." I would go further and say that a state supports a racket even when it does penalize rapists, if it is responsible for the continued threat of rape.

Offers of "protection" are offers that women have dared not refuse. If we refuse the bargain — refuse to pay protection and insist upon moving about without a guardian — we are held responsible for dangers we meet in response to our self-assertion. When we are raped, we hear that we brought it on ourselves, as Hegel said of the punishment visited on a criminal by the state.[27] For we could have stayed home or gone out with a guardian. Our position is in some ways worse than that of the buyer from the crime syndicate. For our success in eliciting offers of protection, the need for which we learn in early childhood, requires that we comport and decorate ourselves in precisely those ways that are said to bring on and intensify the dangers from which we are to be protected. We hear that not to groom ourselves in this way is not to care about our appearance. Belatedly, we find that a male guardian can often protect us from no one but himself, and we are surely at his mercy there. The protectorate tends not to recognize rape by guardians or by males to whom we have once been accessible. Because access, a major face of power, is controlled by the protectorate, those who pay protection are unable to control the need for protection.[28]

Rape Mythology Undermined by Amir's Research

Important to rape as a terrorist institution is the myth that rapists are weirdos lurking in the bushes or stalking beautiful innocent (or naughty) women who walk alone. According to this myth, rape serves only the perverse desires of madmen, always mysterious strangers. In 1971 sociologist Menachem Amir published a study of 646 rapes reported in Philadelphia for the years 1958 and 1960, which did much to discredit this madman myth and the "irresistible impulse" theory of rape as well.[29] Amir found that the majority of the rapes he studied were planned, not spontaneous (in gang rapes, 90 percent were planned; in pair rapes, 83 percent; in single rapes, 58 percent), that nearly half the rapists were personally known to the women they targeted, that a high proportion of rapes occurred in the homes of either the perpetrator or the women targeted, and that 43 percent involved multiple rapists.[30] Defending his *situational*— as opposed to *psychological*— approach to studying rape, Amir reports that "studies indicate that sex offenders do not constitute a unique clinical or psychopathological type; nor are they as a group invariably more disturbed than the control groups to which they were compared."[31] It appears that men convicted of rape are no more mentally disturbed than other men. It does not follow, of course, that other men are not mentally disturbed, or even that they do not rape. On the contrary, such studies raise the question how common rape is among men who regard each other as normal, even respectable.

Amir's research is a turning point. Prior studies focused on the psychologies of rapists and of the women they targeted, assuming that individual rapes had sufficient explanations in individual psychological eccentricity. Patriarchal tradition blames, ultimately, the women in the case — the woman targeted for rape, the rapist's mother, the rapist's wife or "girlfriend" — and reserves sympathy for rapists, who "have a problem." Amir focused on situational aspects, rather than individual psychologies: where the rape was done, when, how, and what were the prior relationships, if any, between the perpetrators and the women they targeted. His findings upset popular mythology about who rapists are, whom they target, and where and when they do it.

Imaginatively, it is a short step from finding social *patterns,* understood as statistical generalizations (which is how Amir understood them), to identifying social *norms* defining an institution by which people guide and evaluate their behavior.[32] The alternative to separate explanations of individual rapes is not necessarily a conspiracy, although Amir's study certainly turned up enough conspiracies. A more interesting alternative is that of a sexuo-political institution, the rules of which, learned by example and precept, are presented as though they were empirical generalizations about women and men, anthropological claims about female and male nature.

Combining Amir's research with Susan Griffin's protection racket theory and the view of Barbara Mehrhof and Pamela Kearon of rape as an act of terror yields the idea of rape as a terrorist institution. This is a relatively optimistic view. It demystifies rape. It does not rest on conjectures about the mysteries of male biology but presents rape as learned behavior. It suggests that rape, like slavery, can be abolished, however inconceivable that may seem to those whose material well-being and sense of self-esteem now depends on its existence.

Doublethink and Clandestine Outlaw Institutions

Although they may be supported in various ways by the state, rackets are outlaw institutions. That is, the behavior central to them is officially illegal. Outlaw institutions involve clandestine operations. The sense in which agents carrying out clandestine operations participate in institutions generating the operations can be problematic. Some agents are clear that they are committing, condoning, or supporting rape, but not that it is part of a political operation. Other agents seem unclear about whether what they did was rape. Many do not care.

The clandestine nature of the institution is part of the explanation why many do not imagine that they are taking part in an institution. Some, manipulated by others, may not be aware of roles they play. Secret terrorism authorized by institutions that have governing bodies can help us get a fix on how terrorist policing institutions work. Participants in secret state practices or crime syndicate operations act with varying degrees of awareness that they are participating in a large and complex institution. Institutions with clandestine operations launder evil deeds like dirty money, passing them through a series of agents with ever-decreasing information about what is being done and why. Agents who administer violent deaths and torture are sometimes paid or coerced outright. But sometimes they are punished, instead of rewarded, by those whom they have served, as a public disavowal of responsibility by the latter. Unpunished rapists may be like hangmen doing the dirty work of others who while not admiring them for it nevertheless make certain that they are enabled to do on doing what they do.

What George Orwell called "doublethink" is a common institutional tool of manipulation.[33] "Doublethink" makes a thing seem its opposite, as when "peace-keepers" becomes the term for weapons. The rules of rape use doublethink to shield participants from having to recognize rape when doing so might be counterproductive. Consequently, women often find it impossible to convince others that a rape was really a rape. The problem is not, as it is so often presented, that there is a slippery slope from polite refusal to teasing seduction on women's part. The problem is that women's wills in rape situations become irrelevant. Despite clear demonstration of undisputed, unwanted violence, the rules of rape can block recognition that a rape was committed, especially when the assailant is no stranger to the woman he targets.[34]

Consider the following case, known to me personally from a little more than a decade ago. I choose it because it is not unusual and so is helpful in making a general point about rape. A female university student did not understand until fully a week later that she had been raped by the male student with whom she went home to study, even though she was well aware that he forcibly detained her, threw her to the floor, pinned her in place by methods that I will spare you, and sexually penetrated both ends of her body, causing her physical injuries and loss of blood. How could she not know that she was raped? She was apparently in shock afterward. But that was not why. The problem was, as she put it, that *she went voluntarily to his apartment,* in response to his invitation. Women who do this hear that they have "asked for it." This woman heard that not only from her assailant but also from the hometown law enforcement officer to whom she first reported the rape, at her mother's insistence, after returning home to recuperate.

In the city where the assault actually took place, police have been taught not to disregard a rape charge for that kind of reason. Hearing this from the rape crisis hotline, the student went to the district attorney. Nearly two years later, I watched the jury return a verdict of "not guilty." The defense attorney denied *only* that the woman had withheld consent. He argued that because she was angry (by then, she was) instead of ashamed (she no longer was), his client had probably made her feel rejected and that she had probably invented the rape charge as revenge.

The thing to notice is what makes it standardly impossible to answer the question what really happened and how this impossibility functions in a terrorist practice. Doublethink turns rape into something the perpetrator and target did together or into an "event" that "happened between us," as the man in the above case put it to the woman who later charged him with rape. This is achieved by rules defining "consent," or rather, defining it out of existence.

The Rules

The first rule of institutionalized rape, still embedded in older legal definitions, is that husbands cannot rape their wives. Or, alternatively, husbands are permitted to rape their wives with utter impunity. Notice that it does not matter which way you put it. The idea gets across. The rule permits husbands carnal access regardless of their wives' wills. Many of the rules of rape are unwritten, although this first one is still found explicitly in jurisdictions not yet affected by feminist criticism. As a result of liberal feminist criticism, some jurisdictions now use the language of "sexual assault," breaking down the possibilities into degrees of seriousness, and have abandoned the term "rape." Yet many of us retain the term "rape" because it conveys, in a way that "sexual assault" does not, who historically has assaulted whom and who continues to be the main target.

When rape is defined as forcible carnal knowledge by a man of a woman *not his wife,* nothing a man does to the woman married to him is allowed to count as "real" rape. If we understand "forcible" in its ordinary sense, this is doublethink. Wives *can* be sexually forced, "accessed" against their wills. It is not rape only if wives are *normatively disabled* from withholding consent.

This is an example of rules that define categories of women who are not allowed to count as rape targets, at least for certain men. No matter what the men do to them, it is not really rape, because the rules give the woman's status itself the value of consent. Other such status examples are prostitutes, women who are not "virgins" (including women previously raped), and women who have had past voluntary sexual relations with a particular man (where nothing he does to her afterward counts as "real" rape).

Another kind of rule gives female appearance, rather than status, the value of consent. Consider the rule that women who dress or move "provocatively" are "asking for it." There are basically two ways for women to "provoke" male sexual aggression. First, there is the "sexy" way, where our clothes and manner accent femininity. Second, there is the "castrating bitch" way, where our clothes and manner manifest, rather, a refusal to make a feminine or "sexy" display of femaleness, and we consequently need to be "taught our place." It might seem, then, that the implication is that women should wear nothing. Yet we hear that this is the most "provocative" of all — except when it is disgusting.

Most interesting, perhaps, are the situational rules, such as the rule that a woman *alone* is "asking for it." There are three ways of being alone. First, there is the straightforward, ordinary sense of being unaccompanied by anyone at all. But, second, women who are accompanied by other women are represented as being "*all* alone," which sounds even more alone than before (although it is often the safest situation).[35] Third, a woman may be *alone with* a man. "Alone with" sounds like a self-contradiction. Yet the description is apt. A woman alone with a man is physically present with someone — as the female student was physically present with the male student in his apartment — who is not, however, presumed to be with her in the sense of being on her side. The alternative to these three ways of being alone is to be accompanied by a guardian — who can, of course, do anything he pleases without its counting as rape.

The above rules confer the value, or part of the value, of consent upon a woman's status, appearance, behavior, or situation. Still others confer that value simply upon the female body itself and upon its involuntary experience. Contemporary patriarchal society treats the female body itself as provocative. There are rules to the effect that a woman who is sexually aroused is willing and that one who experiences pleasure is likewise willing. As empirical generalizations, these claims are false. But they are not simply false empirical generalizations. They are political norms, redefining "consent" and thereby the meaning of "rape."

Yet another rule is that consent once given cannot be withdrawn.[36] We have already seen this implicitly in the cases of some statuses, such as marriage, that may be acquired through consent. But it also comes into play on an ordinary date if a woman wishes to change her mind in the course of an evening. Contrast this with accepting an invitation to have lunch together. If I no longer feel like eating when the time comes, I may just keep you company or drink something while you eat. It is difficult to imagine wanting a companion to eat anyway, just because she agreed to earlier, if she no longer wants food when the time comes. Force-feeding as a way of handling such disappointment would hardly be found natural or excusable. Yet the rules of rape legitimize its analogue regarding sex.

Related to the rule that consent once given cannot be withdrawn is the rule that men once sexually aroused are no longer responsible for their conduct. As an empirical claim, this is less plausible than the analogous claims would be about men who are hungry or thirsty. For self-gratification is readily obtainable in the case of sexual arousal. The claim that sexually aroused men are no longer responsible for their conduct makes sense, however, once we recognize it as not an empirical claim but a political norm. Men sexually aroused are, by the rules, *absolved* of responsibility for their behavior.

Considered one by one, most of the rules do not ask the impossible. They thus create the impression that failing to meet their requirements is avoidable. Yet looking at the requirements only one by one and drawing such a conclusion is like looking at the individual bars of a cage and concluding that since no one of them could possibly confine anyone, there is no trap.[37] In the ways that they work together, the rules of institutionalized rape leave no alternatives by which women can be genuinely secure against sexual violation by men. Trying our best to live up to them still leaves us at the mercy of men (as men have long believed they were at the mercy of their God), who can always find a "violation" if they wish, but who may spare us if we are evidently trying to be "good," that is, if we are sufficiently deferential. Curiously, the result has not been to rob most women of motives for trying to please. Inexperienced women may not appreciate the incoherence of the big picture. But even experienced women often see no better alternative than trying to please those in power, accepting the humiliating position of being "wrong" no matter what, and striving by ingratiation to reduce the likelihood of abuse.

The most blatant rule, summing up the spirit of institutionalized rape, is that when a woman says no she means yes. What must she do or say, then, to mean no? Nothing she *says* counts for much. Historically, she was expected to resist physically to her utmost, which has also been a turn-on for the rapist. If both no and yes mean yes, neither means anything. The net result is that women are politically disabled from withholding consent to male sexual access.

While most rules make it impossible for women to withhold consent, a few do just the opposite: girls cannot give consent — clearly, a political norm, not an empirical claim. Likewise, the unofficial racist rule that white women cannot consent to black men is a transparently political norm. Like the others, these rules also divorce consent from the will.

But their functions are different. Rules that disable women from giving consent enable some men to control other men by marking certain females as off limits to them. Such rules may seem to offer women real, if limited, protection. However, white racist rules have been designed to protect the "purity" of white people, not to protect women. In so doing they control white women as well as men of color, barring both from interracial relationships. Jailbait rules, which might also seem to offer young women some real protection, are designed to protect female marriageability against theft by potential guardians. Yet such rules have not protected girls from abuse by adult men in their homes.

Rules that disable women from withholding consent help to make sense of myths about rape that are otherwise puzzling and even mutually contradictory although simultaneously believed. For example, rape is popularly considered both normal and impossible. When I was an undergraduate, one of my philosophy professors told the "joke" in lecture that it was impossible to rape a woman because a woman with her skirt up can run faster than a man with his pants down. The myth that it is impossible to rape a woman usually is understood to mean that no man could physically succeed with a woman who really did not consent. Taken empirically, this claim appears to deny that women are forced at gunpoint or knifepoint or by gangs to submit to acts to which they would otherwise not submit. But guns, knives, muscles, and so forth are irrelevant to the question of consent. It was sufficient that the woman either was or was not wearing clothes that highlighted her femaleness, that she was alone either with or without other men or women, that she said either yes or no, and so on. If it is impossible to rape a woman, that is because the rules of rape discredit her refusals. They thereby make a certain sense of the myth that only a mentally disturbed or retarded man would commit rape, that the act is not normal. Unless he is a victim of racism, a man would almost have to be mentally disturbed or retarded not to be able to fit his behavior under some rules or other whereby nothing he did would count as rape. Because of those rules, however, rape also appears normal, because it is very ordinary. For, women who are unable to withhold consent are also unable to give it.

The rules also make sense of male paranoia regarding women falsely crying "rape." Offhand, this paranoia is puzzling, considering how much rape goes unreported and how women have been treated when they did report it. However, since the rules do not meaningfully distinguish between women who really do consent and women who do not, it should not be surprising that men wonder whether women have any way to make that distinction in reporting what men did to them.

Stopping Rape: Mill's Liberalism, Femininity, and What's Wrong with Terrorism

It is commonplace among feminists that *preventing* rape should not be women's responsibility. Preventing rape should be the responsibility of those who commit it, support it, or are served and empowered by it. Women's energies are needed for healing, mutual support, and getting on with our lives. Yet women surely have an interest in *avoiding* rape and rape terrorism.[38] Exposing the rules of the institution is helpful toward this end, suggesting strategies of avoidance, such as separatist experiments communicating that women who say no mean no and demonstrating that women together are not alone. Self-defense instruction for those of us raised to be physical cowards and incompetents can be valuable, even life-saving, in the short run. Yet, although it helps to counteract terrorism by instilling confidence, belated self-defense instruction does little to address the institutionalization of rape.[39] Women's transit organizations, rape crisis centers, and battered women's shelters, all heavily dependent on volunteer work, confront the protection racket directly by offering alternative sources of protection so that women need not seek protection from those who create or benefit from the existence of the danger. The critic who found women's working conditions more harmful than "typical acts of rape" could still make the point that if women cease to *value* the "sexual purity" that has made rape, historically, reduce women's value to men, there is *one less thing to fear* from rape. Reassessing the significance of rape is one among many strategies for avoiding rape terrorism.

Despite the belief that preventing rape should not be women's responsibility, many women are in fact taking aggressive steps to combat it, in addition to learning to avoid it. The most popularly controversial strategies of combatting rape are probably the feminist attacks on media propaganda that set up women for rape by conveying to men the message that women like to be manhandled and by encouraging girls and young women to develop positive fantasies of being raped. Pornography is a major vehicle of this propaganda, not only dirty books and magazines but also pornographic scenes sprinkled commonly throughout fiction, modern theater entertainment, and commodity advertising. A little more than a decade ago a low-budget, documentary film entitled *Rape Culture* showed scenes glorifying rape from popular movies in the United States, including *Gone with the Wind, Straw Dogs,* and *Butch Cassidy and the Sundance Kid.*[40] In each, rape is presented as thrilling and fulfilling for a woman. Scarlett O'Hara is never more radiant than the morning after Rhett Butler rapes her. In *Straw Dogs* the rapist beats up a woman and drags her about by the hair before he finally rapes her, and at the moment of penetration, her agonized face melts into ecstatic pleasure. These scenes remind us how women learn to develop the kinds of rape fantasies that facilitate actual rape.

One may wonder whether such rape fantasies fit the idea of rape as a terrorist institution. Some, of course, clearly do. Not all rape fantasies are of being raped; many (as noted in Chapter Three) are of killing the rapist or getting various sorts of revenge. Yet even the fantasies encouraged by pornography fit the idea of rape terrorism. The word "rape" is not used in the scripts of the film scenes mentioned above. Rather, these films present the rapist as a woman's protector. The fantasy that pornography teaches women to enjoy is of rape by a "prince" who then protects her from other men, who are sources of terror. The "prince" is the "good rapist," although even he was a source of terror prior to the act.[41]

Since at least the late 1950s many philosophers have defended pornography by appeal to the liberty principle of John Stuart Mill, a use of that principle that Mill seems not to have foreseen.[42] His liberty principle is that interference in someone's conduct (other than by persuasion and argument), whether by the state or by an individual, is not justified except to prevent that agent from harming yet others. He interprets "harm" as injury inflicted without the informed consent of those on whom it is inflicted. Mill applied his principle to religious and political censorship as well as to undefined "experiments in living," but he did not explicitly apply it to such things as pornography or prostitution. Those who make the latter applications tend to assume that viewers, users, and those participating in the production and exchange of pornography or in prostitution are not harmed in the relevant sense, as long as they are consenting adults, and that no one else need be harmed because no one else need be involved.

Mill himself, however, was not content to rest his evaluations of women's choices at this level. In *The Subjection of Women* Mill argues that the fact that adult women seem to consent to certain arrangements, such as marriage without the possibility of divorce or being denied the political franchise, is not sufficient to conclude that they are not harmed by those arrangements.[43] He gives several reasons why not: One is that what is interpreted as consent (frequently, only a refusal to protest) is often motivated by the realistic fear that protest will bring reprisals. Another is that so-called consent often is no more than a ranking of alternatives in the construction of which the chooser had no part, none of which is tolerable but one of which must be chosen and is therefore chosen as least intolerable of a set of bad options. Still another is that many desires and ambitions underlying so-called consent are socially constructed by practices that stifle rather than foster women's development. In pursuing such questions as "Why are there no great women artists?" and "What if women don't *want* to vote?" Mill was led to inquire into the foundations of women's apparent consent to exclusionary practices and into the social processes by which ill-founded views of women's nature are constructed. His liberalism is, in principle and in practice, significantly shaped by these inquiries. Studies of the clandestine and domestic terrorism to which women have been subjected for centuries would be more in keeping with Mill's social ethics than defenses, in the name of his liberty principle, of the sale and inhumane portrayal of women who consent, or appear to consent, to such things.

In the essay on liberty Mill also has important things to say about character. He argues that individuality is "one of the elements of well-being," understanding this to require the development of our "faculties of perception, judgment, discriminative feeling, mental activity, and even moral preference" and the development of strong, energetic natures.[44] He maintains that "it really is of importance, not only what men do, but also what manner of men they are that do it."[45] Applying the same points to women, we can see some of the costs of rape terrorism to female development.

Bat-Ami Bar On, in her essay on why terrorism is morally problematic, points out first of all that terrorism produces fearful people. Fearful people become contracted; their sense of agency is diminished and thereby their sense of themselves as deserving of respect. Citing the work of Leo Lowenthal, Marilyn Frye, and Kathleen Barry, she explains how terrorism "interrupts the causal relation between what people do and what happens to them."[46] Comparing terrorism with torture, she argues that it produces an alienation from self and a sense of self-betrayal. She concludes that what is most importantly wrong with terrorism is not that it violates the conventions of just war (although it does) but that it is *cruel* to the terrorized in that it erodes their selves and breaks their wills.[47] It is, in short, evil treatment, radically evil treatment.

Her description of the character of those shaped by terrorism sounds, abstractly and in unadorned language, like a description of feminine character as it develops in a rape culture. Women have been mocked by men since the time of Socrates for a lack of courage, strong will, initiative, integrity, self-respect — the very things Mill found important to the development of what he called "individuality" as "one of the elements of well-being." It is not enough to call attention to the fact that there are many women of whom these things are not true and that there are also male cowards. It is important to note the patterns and search for explanations of them. Many male cowards are survivors of other oppressive practices. What is so disheartening about most pornography, even so-called soft core pornography and even when it is produced by women who apparently give their consent to be used in its production, is that it presents to the public this fragile, compliant feminine character in very young women as a sexual turn-on. Finding pleasure in such portrayals calls to my mind the idea of finding pleasure in the "music" produced by the brass bull of the tyrant Phalaris of Acragas (early sixth century B.C.E.). The bull's "singing" was produced by the screams of victims roasting inside.[48] One would hope that, for the most part, only those ignorant of what they were hearing could enjoy it, that sadists like the tyrant are rare. Likewise, one would hope that only those unappreciative of the history of rape terrorism could find the pornography that glorifies its end result a source of pleasure. And yet, Bat-Ami Bar On also finds that terrorism forms the terrorizer as well as the terrorized, with the result that it produces not only fearful people but also cruel ones.[49] Mill did not support the practice of abstracting from histories of cruelty in order to experience pleasure. Nor should we.

GRATITUDE AND OBLIGATION

The ravages of terrorism discussed in the last chapter are not the only forms of moral damage that women have sustained. I mention in Chapter Three the misplaced gratitude many women experience toward "protectors" who may do no more than refrain from abuse. There I rely on an intuitive sense of what was misplaced about such gratitude. In this chapter I offer an ethical analysis of gratitude and its affiliated sense of obligation, assuming the burden of distinguishing between well-placed and misplaced gratitude. In so doing, I also explore the views of some influential philosophers on the ethics of gratitude.

Gratitude is a more important topic than we might think were we to judge solely by the attention devoted to it in the past by moral philosophers.[1] Perhaps it is especially important for those who have most needed others' services. A reason why it has not received more attention may be that those writing on it have not experienced that need acutely or in a sustained way. Further, one might think gratitude less important than other topics because it may seem only a matter of how we feel, whereas often action seems more urgent than feeling. Gratitude is, however, intimately bound up with action by way of its special sense of obligation — a sense that often seems paradoxical. The paradox of *debts* of gratitude is a central focus of this chapter.

The sense of being obligated through gratitude toward protectors has played a large role in shaping the lives of women in rape cultures. But the ethics of gratitude is also important to the ethics of friendship generally. In particular, it is important to understanding the ethics of friendship between parties who are distinctly unequal in power. Those who are relatively powerless may develop a certain misplaced gratitude to those with power over them — gratitude for ordinary decencies, for less abusiveness than was possible, and, as I note, even for genuine benefactions. Recognition of *misplaced* gratitude is all but nonexistent in philosophical literature. Gratitude is almost always contrasted there simply with *in*gratitude as a fault. Perhaps undeserved gratitude seems harmless or even beneficial to others and therefore not cause for concern. But it can indicate a misjudgment of others, a lack of self-respect, or both.

The remainder of this chapter is divided into four sections. I begin by noting a paradox about debts of gratitude. The first section looks at the debtor paradigm of obligation as the source of this paradox. This paradigm appears incongruent not only with gratitude but with informal and personal relationships generally. The second section examines in greater detail the problems suggested by the paradox of a "debt of gratitude" and considers the relevant views of Kant, Aristotle, and Hobbes. I conclude that Hobbes's natural laws of gratitude are more promising with respect to resolving the paradox than the accounts found in Kant and Aristotle, and that Hobbes's natural laws seem to invoke an alternative to the debtor paradigm of obligation. Building on Hobbes's account, the third section proposes a trustee or guardian paradigm of obligation as more congruent with gratitude and friendship than the debtor paradigm. In this paradigm obligations are not closely correlated with others' rights but nevertheless define ethically significant relationships between individuals.

In clarifying the contrast between the paradigms of the debtor and the trustee, I develop further the distinction between formal and informal obligations introduced in Chapter Three in the discussion of Carol Gilligan's discovery of different moral voices. There I suggested that what Carol Gilligan is inclined to call the voice of care may be better understood simply as a focus on personal and informal relationships (or aspects of relationships) and that what she is inclined to call the voice of justice may be better understood simply as a focus on more formal and impersonal relationships (or aspects of relationships). Each kind of relationship gives rise to obligations. Here I argue that the trustee model congruent with gratitude tends to fit informal obligations and that the debtor model is more natural for many formal or impersonal obligations.

The final section of this chapter uses the trustee paradigm to clarify how gratitude can be misplaced by those who are relatively powerless (such as women in a misogynist society or people of color in a white racist society) in relation to benefactors who have power over them. I also consider the possibility that "*debt* of gratitude" may accurately reflect the complexity of relationships to powerful benefactors. Being able to assess the obligations felt by the relatively powerless is important to evaluating women's voices, to the project of sorting out what women's voices may have to offer moral theory and what it would be better for women to overcome.

The Debtor Paradigm of Obligation

The idea of a debt of gratitude is paradoxical. If that for which gratitude is due was neither for sale nor on loan but was in some sense gratis, what sense does it make to feel indebted for it? How can one repay such a debt without transforming the transaction into one in which there is no room for gratitude? What kind of debt is this?

Friedrich Nietzsche cited the economic contract between buyer and seller as an ancestor of the moral concept of duty.[2] He found an origin of guilt in the debtor-creditor relationship. Guilt (in German, *Schuld,* which also means "debt") is an unpaid debt. To avoid guilt we pay our debts, what we owe, do as we ought. Perhaps economic history can also illuminate debts of gratitude. The anthropologist Marcel Mauss found entire economies structured around the "gift" relationship.[3] Such "gifts," however, are as paradoxical as our debts of gratitude.

Being in debt is only one paradigm of obligation. For nonutilitarian theories of right, however, it has become *the* paradigm ethical relationship. Kant treated moral obligation as a supreme indebtedness, an owing of duties to someone or other, if only to ourselves. When we cannot specify what must be done to carry out the duty or the party to whom the duty is owed (as in the case of the "duty of benevolence"), we have an "imperfect duty," an imperfect debt.[4] No one is entitled to collect it. We owe it nonetheless. Fulfilling obligations on this paradigm is a matter of settling accounts. Moral problems become conflicting debts: Payment of one interferes with payment of another. And so a central problem, if not *the* central problem, of the descendants of Kantian ethical theory has become the determination of what we really owe in such cases. For, according to Kantian and post-Kantian moral economics, we cannot really owe what we cannot pay — with perhaps one exception: a debt of gratitude.[5]

A morally good person on this paradigm is a competent, scrupulous, even imaginative moral book balancer whose basic concern is to stay as much as possible "in the black." Theorists disagree on the fundamental principles of moral book balancing — even whether there are any — but widely agree that keeping the books tidy is either the most important business of life or else that without which the rest of our businesses matter little. Moral book balancers take this task seriously. Some think only conscientious balancers deserve happiness. Few are confident of the requital of such desert. Still, the worthiness to be happy is a powerful source of pride. The books can be balanced, more or less, without further incentive.

Those delinquent in their payments are guilty and may be forced to pay their debts through punishment, which is thought also to encourage a more businesslike attitude for the future. And what a future. Moral book balancers cannot look forward to the day when all their debts are paid off. There is always the "ought" and "ought not," no matter how many payments have been made. One cannot even get ahead by overpaying. Supererogatory conduct releases no one from those perennial perfect debts.[6] And what a perfect debt it is that one can pay and pay and yet continue to owe. Nor may one avoid incurring debts. It is said belong to one's human nature to be so liable.

Is it any wonder that moralists are sometimes despised? It can be insulting to be reminded of our debts. Taking the initiative with payments is a major source of pride remaining to a debtor. Who would rob us of that by reminding us what we owe?

The Kantian sense of obligation is a sense of duty. If duties are debts, for what are they owed? Perhaps Elizabeth Anscombe was right that much modern ethics is the remainder of a Divine Law-giver morality with the Law-giver absent.[7] On the Divine Law-giver theory, we could say for what we were indebted. Without the Law-giver, we seem left with duties traceable neither to benefits received nor to goods taken, damaged, or consumed. We think everyone due minimal decencies from everyone. Thus we seem forever each other's debtors — an odd relationship: debtor-debtor, not debtor-creditor.

In these respects, debts of gratitude and John Rawls's "duties of fair play" (discussed near the end of the next section) make more sense.[8] Here we feel indebted for benefits received. Yet the sense of obligation associated with gratitude has its own peculiarities: Although it often brings out the debtor in us, it fails to make clear the nature of the debt or how we are to pay it. And we may come to feel deeply indebted to friends. Yet it is said that friends do not worry about book balancing.

The debtor paradigm works best for relatively formal obligations. It presents problems for informal and personal relationships. These problems infect ethical theories structured around the debtor paradigm. Some moralists—Kant, Henry Sidgwick, W. D. Ross—speak of *duties* of gratitude, for example.[9] Thus they find a place for right and wrong responses to a benefactor or friend. An awkward place. Yet how else is the fault of ingratitude to be acknowledged? And what better way to guard against it than to prescribe activities—requiting benefits, returning favors, and so on—as one's duties of gratitude, which any conscientious person can dutifully carry out?

But if being befriended imposes a debt, and debts are to be paid, then what is awkward about duties of gratitude? Well, sometimes these "debts" are not to be paid too quickly. That can be ungracious. Sometimes it seems they are not to be paid at all but only acknowledged. Or, is that how one pays them? (Like paying respect?) What kind of debt can one sometimes pay simply by acknowledging it?

The Debt of Gratitude

There are at least two problems regarding debts of gratitude. One is what it means to pay such a debt, even whether it is, literally, payable. The other is that payment, however explained, is supposed to be from a sense of gratitude, not from a sense of duty. Doing it from the sense of duty seems to betray an absence of gratitude.[10] Yet, how can it be inappropriate to acknowledge or pay a debt from a sense of duty?

Consider the motivational problem first. A duty to *be grateful* sounds like a joke. Do we also owe comedians debts of laughter? Perhaps the comparison is offensive. Debts of gratitude are borne solemnly. We seldom hear jokes about them. This suggests, however, that the obligation does involve not only what we do but also the spirit with which we do it.

According to Kantian ethics, I can conscientiously fulfill my obligations even if my heart is not in it. That is often true. Yet I also think I can be obligated to be a good sport, a good colleague, a gracious host. I am not obligated to give a mere show of these things. I am supposed to be these things "from the heart," which seems impossible if I feel bound. Or, can the heart itself be bound? Bondage of the heart sounds like loyalty. So let us consider how the heart might become bound.

To be grateful, must I not first be in some measure gratified? I can hardly be bound to be that. That is, I can hardly be bound to be gratified by others. And if I gratify myself, I have only myself to thank. To deserve my gratitude others must succeed in gratifying me somewhat. There is luck here, if only in the "fit" between us. Whether others succeed in gratifying me is not simply a function of their efforts or intentions, nor of mine.

The basis of debts of gratitude may yield a clue to what is owed and thereby to how, if at all, it is payable. I may owe a debt of gratitude as the result of a gift, a favor, a rescue, support and encouragement, recognition, sympathy, any number of things people do for me or give me beyond what they owed me. My gratitude rightly dissolves if I find the deed was done for a reward or for some other ulterior motive (although the sense of obligation may remain). In an illuminating paper on this topic Fred Berger said that gratitude responds to another's *benevolence,* more specifically, *to the valuing of oneself* presupposed in another's benevolence: Gratitude acknowledges and reciprocates that valuing, thereby demonstrating that one does not value the benefactor merely as useful for one's own ends.[11]

It should be noted, however, that gratitude need not be deserved to be in order. Gratitude is not always *to* someone, although it is *for* something. I may be grateful that the weather "cooperated" with plans for the picnic, or that the highway patrol officer was distracted as I sped by, without being grateful to anyone for either event. It was this kind of gratitude that Nietzsche embraced as a sign of health. My interest, however, like Berger's, is in deserved gratitude.

Berger's account is an excellent beginning. But he did not take on the question what it means to be obligated in such a context. Of course, the debtor in us does not surface for every little thing — being given the time of day, for instance. (Is saying "thank you" paying a debt?) It comes out for important things and for things done out of special concern. But here come the difficulties. Sensitive benefactors may want their beneficiaries *not* to feel indebted to them, for it alters their relationships. In the Talmud, on account of such alterations, the highest form of alms-giving is said to be when donor and recipient are unknown to each other.[12] In the Talmud, also, however, alms-giving is said to be inferior to kindnesses or benevolences as forms of charity, and in the latter, the benefactor and beneficiary are usually known to each other.[13] Here it is clearest that one is *not* to pay — even that one *could* not. Caring is not for sale; we must not put a price on another's concern. Nor is one to pay for a gift, which makes reciprocal gift-giving delicate. To pay is to reject as a gift what was offered, which can be unkind if not the result of misunderstanding. Yet, even after expressing appreciation or reciprocating, one may feel indebted. What is the meaning of this feeling indebted?

Aristotle, Hobbes, and Kant suggest answers to this question. Neither Aristotle nor Kant, however, offers an answer congruent with gratitude. Kant thought that, literally, one never could pay such a debt, that is, that one never could pay it *off*:[14] Perhaps, then it should not be surprising that Kant's account does not fit well with gratitude. Eternal debts may weigh more heavily than temporary ones, and heavy debts undermine gratitude. Both parties' positions seem unenviable: If it is futile to try to pay off the debt, it is also offensive to make much of it, and givers might anticipate this. How, then, can caring impose such debts? How does a thing of joy become a burden forever? Or, so it sometimes seemed to Kant.

> If I accept favours, I contract debts which I can never repay, for I can never get on equal terms with him who has conferred the favours upon me; he has stolen a march upon me, and if I do him a favour I am only returning a *quid pro quo*; I shall always owe him a debt of gratitude, and who will accept such a debt? For to be indebted is to be subject to an unending constraint. I must for ever be courteous and flattering towards my benefactor. . . . I may even be forced to using subterfuge so as to avoid meeting him. But he who pays promptly for everything is under no constraint.[15]

In the *Doctrine of Virtue* Kant did caution that one is "not to regard a kindness received as a burden one would gladly be rid of (since the person so favoured stands a step lower than his benefactor, and this wounds his pride)" but that one should "accept the occasion for gratitude as a moral kindness — that is, an opportunity given one to couple gratitude with love of man."[16] Thus he shrank from accepting the implications of his own account of the nature and basis of gratitude. That account, however, betrays a different attitude.

Kant was in a bind. For he also held we have an imperfect duty of benevolence, exercise of which puts others in debt to us.[17] He considered it meritorious to carry out this duty, although also contrary to one's duty to oneself to accept favors unnecessarily.[18] It almost seems that benefactors have more basis for gratitude to willing beneficiaries for providing occasions for meritorious benevolence.

Kant analyzed the benefactor-beneficiary relationship as an inequality of love and respect. The benefactor, he said, stands in a relationship of love to the beneficiary ("*moral* love," not "*pathological* love"), whereas the beneficiary stands in a special relationship of respect to the benefactor, but not one of love.[19] He also analyzed friendship as *equal* mutual love and respect.[20] The astounding implication appears to be that ideal friends never actually help each other. To do so would ruin the friendship. Apparently, each should realize that the other stands ready to help and hope that help is never needed.

Kant accepted this implication for material favors but, oddly, missed it for the emotional support offered by a listener who can be counted on not to betray confidences. Mutually exchanging confidences is what he thought ideal friends do instead of "favors." Apparently he thought good friends never have occasion for gratitude to one another: Love is never having to say, "Thank you." Something has gone wrong.

Although Kant's views depart from common sense, even common sense recognizes some debts as unpayable. Consider that unpayable debt of gratitude to a wife, frequently encountered in academic book prefaces of a couple of decades ago. Why was the debt unpayable? It is clear if she had died or if misfortune prevented him from reciprocating. Such "debts" seem unpayable not in principle but only contingently. But often she was still alive and typing. Yet, unpayable in principle may be exactly what is meant. (The pun is appropriate: He may have felt he was paying interest forever, never reducing the principal.) The point is not that the debt was too large for his means but that it felt undischargeable, unforgivable, interminable, like a perfect duty — owed forever.

An unpayable debt of gratitude may leave one feeling forever guilty, and, therefore, unworthy. Consider Nietzsche's account of the Christian's relationship to God. In assuming the penalty for their sins, God's Son left the rest of His children an eternal debt of gratitude. It would have been nobler, said Nietzsche, to assume the guilt.[21] The holy Christian God, unlike the noble Greek gods, plunged His children further into debt, by the same token preventing their ever paying it off. Similar logic, perhaps, explains the unpayableness of the debt of many men to women for not holding them to a reciprocation of services, thereby earning eternal (unpayable) "gratitude." They might have done better to exchange confidences.

Aristotle also had views about the dischargeability of obligations to a benefactor. But they leave no more room than Kant's for gratitude. According to Aristotle, a noble person "is apt to confer greater benefits in return; for thus the original benefactor besides being paid will incur a debt to him, and will be the gainer by the transaction."[22] Emerson's way of putting it was: "You cannot give anything to a magnanimous person. After you have served him, he at once puts you in debt by his magnanimity."[23] Noble people, said Aristotle, are ashamed of receiving benefits. Instead of gratitude, we have here a game of One-Up, as never-ending as the game of revenge (perhaps even a relatively benign form of it).[24] A good example of One-Up is found in Ruth Benedict's account of the custom of the potlatch among the Kwakiutl of Vancouver Island. The shame feared by the Kwakiutl is clearly not of receiving gifts, however, but of being unable to make an even greater return (so as not to end up in another's debt).

Ultimately, Kant's position is the same as Aristotle's. Both were troubled by the threat to one's pride posed by indebtedness. Both proposed to resolve the problem by repayment. Kant defined gratitude as "honoring a person because of a kindness he has done us" and maintained that gratitude is "a *holy* duty," that "the obligation with regard to it cannot be discharged completely by an act in conformity with the obligation (so that no matter what he does, the person who is under obligation always remains under obligation)."[25] Thus, the beneficiary pays tribute eternally in the coin of respect, thereby excelling in humility — One-Up again, with a Christian twist.

Both philosophers distinguished repaying a benefactor from paying a seller and from repaying a loan, thereby making some progress with the paradox of a debt of gratitude. Both answered the first problem mentioned above, namely, the problem of what it means to pay a debt to a benefactor. But neither preserved the spirit of gratitude in doing so. Aristotle's magnanimous beneficiary preserves, rather, the spirit of competition, and Kant's account preserves the spirit of Stoic discipline.

The problem appears to be the sense that indebtedness threatens one's pride. Aristotle's focus is on the benefit, a symbol of power. For moral book balancers, pride rests on spiritual credit. Kantian gratitude appears to be a credit-giving that allows the giver to earn credit by giving it. But this is not what gratitude is.

"Giving credit" is ambiguous. In "giving credit where credit is due," I may simply acknowledge a source. Pride keeps me from taking credit for others' achievements. I may not intend gratitude, although I may also not be eager to clear up ambiguity concerning that fact. I may not be merely indicating a source, however. I may also be giving credit in the sense of paying tribute, honoring, or praising.

Yet, gratitude is not praise. Anyone — beneficiary or not — can praise an admirable effort or achievement. In giving the Good Samaritan credit for helping the stranger, I pay tribute (hats off) but do not acknowledge a debt of gratitude. Only the stranger, if anyone, has such a debt. (If others also feel grateful, perhaps they identify with the stranger.)

In defining gratitude as "honoring a person because of a kindness he has done us," Kant confused gratitude with giving credit in the sense of *praising*. The basis of this honor, he said, is a certain "*priority* of merit: the merit of having been the first in benevolence."[26] Except for the part about being first, Kant's account so far seems to agree with Berger's. But how is it that the merit of benevolence provides a basis for gratitude? Kant saw it as a purely objective merit. His valuation of the benefactor's good will was independent of the empirical fact that someone actually benefited from it or even that someone actually valued it. Anyone can respect Kantian merit. From Kant's account of the nature and basis of gratitude, it is impossible to see why only a beneficiary or intended beneficiary (if anyone) becomes obligated. Berger's account, on the other hand, relates the desert basis of gratitude to the fact that someone has been gratified in such a way that without appropriate acknowledgment, the latter might appear to value the benefactor only as someone who happened to be useful. If Berger was right, being first seems not in itself important, although it may be evidence of the relevant valuation. And that seems right.

The view of gratitude as praise for taking the initiative may underlie a common embarrassment about receiving gratitude, especially for anything done out of love. Praise for that reveals that what was done was not appreciated for what it was. Those who deserve our gratitude are better prized than praised. The credit we give acknowledges that their good will was of value *to us,* that they pleased us, for example. It is not an entirely objective assessment of their character.

Kantian gratitude lacks warmth. Yet its coolness matches the coolness of Kantian benevolence. At least, whatever heat there is seems not to be directed toward the other in either case. The benefactor is only acting from duty, albeit imperfect duty. And so, perhaps, praise is what the Kantian giver deserves.

Good deeds, however, are not commonly thought to deserve even eternal praise. Why might Kant (and not only Kant) think that one's responsibilities to a benefactor are eternal?

The idea that a debt of gratitude is forever may stem from the truth that the nature and duration of a beneficiary's responsibilities may be determined more by the benefactor than by the beneficiary. There is an interesting bit of luck here, although which determinations are the lucky ones defies generalization. Some obligations to a beneficiary may last as long as the benefactor does not abuse the beneficiary's good will. Carrying them out need not terminate them. To see this, let us consider what they are.

Hobbes has a modest account in his natural laws of gratitude. In *De Cive* 3:8 he says: "[You are to] suffer not him to be the worse for you, who, out of the confidence he had in you, first did you a good turn [, and] [you are to] accept not a gift, but with a mind to endeavour, that the giver shall have no just occasion to repent him of his gift."[27] And in the *Leviathan* 15, he says: "[One who] receiveth benefit from another of mere grace [is to] endeavour that he which giveth it, have no reasonable cause to repent him of his good will."[28] These "laws" need interpretation with stories about what counts as accepting a benefit and what counts as reasonable cause for regret. They seem more promising, however, for happily resolving the paradox of a "debt" of gratitude than the accounts of Kant and Aristotle.

They do not require us to reciprocate a favor, for example, unless failure to do so makes it *reasonable* for another to regret doing the good turn. Some responsibilities are naturally carried out in relation to still other persons: A hitchhiker may pick up future hitchhikers, for example, or a student give help and encouragement to newer students. Not doing so might give their benefactors reasonable cause to regret the relevant good turns. Another more serious cause for regret is taking unfair advantage of one's benefactor, using the benefit to put the benefactor at a disadvantage. Here "cause for regret" may understate the case. Such betrayals can seem treasonous. A beneficiary's responsibilities not to do such things may last indefinitely.

In this respect, a beneficiary's responsibilities differ from those of a borrower or contractee. The borrower's responsibility is to return what was borrowed, the contractee's to fulfill the contract. Once done, it matters not, as far as the obligation is concerned, whether the creditor or other contractees reasonably regret the transaction. It may matter from some points of view, but not to whether the responsibility is discharged.

Carrying out the Hobbesian responsibilities *need* not demonstrate gratitude, any more than repaying a loan need demonstrate honesty. However, the Hobbesian responsibilities cohere well with gratitude; one can act from a sense of their significance and yet preserve the spirit of gratitude. They are too abstract to be readily enforceable. They require judgment and discretion from the beneficiary. If gratitude is naturally demonstrated in carrying them out, perhaps that is enough to justify Hobbes in calling his formulae laws of gratitude.

The responsibility that Hobbes describes is more abstract than but still very much in the spirit of the "duty of fair play" that Rawls said is correlative to the right defined by H.L.A. Hart's "mutuality of restrictions":

> When any number of persons engage in a practice, or conduct a joint undertaking according to rules, and thus restrict their liberty, those who have submitted to these restrictions when required have the right to a similar acquiescence on the part of those who have benefited by their submission.[29]

Thus the duty of fair play is the duty to acquiesce in restricting one's liberty according to the rules when one has benefited from the similar acquiescence of others. Rawls adds that the rules in question are just and that one benefited voluntarily (or at least without protest) as parts of a jointly sufficient condition of incurring the duty of fair play.[30] In "Justice as Fairness" Rawls thought Hobbes had confused gratitude with fair play.[31] The content of the "duty of fair play" is apparently specified by the rules of the practice and correlated with others' rights. Responsibilities of gratitude, however, are relatively unspecific. The benefactor does not have a *right* to one's acting in accord with them but only *deserves* it (or does not). Perhaps, however, it is only in formal practices that fair play is a response to rights. In informal practices, such as hitchhiking, without well-defined rules and penalties for non-compliance, the compliance of others may be an appropriate basis for gratitude. It may be more realistic here to speak of deserts than of rights.[32] For informal practices there may be no difficulty with the idea that failure to "play fair" manifests *in*gratitude. The question suggested by the paradox of the debt of gratitude is, rather, whether playing fair can manifest both gratitude and a sense of obligation. An affirmative answer seems to require an alternative to the debtor paradigm of obligation, to avoid the problem of endangered pride. Hobbes's gratitude is a response to a judgment implicit in the benefactor's deed that supports the beneficiary's self-esteem. His account explains why only a beneficiary or intended beneficiary (if anyone) becomes obligated. Hobbes said the benefactor had confidence in the beneficiary. Such transactions seem likely to be mutually gratifying, not to pose a threat to the beneficiary's pride.

Hobbes's laws of gratitude suggest the idea of a trust. This, in turn, suggests an obligation that is not strongly correlated with rights on the part of others, which is also the kind of obligation needed generally in Hobbes's state of nature. To see what this means, let us consider the concept of obligation.

The Trustee Paradigm and Informal Obligation

Contractual bonds are not the only ethically significant interpersonal ties. Where they exist, there may be others that run deeper. A debtor may have cause to be grateful for the extension of credit. Does the debtor then owe two debts? Moral book balancers may say so and consider that paying interest takes care of the second debt. If so, the case is altered. For then there seems no basis for gratitude.

A bond more coherent with gratitude and friendship than that of the debtor is that of a trustee or guardian, especially one who is not under contract. Owing gratitude is more like having accepted a deposit, than like having taken out a loan. In taking out a loan, I am extended credit. My position is inferior to that of my creditor in that I am subject to nonreciprocal constraints — at least sensible creditors so arrange matters. By contrast, in receiving a deposit, I already have credit. I do not have to prove myself; my judgment is relied upon. Deposits are a source of pride. As a beneficiary, I can regard myself as the "trustee" of another's good will or concern. I cannot literally return another's good will (although that is what we say), but I can reciprocate it.

If I am a trustee or guardian, I am obligated. I owe it to those whose trust I have accepted to act responsibly on their behalf. But I am not thereby a debtor. My position is not characteristically inferior. Within the relationship I am to a great extent not subject to constraints, despite the fact that I am under obligation. To be penalized for serious abuses, I must be relieved of my position. Carrying out the obligations of a trustee or guardian does not necessarily result in their discharge; it may have no tendency to terminate the obligation. If someone has deposited something with me for safekeeping, I carry out my responsibility as long as I keep the thing safely, and who knows when or whether the other will return for it? We do not always tie down these things, although we can.

Like Kant's "imperfect duties," these responsibilities tend to be abstractly defined. They allow room for latitude. They call upon discretion and judgment to a greater extent than what Kant called "perfect duties" (and later called "juridical duties" by contrast with "ethical duties").[33] They are fulfilled satisfactorily if others have no reasonable cause to regret the trust.

Let us distinguish here between an *obligation* as a bond (ligature), on one hand, and, on the other, a *duty*, as a kind of responsibility the discharge of which can fulfill an obligation (an obligation "content," so to speak; what is due). Strictly speaking, it is duties that are owed; obligations are not owed but are the bases of duties. Duties are often correlated with others' rights. But not everything that we owe is such a duty. We can owe what others only deserve from us without having any right against us. Deserts can create ethically significant ties, desert of gratitude, for example.

If I fail to carry out a duty to others who had a right against me, they may justifiably feel wronged. One is not surprised if they complain about it. They may remind me, apply pressure, in some cases compel me to perform or insist upon compensation. Such things do not compromise their self-respect but, if anything, vindicate it. We say they are within their rights. If I violate others' rights, I owe them at least an explanation, often more. Their interest is primarily in the thing to be done, and the obligation is satisfied when it is done or adequate compensation made.

Actual constraint is not called for until the obligated party fails to perform. It is not all right to prod people to fulfill their obligations when they have not had a chance to do so on their own initiative. In one sense a debtor is a transgressor — as in "forgive us our debts [trespasses] as we forgive our debtors [those who trespass against us]," hardly a request to be released from one's obligations but only from the penalties of having defaulted. Likewise, "paying one's debt to society" suggests punishment by the state, not obedience to it.

The responsibilities of trusteeship and guardianship are not closely correlated with others' rights, even when the trustee or guardian is under contract. If Hart was correct that rights correlated with others' duties are *justifications for interfering with the freedom of others,* obligations do not always involve such rights.[34] It is one question whether I have an obligation and another whether anyone can justifiably hold me to it. Even where my obligation creates the presumption of such a right in others, they can promise not to hold me to it, thereby surrendering their justification for restricting my freedom but *not* thereby terminating my obligation.

In not being held to our obligations, we are treated as more responsible. "I won't hold you to it" means that if you don't do the thing, I won't compel you or insist upon compensation or explanations or put pressure on you or even complain. Now your responsibility is increased — not in that you "owe" more but in that you are now entirely responsible for getting yourself to do the thing. (This needs qualification, however; even though *I* have promised not to exercise my right against you, I still *have* the right, and others, such as the state or my children, may be justified in acting on my behalf.)

Genuinely to release others from an obligation is to change the presumption that their failure to act in certain ways would wrong someone. One may be released from a promise or have a debt forgiven. This is communicated better by "Forget it," than by "I won't hold you to it." Honors systems impose tremendous obligations, and one is not to forget them.

In some cases when others are not justified in holding one to an obligation, they may have, as we say, "a right to expect" but not a right *simpliciter*. It still can reflect poorly on the obligated person not to do the thing without adequate explanation or compensation. When others rely on us to carry out responsibilities without constraint, we are likely to feel an even greater sense of obligation.

Hart's account of the bond of obligation did not accommodate these facts. He said that the bond of obligation is like a rope tied around the obligated party, the ends in the hands of another who is free to use them or not.[35] This image captures the idea of being under constraint *to fulfill* an obligation, but not simply *having* one. Being obligated does not necessarily imply that others are free to pull strings.

The bonds characteristic of our relationships to friends, former friends, neighbors, kin fit the pulling strings model poorly. Yet we refer to them as obligations and as responsibilities. These are the obligations (responsibilities) to which women refer so often when speaking with what Carol Gilligan calls "the voice of care."[36] Like the debtor-creditor bond, these obligations have bases in the histories of the persons so related. Ideals of universal sisterhood and brotherhood attempt to regard everyone as so bound. But these ideals are problematic. Although belief in God the Father makes some sense of universal siblinghood, even believers reinvent distinctions between those to whom one has special obligations and others.

The bond between the doer and receiver of a favor is such a special relationship. One may need to ask permission to do a favor. The other may not wish to become obligated. People can wonder why someone wants to do them a favor. If others want to help me only because they see me as unfortunate, I may be offended rather than grateful, feel pitied rather than cared for. Such help is not gratifying. It is otherwise if others wish to help me because of something about me that would make it regrettable if I should not receive help. Then I am not identified simply as an unfortunate but as someone worth helping. I may be happy to be obliged. If we can accept anything done out of love, it is not, as Ralph Waldo Emerson said, because that is a way of receiving it from ourselves but because love supports our self-esteem.[37]

In complaining of a tendency in moral philosophy to extend "obligation" to cover anything that one "ought," morally, to do, Hart reminded us that outside the profession of philosophy "obligation" refers to special relationships.[38] Richard Brandt also reported evidence in ordinary language of such a use of "obligation," which led him to distinguish two basic contexts in which the concept of obligation has a place: the context of promises or agreements and the context of accepting benefactions.[39] The latter seems fundamental in that willingness to accept another's word manifests a good will that does not itself rest on respect for contracts or promises. Such good will is, or can be, a benefaction. Promises and agreements ground duties correlated with rights, while accepting benefactions grounds responsibilities in relationships that are often highly informal.

However, Hart's tendency, natural to a philosopher of law, was to recognize only relatively *formal* obligations, namely, those closely correlated with rights on the part of others. The debtor is a paradigm of formal obligation; friendship, a paradigm of *informal* obligation. In becoming a benefactor one characteristically befriends another. The obligations of friendship are not closely correlated with rights, but they are still special, ethically significant relationships. Perhaps most of our obligations, in the sense of special relationships to specific individuals, are of the informal sort.

Formality applies to definition and structure. It facilitates control, provides assurance. Concern about control suggests a lack of trust and confidence or inability to predict and plan. Within boundaries, formality is a matter of degree. An obligation may be well-defined in some respects — such as the amount of money to be repaid — but not in others, such as the time of repayment. The latter unspecificity, however, is sufficient to hinder enforcement of the obligation and so gives a good reason for classifying it as informal.

Formality is not the same as legality. Both legal and extra-legal relationships give rise to obligations of varying degrees of formality. The mutual obligations of spouses, for example, are relatively informal, despite the formality of the status of spousehood. Obligations of outside parties to a married couple, considered as such (as a married couple), tend to be more formal than most of the obligations of spouses to one another. Thus, marrying formalizes certain obligations with outside parties and substitutes informal for formal ones to one another; divorce cancels certain formal obligations with outside parties and substitutes certain formal ones for informal ones to each other.

The obligation of a beneficiary to a benefactor is relatively informal even when it is legally defined. As in marriage, legally defining the relationship — for example, in wills, trusteeships, and insurance policies and in medical donor-donee relationships — ties down outsiders' obligations to respect it and substitutes certain informal obligations for formal ones between benefactor and beneficiary. Procedures by which these relationships are instituted and dissolved tend to be more well-defined than the responsibilities within the relationships. The threat of dissolving the relationship may be the major sanction of its internal responsibilities.[40]

In paying a debt, I discharge that obligation. I am no longer bound to my former creditor; that special relationship is concluded. By contrast, living up to informal obligations tends to confirm, or reaffirm, the special relationship involved rather than to bring it to a close. As I live up to my obligations to friends and associates, we become closer friends and associates. Our ties deepen, become stronger. This may be the most important difference between formal and informal obligations.

Often we think those to whom others are informally obligated are not entitled to complain of the latter's failures, that it would reflect poorly on them to do so, although perhaps not that it would reflect similarly poorly on still others to do so on their behalf. Complaining on one's own behalf may be too much like complaining of one's own judgment. Francis Bacon put this and related points well, in pointing out important services that friends can render.

> How many things are there which a man cannot, with any face or comeliness, say or do himself? A man can scarce allege his own merits with modesty, much less extol them; a man cannot sometimes brook to supplicate or beg; and a number of the like. But all these things are graceful in a friend's mouth, which are blushing in a man's own. So again, a man's person hath many proper relations which he cannot put off. A man cannot speak to his son but as a father; to his wife but as a husband; to his enemy but upon terms: whereas a friend may speak as the case requires, and not as it sorteth with the person.[41]

These sensitivities tend not to arise where our obligations with another are formal.

Yet another difference between formal and informal obligations is that paying the penalty for defaulting on a formal obligation is supposed to restore one to (informal) good terms with others. In the case of informal obligations, however, the chief "penalty" is alienation. A delinquent debtor remains a debtor, but a poor friend is close to not being a friend at all. There is a form of alienation for debtors, however: bankruptcy. Although formally institutable by the delinquent, this step may have the informal consequence of the former debtor's inability to obtain future credit.

Social obligations tend to be informal, although the possibility of taking a debtorlike attitude toward them makes them ambiguous. In accepting a return dinner invitation, for example, one may wonder whether the intent was to discharge the obligation or to cement a friendship. This seems a desirable ambiguity on the whole. It allows us to treat social obligations as (mere) formalities if we wish. Debt-paying, balancing accounts, can be an important defense against unwanted intimacy, a defense women lack in relation to men in sexist dating practices.

The obligation to follow etiquette is an informal obligation of polite society, which is a bit confusing because the requirements themselves are highly formal (well-defined). A clue to the informality of the obligation to attend to etiquette is that the penalty for disregarding it is estrangement from polite society—which may explain why some people are more devastated by their breaches of etiquette than by their violations of some moral obligations. For concerned members of polite society, these rules achieve the requisite predictability without sanctions other than the threat of alienation. Miss Manners says one is not to correct others on etiquette unless they request it; this is itself a requirement of etiquette.[42] Etiquette is not only formal but also impersonal, like justice.

When we choose to regard an obligation of gratitude as imposing a debt, perhaps we are regarding it as like the bond of a debtor to a creditor who has said, "I won't hold you to it." This has an important consequence: If the debt were paid, the special relationship by which one had incurred it would be terminated, and yet one would be on good terms with the other.

It is a disadvantage to be in debt. We do not incur debts for their own sake. We may take on debts for the sake of building a credit-rating, which presupposes that we expect to pay them off. Debts are not ordinarily a source of pride, even if paying them off is. One's self-respect demands that one do what one can to pay off one's debts, to conclude relationships that subject one to nonreciprocal constraints. We prove ourselves reliable and maintain self-respect in extricating ourselves from such relationships.

This clarifies why a benefactor may be offended at one's feeling indebted. The benefactor may feel rejected. It is as though one had said that one would prefer to conclude the relationship, that it is not a source of pride or joy.

The paradigm of trusteeship, like that of the debtor, is economic and often legal. Trustees may be book balancers (as when they are in charge of finances) but they need not be (as when they are in charge of children). Guardianship suggests the economy of the house rather than the marketplace, and so perhaps less book balancing. As metaphors these paradigms, too, have limits. We do not ordinarily solicit deposits or charges, whereas it is not uncommon to ask favors. And we benefit others by accepting deposits or trusts, whereas we are benefited in accepting favors. A trustee or guardian is someone to whom others may be grateful, whereas a beneficiary is, presumably, grateful to others.

Yet even these things are not totally surprising. We are grateful to those willing to become obligated to us, who can regard such relationships as a source of pride or joy. On the debtor paradigm, the original favor doer seems without basis for gratitude for a return favor; what is returned does not even seem describable as a favor. It is a joke to say we are gratified to see people pay their debts — we are relieved, sometimes impressed. Gratitude itself, however, is among the things for which gratitude is felt. Those "happy to be obliged" thereby gratify us as well. Max Scheler maintains that "love (once it is somehow perceived), evokes a loving response."[43] Something like that seems true of gratitude.

Misplaced Gratitude and the Debt of Gratitude

With these distinctions in mind, let us return to the gratitude of those who are relatively powerless and in need and to their "debts of gratitude" to those more powerful who are able and willing to help them out.

The trustee paradigm helps clarify misplaced gratitude. Relatively powerless people are unlikely candidates for "trusteeship." The "confidence" of the powerful in them is not likely to be of a kind that enhances their self-esteem — "confidence" that they will not rebel against injustice, for example. Historically, from the protection racket of rape cultures to the "white man's burden," the powerful and privileged have *imposed* their guardianship on the relatively powerless, for whose disempowerment they have often been also responsible. Yet they have also often felt that those who fell under their protection should be grateful for such "care." If these guardians were trustees, they were each other's trustees, not trustees of powerless of whom they took charge.

Even when all this is true, there is more to be said. The benefactions of the powerful often are truly manifestations of generosity rather than calculated investments. Generosity differs significantly, however, from benevolence, kindness, and charity.[44] Recall that on Fred Berger's account, gratitude is a response to *benevolence,* specifically to benevolence that embodies a certain valuing of the beneficiary. It is not a response to generosity as such. Generosity is liberality, which, when a virtue, is a matter of knowing when to give (to let go) and being good at doing that.[45] Those who are generous are not, as such, overly concerned with conserving resources, nor even with being able to satisfy their own needs or wishes, and in the same way, they are not particularly concerned about the needs or wishes of others, either. There may be no real confidence reposed in the recipient of generosity, no judgment especially supportive of the recipient's self-esteem. When the powerful are generous, it may be simply that they enjoy giving. Their generosity supports their self-esteem by demonstrating their wealth and power. Generosity can be accompanied by insensitivity to others' wishes with regard to becoming obligated. Certainly the very powerful can afford not to care whether others are obligated or not.

Still, there is a sense in which gratitude regarding such benefactors need not be totally misplaced. Provided they were not the cause of our need, we may be grateful that even insensitive benefactors are there without being grateful *to* them. And we may incur informal obligations to reciprocate where we can, even if we rightly do not find that they deserve our gratitude. But to think that we owe "benefactors" who disregard our wishes not to become nonreciprocally obligated, who would place us in need and eliminate all other sources of help, or that we owe "benefactors" who would even voluntarily support those who maintain us in such need is to misjudge them and to fail to respect ourselves. We misjudge benefactors when we infer their benevolence simply from their generosity. Genuine benevolence as a concern for others' well-being is incompatible with disregarding their willingness to become obligated. Those who lack such regard thereby lack respect. And a willingness on our part to *become* obligated to others despite their lack of respect for us raises the question whether we lack self-respect.

To those who are powerful it may seem natural that others should want to serve them and gain status through the association. It also may seem natural to the powerful that others should be grateful, insofar as gratitude is a happy recognition of sources of good fortune. Those who are powerful, at any rate, have no general interest in rejecting the gratitude of others, nor in discouraging their sense of obligation.

Where gratitude is genuinely due another, the "debt" in a debt of gratitude refers to responsibilities gratefully incurred. I have argued that such responsibilities, unlike literal debts, are informal and the metaphor of a debt therefore misleading. The metaphor of a trust comes closer to capturing the obligation involved. This metaphor is helpful in assessing our informal obligations to others insofar as it directs us to consider whether we are, indeed, trust-holders for them or whether, on the contrary, they have either found or placed us in circumstances that left us little choice but to "trust" *them* with all that we have and all that we are.[46] If, after all, it is others who hold *our* trust, it is they who should first of all feel obligated to us. Perhaps we may judge our reciprocal obligations by how well they honor theirs.

One may wonder, however, if "debt" is inapt for obligations of gratitude, why "debt of gratitude" is what we say. Perhaps we are careless with language. But there is a more interesting possibility. It is possible to hear the metaphor of a "debt of gratitude" as ambivalent or ambiguous rather than simply as paradoxical. Gratitude manifests pleasure, even joy. But debts are burdens. As Emerson noted: "The law of benefits is a difficult channel. . . . We wish to be self-sustained. We do not quite forgive a giver. The hand that feeds us is in some danger of being bitten."[47] One may be grateful for the opportunity to get out of difficulty by incurring an obligation and yet not find the resulting relationship with the benefactor gratifying. Or one may not yet know whether the relationship will turn out to be gratifying. Perhaps "*debt* of gratitude" captures the combinations of attitudes and feelings appropriate to such circumstances—in one case, being happy *and* obliged; in the other, suspension between that and being happy *to be* obliged. Only the latter seems a promising beginning of friendship.

WHAT LESBIANS DO

> Character — the willingness to accept responsibility
> for one's own life — is the source from which
> self-respect springs.
> —Joan Didion, *Slouching Toward Bethlehem*

> A paradigm case of taking responsibility
> for one's sexuality is coming out as a lesbian.
> —Joyce Trebilcot, *Dyke Methods*

If gender is a source of moral luck for those of us raised with the legacies of patriarchy, it may seem that sexual or erotic orientation is likewise a source of moral luck, given the heterosexism of patriarchies. There is certainly luck, good and bad, in finding others of one's sex erotically attractive. Although there is at present no consensus on the question whether there exist genetic predispositions to this experience, surely luck is involved in whether our early erotic experiences are painful or pleasant, whether we find them rewarding or the opposite.[1] Incalculable social energy has been expended on stifling and hiding same-sex erotic intimacy and pair-bonding, cultivating heterosexual intimacy, finding diversions from erotic temptation in socially accepted celibacy.[2] It has been easier for most lesbians or gay men to pass as heterosexual than to pass as the other sex, even though some have done both.[3] Although there is surely luck in the success of such endeavors, that is not what this chapter explores. The luck that interests me here is that involved in recent attempts by lesbians who embrace femaleness to *take responsibility* publicly for a lesbian erotic orientation. Although some of what I say applies also to gay men and to people whose commitment is heterosexual, their positions in heteropatriarchy differ enough from those of lesbians that not all of what I have to say about lesbians will also apply to them.

Coming out as a lesbian, in the context of heteropatriarchy, is a paradigm of taking responsibility for oneself. Taking responsibility is, in general, a source of self-respect. Taking responsibility for oneself can be a major source and support of one's self-respect. This is why many with socially stigmatized identities come out and why others — outed, discovered, or prompted initially to come out for other reasons — embrace that identity publicly.

The expression "coming out" has an older and a more recent meaning. I intend the more recent meaning when I use the expression. In the older sense, one came out by entering into an overtly lesbian relationship (hardly a public one). "Coming out" in the 1950s meant "getting involved for real" as opposed to merely fantasizing. This sense lingers on in the expression "bringing [someone] out" as applied to making love with a woman who has not previously made lesbian love. In the years prior to World War II, according to George Chauncy, "coming out" — a play on the debutante's being formally introduced to the heterosexual society of her cultural peers — referred to gay men's formal presentation to gay society at drag balls. "Gay people in the prewar years," he says, "did not speak of *coming out* of what we call the 'gay closet' but rather of *coming out into* what they called 'homosexual society' or the 'gay world,' a world neither so small, nor so isolated, nor, often, so hidden as 'closet' implies."[4]

In the more recent sense of the expression, however, coming out is a usually informal individual act of communication, an identification of oneself as lesbian or gay to one or more others, although it can also be done in a formal and public way. Asking to whom a lesbian is out is not asking who her lovers are but, rather, to whom has she *identified* herself (or to whom she has been identified) as lesbian. Being "outed" is being exposed, involuntarily. Coming out is often done in self-defense or for political reasons — to make extortion impossible, to make oneself accessible to others like oneself in order that combination for political purposes be possible, and so forth. It might be thought that the more recent sense includes the older one, at least in the sense of becoming involved in a real (as opposed to imaginary) relationship. But it is not clear that that is so. Perhaps neither sense presupposes the other. Women have entered into overtly lesbian relationships without admitting to themselves that that is what they were doing, certainly without embracing a lesbian identity. And women sometimes embrace lesbian identities today on other grounds than experience with relationships commonly recognized as lesbian. Some identify as lesbian celibates.

Both senses of coming out, however, presuppose certain kinds of social contexts in which "lesbian" has recognized meanings. Here is where we find the luck that interests me. To be able to take responsibility for our identities as lesbian, we need social cooperation. As noted in Chapter Four, Nel Noddings observed that how good one individual can be depends greatly on how others receive what that individual does.[5] Although she did not appear to be thinking about social norms when she made that observation, how others treat us is often relevantly describable only in terms of social norms. Whether I am even *able* to take responsibility for myself can depend on the existence of certain socially shared norms. I often feel that I am lucky to live at a time when the meanings of "lesbian" are in as much flux as today. Because of the current fluidity in the meanings of such terms as "lesbian," coming out in the more recent sense enables us to challenge common understandings of what lesbians do. The title of this chapter is meant to be ambiguous: one of the things many lesbians do is take responsibility for ourselves. I get to other things that we do later.

Until recent challenges to courts' refusals to allow lesbian adoption and child custody, lesbian feminism has had little to do with taking responsibility for reproductive institutions. From the perspective of human reproduction, it appears puzzling, even downright perverse, that lesbian relationships have been generally dealt with in law and in psychiatry as though they were *sexual*. In this chapter I argue that for purposes of taking responsibility for ourselves, lesbian relationships are better conceived as *erotic* than as sexual. Understanding coming out as taking responsibility for erotic rather than for sexual intimacy removes certain conceptual bases for regarding such behavior as perverse or even deviant.

There are three possible confusions that I wish to dispel at the outset. First, it is no part of my argument that lesbian relationships characteristically are or should be more spiritual than physical or more spiritual than heterosexual relationships. However physical, sensual, or orgasmic, I argue that they need not be and probably should not be considered sexual. Second, I am not advocating that lesbians refuse responsibility for reproduction. My thought is, rather, that taking responsibility for reproduction should be a project conceptually distinct from taking responsibility for erotic intimacy. Third, I am not rejecting identity politics. I am skeptical specifically of the politics of sexual identity where "sexual identity" can include an orientation toward members of the same sex as lovers or intimate partners.

The remainder of this chapter has three sections. The first section takes up the care-taking sense of taking responsibility introduced in Chapter Two and distinguishes it from other senses in relation to coming out, so as to avoid a certain misunderstanding. The second section examines the social construction of sexuality as the institutionalization of activities surrounding reproduction together with activities that have come to be associated with reproduction by way of socially constructed norms. The final section distinguishes the erotic from the sexual and argues that, in certain respects, eroticism offers lesbians a better standpoint than sexuality for taking responsibility for intimate relationships.

Taking Responsibility

In the context of relatively formal obligations, in which obligations give rise to duties correlated with others' rights to whatever we have a duty to do, responsibility is a triadic relation of the form, "A is responsible to B for x," or "B can hold A responsible for x," where "A" and "B" range over persons and "x" ranges over actions or events. The interest of moral philosophers in this kind of responsibility has been primarily in the assignments of such things as credit and blame, punishment and reward, and in some parties holding others to certain conduct, if only requiring them to justify or explain themselves. If A is responsible to B for x, then B has a corresponding right against A regarding x. So understood, taking responsibility is about recognizing justified limits to our freedom set by the rights of others. It is about the distribution of social control. The accountability and credit senses of taking responsibility fit this pattern. And that for which we take responsibility in these senses is usually an action or event, paradigmatically something we have done or failed to do.

Responsibility can be taken for things, for beings, and for states of affairs, as well as for actions or events. Where the object of responsibility is not an action or event but is something that has a welfare, or requires upkeep or maintenance, or is an ongoing venture that can succeed or fail, the responsibility relationship may be simply dyadic, of the form,

"A is responsible for x." The administrative and care-taking senses of responsibility often fit this pattern. Obligations of the administrative and care-taking responsibilities often fit the trustee model, as developed in Chapter Six, better than the debtor model. This may not be obvious, however. The trustee model of obligation may seem triadic, in that one party A holds something x in trust for another party B. However, what A held in trust in the examples under consideration in Chapter Six was B's goodwill. This x is not detachable from B. Thus the relationship is basically dyadic. A is responsible for something about B, but B does not have a claim against A in regard to it. A trustee relationship *can* be triadic; I can hold your funds in trust, for example, in which case you certainly can have a claim on me for them. But a trustee relationship need not be triadic. It can be dyadic, as in the case of obligations of gratitude, where what I hold in trust is your goodwill. In that case I take on the responsibility to see that your goodwill was not misplaced.

Gratitude is not the only example of informal obligation for which the trustee model is more appropriate than the debtor model. Taking responsibility for oneself is another case in which one takes on a trust. In this case, one entrusts oneself with the care of oneself and takes on the responsibility to make oneself good. This has nothing to do with regarding oneself as answerable to anyone else. That would be taking responsibility in the accountability sense. What I have in mind by taking responsibility for oneself in coming out as lesbian is not a matter of justifying oneself to others or even of justifying oneself to oneself. It is not really about justification. It is about care-taking and about pride. It is a matter of taking charge of oneself and undertaking to make something of oneself.

When we take responsibility for things, beings, or states of affairs — for what has a welfare — our focus is on such things as development, maintenance, protection, care-taking, and supporting, rather than on interpersonal control or limiting freedom. If you take responsibility for the house and I take responsibility for the car, each of us is concerned with the care of the thing in question, regardless of whether we can also hold each other answerable and regardless of whether anyone else can hold either of us answerable. As the work of Carol Gilligan and Nel Noddings indicates, modern moral philosophers have paid far less attention to responsibility as care-taking than to responsibility, as holding people answerable and as the correlative of rights.[6]

Taking responsibility for something with a welfare requires the ability to do such things as influencing, guiding, shaping, maintaining, developing, defending, protecting, supporting. These activities can involve exercises of control. But control in this context is a means to the further end of well-being. When responsibility is conceived as a tradic relationship, as the correlative of rights, the parties' interest in control is not simply as a means to something further. Where rights are at stake, the parties involved have an interest in maintaining a certain distribution among themselves of control over each other. There is a focus on control here as important in its own right.

Joyce Trebilcot points out that taking responsibility for something does not require that we identify ourselves as its author, originator, or cause.[7] We may identify ourselves, rather, as backers, supporters, maintainers, developers, protectors. In so doing, we become committed to the value of that for which we take responsibility — not necessarily to its success (although that is a possible value), but to making something of it, maintaining, or protecting it and to making good on failures to do so.

Taking responsibility in this sense is captured by the metaphors of standing behind, backing, supporting, all of which convey the ideas of giving or being prepared to give added substance to something and being committed to its value. In supporting ourselves, we enter into our own development in a positive way. We may not have been behind a thing to begin with, but we can stand behind it now and for the future. Such undertakings reveal something of our character in revealing our commitments, what we value, and what we are prepared to do about it. They not only *reveal* character but also are partly *constitutive* of it.

Because coming out as lesbian has been conceived by feminists in terms of taking responsibility for ourselves, many of us have not been happy with the popular liberal view that toleration is the appropriate response to variety in physically intimate relationships, which is usually defended on the ground that individuals' predilections in such matters are no one else's business. In coming out as lesbians we have been prepared to stand behind our intimate relationships in as public a way as heterosexuals do in marrying — although we have not necessarily been prepared to stand behind them as permanent relationships, and many of us would not be eager to place in the hands of law power to enforce them. Both lesbians and gay men are likely to view coming out as a major step in the development of character. The liberal toleration view suggests that physically intimate relationships outside of marriage are nothing that one could or should stand behind. Ignoring them is an act of toleration whereby a point is made of overlooking what might otherwise prove troublesome. Tolerating is a way of excusing, and excusing presupposes something unfortunate to be excused. From the liberal point of view, coming out, then, looks like a display of bad taste, or at least, ingratitude to the liberal spirit of others if not an offense against public decency. On the other hand, if coming out is understood as an act of taking responsibility, the tolerant reception is what looks offensive. Toleration here communicates a negative value judgment together with a decision not to regard the agent as responsible, an attitude bound to be received as condescending under the circumstances.

Although taking responsibility involves being committed to the value of something, we can sometimes take responsibility for what turns out badly as well as for what turns out well. The value to which we are committed need not be pragmatic, and failure is not necessarily incompatible with goodness. We may be committed to the value of something as an embodiment of ideals we believe in, despite its lack of success. But if the way in which I am taking responsibility is by identifying myself in a certain way, then a certain success is required: I do not manage to identify myself to others in a particular way if they fail to or refuse to recognize me in that way.

Also, taking responsibility for something need not commit one to the idea that the thing is good throughout. If I take responsibility for my life, for example, I take responsibility for bad parts of it as well as for good parts. I do not deny that there are bad parts. Nor do I merely own them as mine. It means such things as that I am committed to not being defeated by them and to such things as repairing or compensating for damage I do, seeking to understand the causes, converting misfortune into opportunities for positive development—in general, to exercising care (not to be confused with caution) in the way I lead my life. Taking responsibility, in this sense, requires faith and hope. It is incompatible with cynicism and despair.

Taking responsibility for oneself is also a matter of degree. It would be silly and arrogant to take responsibility for everything that we are and do. Nor is it possible. One has to be in a position to stand behind something.

When are we in a position to back something, to stand behind it? Being in a position to stand behind something requires being able to carry out tasks that constitute backing it, making it good. Except for my ability to defend a thing's existing or realized values, I am unable to stand behind something when I cannot affect it and when I can neither repair nor compensate for the damage it does. As will become apparent, my abilities to do some of these things may require social cooperation. They may require that my action receive a certain uptake on the part of others. But also part of what it can mean to be in a position to back something is that backing it would be a good thing for me to do, that it would be worth my while. I am not in a (good) position to back something that is not already good unless I can make something tolerably good of it without expending more effort than it is worth.

In an essay on self-respect for *Vogue* magazine, Joan Didion presents being responsible for oneself as taking a certain attitude toward one's choices. "People with self-respect have the courage of their mistakes," she writes. "They know the price of things. If they choose to commit adultery, they do not then go running, in an excess of bad conscience, to receive absolution from the wronged parties, nor do they complain unduly of the unfairness, the undeserved embarrassment of being named co-respondent."[8] Being responsible for yourself, here, looks like being willing to lie in the bed you have made.

Joan Didion seems, in this passage, to understand being responsible as a kind of acceptance. More than acceptance, however, is required to distinguish taking responsibility from resignation. Taking responsibility involves the added idea of backing, and that involves the judgment that the thing in question is worth backing. Taking responsibility for oneself even as an adulterer involves, I should think, an ability and a readiness to do something about the harm, if any, that it caused others, independently of rights they might have to compel one to do so.

For political activists or dissenters, matters are more complex than for agents who simply face failures to act in accord with their own better judgment. Joan Didion's discussion considers choices within a social framework that is not itself under criticism by the chooser. By contrast, Joyce Trebilcot, as a social critic, was concerned not only about individual choice but also about the framework. Political activists may be unwilling to accept much that follows upon their choices because of the context within which those choices were made. Often they feel that others, who support that context, should take responsibility for some of those consequences.

For a political activist, taking responsibility can be an ambitious and risky business. Taking responsibility in the context of practices that we reject requires *doing it at the level of meaning and definition*. This is the predicament of feminists with respect to intimate relationships.

Lesbian relationships are popularly understood as sexual relationships. To explain what it would mean to take responsibility for oneself as lesbian at the level of meaning and definition, I need to throw into question the understanding of lesbian relationships as sexual. For that purpose, I distinguish between sexuality *as an institution* — a set of practices defined by social norms — and sexuality *as behavior and experience* that falls under norms of the institution of sexuality, which define or redefine that behavior and experience as sexual.[9] An analogy may help. Consider taking responsibility for one's crime. Should we not distinguish between taking responsibility for the act performed and taking responsibility for its criminality? That distinction seems unimportant only if we already stand behind the relevant laws and institutions. If I stand behind the law, my choice to disobey it is either backsliding or part of a strategy to improve or correct the law. Taking responsibility for my choice is at the same time a way of backing the law and the system to which it belongs. However, if I do not stand behind the law, taking responsibility for disobeying it is another matter. Although I may not be free to act as though the law did not exist, neither am I required to try to improve it. But then I must be able to rely upon meanings of my conduct that are independent of the legal categories imposed on it.

Analogously, it becomes important to distinguish between taking responsibility for our intimate relationships (fantasies, feelings, behavior, and so forth) and taking responsibility for their *sexual meanings* if we do not stand behind the institution of sexuality that is the source of those meanings. If we are not in a position to redefine sexual social norms, our so-called sexual identities are substantially beyond our control. This is generally true of lesbians in patriarchal society. We are not in a good position to take responsibility for our sexual identities. This is one reason, although as I point out it is not the only one, for lesbians to refuse responsibility for sexual identity. Refusing responsibility for the sexual meanings of our identities as lesbians does not, however, imply refusing responsibility for ourselves *as lesbians,* as long as there are other possibilities where we can have some influence.

In her analysis of taking responsibility for our sexualities, Joyce Trebilcot suggests that a way in which we might go about it is to choose carefully whether to participate in activities currently defined by social sexual norms.[10] For example, a heterosexual woman might choose not to marry any of her lovers. Choosing whether to participate in such activities, however, is not sufficient to give us control over our identities. For the meanings of our choices depend greatly on others' responses to us. Their responses determine which norms will actually take effect. Refusing, on principle, to participate in heterosexual courtship, intercourse, or marriage is ordinarily considered, within the institution of heterosexuality, to be deviant, at the very least, to require justification. That institution defines lesbians as women who make perverted sexual choices. To the extent that the meanings of our choices are determined by the responses of others among whom we live, we seem inevitably to "participate" in sexist and heterosexist institutions as long as we live among their supporters.

If we live in a heterosexist society, then, we need to take responsibility for ourselves not just at the level of choosing to accept or reject options defined by prevailing practices but at the level of practices themselves. This requires changing the meanings of what we do. Taking responsibility here requires *successfully imposing on rituals and relationships meanings that we can stand behind.*

Even if we do this, many others will continue to employ their own definitions of us, as some fundamentalist Christians today, for example, persist in defining adherents of other religions as sinners or heretics. Yet their definitions do not negate our responsibility-taking as long as they do not prevent us from standing behind our own definitions. To do that we need to be able to make something of them, give them effect, implement them.

What is required for us to be able to stand behind our own definitions? To come out as a lesbian requires a context. Not only is a closet presupposed from which to escape, but also there must be places to go, other than into the courts or the psychiatrist's office. To come out successfully, we need a certain range of receptions. Comings out need confirmation. Otherwise we succeed in coming out only as exhibitionists, deviants, criminals, unrepentant sinners, and so forth — not that it is necessarily a bad thing to do that, but to make out why, we need also to come out as something more. When others (not only lesbians) confirm the self-image of those of us who come out, they, too, take a certain responsibility for the meaning of "lesbian" in their offers of such support.

The need for social uptake in changing meanings suggests a certain moral problem in a society in which the existing meanings of "lesbian" are deeply negative. The objection is that we risk exposing those we love to victimization by others in a society that does not yet recognize the changes we would institute. It is absurd to think that you can change the meaning of something just by intending a different meaning when you use it yourself or with your friends. The question arises whether I am recommending something like that here with respect to the existing sexual meanings of lesbian intimacy.

It is one thing merely to intend our actions to have certain meanings and another for them actually to have those meanings. Our freedom to act on meanings we can stand behind partly depends on our success in changing meanings. Since that is a social success, not an individual one, there is genuine moral risk here. There is a risk that the requisite validation will not be forthcoming or will not be sustained and that, consequently, one will not be able to take responsibility for the relationships in question. For an appropriately responsive community is not entirely within anyone's control.

It may be objected that my taking responsibility requires me only to try, not to succeed, because I can embrace the values I find in my relationships whether others recognize them or not. If I am right in my understanding of what it means to take responsibility, however, it is not just a matter of mentally embracing something. What is at stake here is one's ability to provide a kind of support. I do not offer real support as long as everyone else can write off my attempt as perverse.

It is true that in coming out, lesbians may risk exposing others to harm. However, to evaluate that, we must consider the alternative. It is not as though we can responsibly just wait until social conditions appear propitious. For those conditions may be creatable only as the result of others, whose situations are relevantly similar, taking the risk in advance of any such appearance. Some have argued that in such a situation, it would be morally wrong not to take the risk.[11] For the consequences of everyone similarly situated not doing so are disastrous for many. Yet I find more truth in the idea that there is truly moral risk here and that it may be possible only in retrospect to assess with any confidence the morality of taking or foregoing such a risk.

Thus, taking responsibility for ourselves involves moral luck. There is luck involved in the validation requisite to successfully creating meanings. Insofar as taking responsibility for ourselves and our character involves imposing meanings on our lives that we can stand behind, that luck becomes a kind of moral luck.

The meaning of "lesbian" is currently undergoing change from a popular medico-legal conception as a sexual identity to a feminist conception that is now in many respects unclear. The clarification I want to propose involves distinguishing the sexual from the erotic. It is, I believe, coherent with much contemporary lesbian feminist practice, although there is at present no common agreement on vocabulary to describe what is occurring. Despite our widespread continued use of the language of sexuality, it seems to me that we rightly back many relationships as lesbian that are not clearly sexual in any sense of "sexual" worth our support. To clarify that, I turn next to the concept of sexuality.

Sexuality

Should we stand behind lesbian relationships as sexual relationships? Should we stand behind lesbianism as a sexual identity? What is at stake in these questions?

"Sexuality" is ambiguous among at least the following:

(I) femaleness or maleness (a heavily physiological concept)
(II) the institution of sexuality (a heavily political one)
(III) instances of behavior falling under the norms of (II), which relate that behavior to (I).

The question whether to stand behind lesbian relationships as sexual is in part about the sexuality of what lesbians do. The concept of sexual behavior is systematically ambiguous, thanks to the physiological and political meanings of sexuality.[12] "Sexual behavior" seems to have a narrower and a wider sense. The narrower (physiological) sense refers to behavior characteristically instrumental toward or controlling of physiological reproduction. The wider (political) sense includes behavior falling under norms of the historical institution of sexuality, norms defining correct and incorrect behavior for females or for males in a variety of contexts. Such norms define what Kate Millett called sexual politics, insofar as they create and distribute forms of power.[13]

Perhaps all, or nearly all, physiologically sexual behavior is also sexual in the political sense. That is, perhaps all or nearly all such behavior is covered by sexuo-political norms. But not all sexual behavior in the political sense is also physiologically sexual. The institution of sexuality relates behavior in a great many ways to reproduction, and not only to physiological reproduction but also to social reproduction, the reproduction of culture, institutions, ways of life. In so doing, it structures adult intimacy.

Taking responsibility for sexuality, then, is at least ambiguous between taking responsibility for behavior that is instrumental toward or controlling of physiological reproduction, on one hand, and on the other, taking responsibility for behavior that has been defined ("constructed") as sexual by social practices. If taking responsibility for one's sexuality is understood to include taking responsibility for one's sexual identity, it is taken at least partly in the second way.

I question the wisdom of lesbians' taking responsibility for our sexual identities, not only because we are in a poor position to influence the institution of sexuality but also in the way that I would question the wisdom of sodomites' taking responsibility for their criminal identities. Social norms that define sexual identities define too much else in the process. They develop the concept of sexual identity in such a way that "homosexual" inevitably sounds perverted. We should, where we can, take responsibility for our reproductive potentialities and also for our intimate affiliations. But why take responsibility for sexual readings of our intimate affiliations? Why tie responsibility for physiological reproduction to relationships of playful adult intimacy? Viewing intimacy through the lens of sexuality amalgamates these otherwise distinct projects.

Sexual identity is a hybrid concept, partly physiological, partly political. According to John De Cecco and Michael G. Shively, of the Center for Research and Education in Sexuality in San Francisco, sexual identity has four components: (1) biological sex (assigned at birth), (2) one's *conviction* of being female or male (referred to as one's "gender identity"), (3) femininity or masculinity, as defined by social norms, and (4) sexual orientation. Sexual orientation, in turn, is broken down into at least four factors: (1) erotic fantasies, (2) emotional affiliation, and (3) sexual behavior.[14]

Of the four named components of sexual identity, only the first, namely, biological sex (femaleness or maleness), seems uncontroversially genetically determined. Even that claim needs qualification with respect to individuals of indeterminate sex who are nevertheless classified as either female or male. It is a question for feminists whether any of the other factors is worth preserving. In a philosophical feminist critique of transsexualism, Janice Raymond has argued that what Shively and De Cecco, following Robert Stoller, call "female gender identity," namely, one's "conviction of being female," is better understood as one's sense of being feminine, that is, as identifying with the family of psychosocial characteristics normatively associated with being female in a sexist society—which is what contemporary American feminists have usually meant by "female gender" as distinct from "female sex."[15] If Janice Raymond is right, the conception of the preoperative male-to-female transsexual as a woman trapped in a man's body assumes that *real* women are determined by conformity to sex-role stereotypes, which feminists find oppressive. This criticism has implications for male-to-female transsexuals with respect to taking responsibility for their sexuality. If Janice Raymond is right, the meaning of the "woman" that the male-to-female transsexual wants to be is not something that anyone should stand behind. Consciousness-raising is a better solution than surgery.

Perhaps Queer Theory with its ideas on "gender bending" and multiple genders can find ways to make sense of male-to-female transsexual surgery as something other than a (presumably unwitting) endorsement of sexist stereotypes. I have yet to see it done. The case is different for a female-to-male transsexual, given the patriarchal history of identifying human traits as male. The preoperative female-to-male transsexual may find for good reasons that her sense of herself as human does not sit right in a female body in the context of patriarchy. She may not have internalized, even unwittingly, sexist norms of masculinity in her desire to be thoroughly male. But she may find it psychologically impossible to dissociate from femininity the femaleness of her birth body.

The very notion of an identity defined in part by way of sexual orientation is, according to historians of sexuality of the past couple of decades, a relatively recent phenomenon. Labeling *persons* "homosexuals" as opposed simply to marking individual *acts* as sodomitic or sapphic apparently dates only from the late nineteenth century. According to Jeffrey Weeks's history of homosexual politics in Britain, the term "homosexuality" was coined in 1869 by a Swiss doctor, Karoly Maria Benkert, and did not enter English currency until the 1890s.[16]

Formerly, the act of sodomy was prohibited by secular and ecclesiastical law, and the prevailing assumption was that such an act might be committed by any man. As Michel Foucault tells it, with the nineteenth-century medicalization and psychiatrization of sex, the former sodomite criminal or sinner "became a personage, a past, a case history, and a childhood, in addition to being a type of life, a life form, and a morphology, with an indiscreet anatomy and possibly a mysterious physiology."[17] By this he did not mean that people simply discovered that homosexual agents had certain sorts of histories and lifestyles. The idea was, rather, that as people defined themselves through the articulation of social norms, they were thereby "constructing" identities for themselves and others and were even constructing who they, and others, had been.[18]

Thomas Szasz has argued similarly that psychiatrists have simultaneously "discovered" and "created" the mentally ill. The category of mental illness, understood as a basis for commitment to a total institution, he maintains, has functioned in recent times the way the category of heresy functioned during the Renaissance. He presents both "witch" and "homosexual" as identities of deviance defined by way of social norms and considers the homosexual a paradigm modern-day heretic.[19]

Joyce Trebilcot's account of coming out as a lesbian is in a certain respect similar to Foucault's account of the creation of the homosexual identity and to Szasz's account of the creation of the mentally ill. She says it is not simply a discovery but at once a discovery and a creation.[20] By contrast, many contemporary gay liberationists have held that sexual orientation is beyond anyone's control (so far) and have exhibited more often than feminist lesbians a lively interest in the possibility of genetic explanations.[21] They have tended to deny individual responsibility, arguing that laws attempting to regulate sexual orientation and therapies attempting to alter it are irrational and unfair. The social construction of sexuality, however, suggests an alternative to this line of criticism of the law and psychiatry. If Foucault is right, the medicalization and psychiatrization of sex, understood as historical events, created forms of power by defining new relationships. To combat the distributions of power defined by those relationships, perhaps we need to reject the sexual institutions through which they have been defined. If "lesbian" were not politically sexualized, coming out as a lesbian might be compatible with rejecting rather than affirming one's (socially defined) sexual identity in the sense set out by Shively and De Cecco. Even the term "lesbian," unlike the term "homosexual," comes from the history of erotic poetry, not from the history of medicine or psychiatry, and "gay" has likewise a popular folk history associated with music and romance.[22]

What purposes are served by regarding so-called sexual orientations as sexual in any other sense than that indicating the sexes of the parties involved? What purposes are served by regarding love-making as sexual behavior?

Friedrich Nietzsche and Sigmund Freud saw embracing sexuality as overcoming squeamishness about the body. Yet embracing the body does not require embracing a sexual interpretation of its erotic pleasures. At issue for women is a history of being defined and devalued by what has been called our sexuality, either our utility for reproducing patriarchy or our utility for phallic play (recreation). The twentieth-century sexual revolution shifted the emphasis from reproduction to recreation and attempted a revaluation of the recreation from a fraternal, rather than patriarchal, perspective but did little to contest a phallic definition of intimate relationships.

Many rightly question applying the concept of love-making to sex as fraternal recreation. What has not been questioned, however, is the wisdom of viewing erotic behavior as sexual. The homophile movement of the 1950s came close to doing so with its emphasis on the love, rather than the sexuality, of same-sex partners. However, the love emphasized by the homophile movement was not clearly enough erotic. For homophiles, the important distinction was between love and sex, but not particularly between the erotic and the sexual, although perhaps it had the potentiality for that development.

Insofar as the erotic is a powerful bonding agent, it is worth pondering the implications, for maintaining the structure of heteropatriarchy, of conflating it with sexuality. I want to challenge the association of women's intimate bonds with behavior interpreted as variations on or deviations from phallic play or insemination. From the latter points of view, lesbian relationships inevitably appear deviant, substitutes for "the real thing," as perversity in reproductive behavior.

There is a sense in which lesbian relationships could become straightforwardly sexual without being deviant or perverse. With a different social construction of reproduction, lesbian relationships could certainly take on positive reproductive forms, participating in the reproduction of society through giving birth and rearing children. Many lesbians in fact do this, although their careers as reproducers are currently precarious, given present social norms governing reproduction.[23] To be in a good position to assume responsibility for our reproductive potentialities we need a social reconstruction of reproduction worth standing behind. The point is generalizable. To be in a good position to assume responsibility for ourselves, we need to participate in a social reconstruction of ourselves that we can stand behind.

It is not my intention to claim that humanity, or even sexuality, is entirely socially constructed. That it is socially constructed in part, however, is what makes it possible to take the kind of responsibility that I am writing about. To some extent we construct ourselves in that who we are is partly determined by social interaction, typically in accord with social norms, which are themselves constructed by social interaction and revisable by different interactions.[24]

According to a well-known labeling perspective in sociology, social construction, or definition, occurs on three levels: interpersonal reactions, collective rule-making, and organizational processing.[25] All three are involved in the social construction of sexualities. Instead of collective rule-making, I think of *norm construction*. Norms often empower or disable by defining roles and relationships. Instead of organizational processing, I think of *rituals*, understanding by "rituals" what Nietzsche referred to as "the custom, the act, the 'drama,' a certain . . . sequence of procedures."[26] Rituals are often given meanings by social norms. Nietzsche also observed that what endure in the institution of punishment are the rituals (the "drama," he called it) — perhaps such things as arrest, inquisition, trial, beheading, incarceration, flogging. Less enduring are what Nietzsche called the rituals' "meanings," the purposes for which they are used, such things as prevention, deterrence, revenge, reform, expulsion, or a compromise with revenge. The same may be true of sexuality. What endure may be the various rituals referred to as "having sex" — rituals of copulation, sodomy, other so-called sexual acts. Such rituals have borne a variety of meanings, even religious ones. One feminist response to the institution of rape has been the inclination to say that rape is not sex, meaning that the point of the act is not to gratify the desire for sexual pleasure but, rather, such things as putting women in their place or getting revenge on other men. Yet it is undeniable that many of the rituals involved in rape are the same rituals involved in "having sex."

Taking a similar approach to "revenge" in his book *The Wanderer,* Nietzsche describes words as "pockets into which now this and now that has been put and now many things at once."[27] He regarded words and rituals as having lives of their own, so to speak, with meanings that come and go. This seems at least as true of "sex" and the rituals we call "sexual" as of "revenge" and the rituals we call "punishment."

What does it mean to "have sex?" In the sense of "sex" that refers to one's femaleness or one's maleness, one "has it" all the time. But "having sex," of course, refers to behaviors that are not inevitable. "*Having* sex" is a practice defined by the historical institution of sexuality, rather than determined by the physiology of human reproduction. Sexuality as an institution has a genealogical history, an evolution, like punishment. Nietzsche also observed that "all concepts in which an entire process is semiotically concentrated elude definition; only that which has no history is definable."[28] Taking this seriously suggests that what has a genealogy is better understood through its relationships to its many ancestors than through the search for an essence. If "having sex" is defined by an institution that has a genealogy, it may consist in engaging in ancient rituals that are now governed by social norms that relate them to human reproduction. To impose a sexual meaning on such rituals is then to interpret them by way of the norms of an institution that also structures reproduction.

It might be objected, however, that the analogy with punishment breaks down. There is no such thing as plain punishment, prior to social practice. Yet, it has seemed to some that there is such a thing as plain sex, on a par, perhaps, with plain eating and drinking, not yet defined by social practice.[29] Lunching and dining are defined by social practices, but one can eat or drink without lunching or dining. Is there not likewise just plain having sex, prior to its social constructions?

The difficulty is to say what it is. There are, of course, sexual organs, as there are digestive organs. But so-called sexual behavior is not understood as necessarily involving organs. Nor is all behavior that involves sexual body parts sexual behavior. In law and psychiatry, it seems taken for granted that lesbian genital love-making *is* sexual behavior. If lesbian love-making were genital, that would seem a comprehensible — although not decisive — reason to regard it as sexual. But if "having sex" is enacting certain rituals involving external genitalia, or rituals preparatory to those or analogous to them, it can be argued that "having sex" is a phallic concept that cannot be applied without distortion to lesbian love-making.[30] For women have no external genitalia. Lesbian love-making is *never,* strictly speaking, *genital.* What are inaccurately referred to as women's external genitalia are (1) the menstrual canal (neither generative nor an organ), (2) the clitoris, an organ that generates only pleasure (thus not generative in the requisite sense), and (3) the labia (like the menstrual canal, neither organs nor generative). These parts are, of course, female, and so "sexual" in the same sense as a full beard, vaginitis, menstruation, menopause, and hot flashes, none of which enters into the definition of behavior as sexual behavior.

Women's physically orgasmic pleasures have their physiological source in the clitoris, which makes no contribution to reproduction at any point in the life cycle and which continues to function long after reproduction has become impossible. Clidoridectomy does not impair reproductive capacity.[31] What the clitoris is good for is pleasure. The role it plays in human relations appears thus to be a bonding role, not a reproductive one.

It may be objected that the clitoris plays a role in reproduction insofar as it provides pleasure during a reproductive act and thereby facilitates reproduction. There is no correlation, however, between clitoral pleasure and conception. It is therefore misleading to say that such pleasure facilitates (physiological) reproduction. What it facilitates is bonding and perhaps love-making, only one of the rituals of which is ordinarily requisite to reproduction.

Classification of the clitoris as a genital organ betrays a phallic bias: Either the clitoris is misperceived as a little phallus or its pleasures are viewed as a byproduct of copulation or as analogous to those of penile ejaculation — commonly, if mistakenly, identified with male orgasm.[32] If the clitoris is not a genital organ, then its involvement in love-making does not offer a reason to consider that love-making sexual, at least not on a genital conception of sexuality.

Not all conceptions of sexual behavior have a genital focus. Freud offered an account of infant sexuality as polymorphously perverse, meaning that nearly any part of the body can be "sexualized" by becoming a focus of repeated vigorous muscular activity, such as sucking, with the result that a tension is regularly created there which needs to be relieved and can be relieved by muscular activity, such as sucking or pulling or rubbing.[33]

But what does it mean to call this production and relief of tension *sexual*? Freud seems to have thought the energies involved were sexual energies. But that only pushes the question back a step: What does it mean to identify *energies* as sexual?

Two kinds of answers suggest themselves: either their *sources* are sexual or their *directions* are sexual. Nongenitally focused conceptions of sexual behavior, such as Freud's, attempt to define sexual behavior in terms of either motivation or teleology rather than in terms of body parts. The search for a common motivation, however, has proved as futile as the search for other common denominators. The likeliest teleological candidate is the purpose of furthering the life of the species.[34] By this criterion, however, research into health care, ecology, and environmental ethics may be clearer instances of sexual behavior than lesbian love-making.

For Aristotle sexual pleasure is pleasure in certain kinds of touching.[35] This view is similar to Freud's and enters into a popular notion of sexuality today. It is this kind of view to which I turn next. The view of sexuality as touching for pleasure probably confuses the sexual with the erotic. Disentangling the erotic from the sexual is an important step in taking responsibility for lesbian relationships, even if some ultimately want also to move beyond the erotic.

The Erotic

"Erotic" is popularly employed as a euphemism for "sexual," especially in the context of art and pornography. However, the meanings of "erotic" and "sexual" are distinct. "Sexual" is either a biological concept or a sociopolitical one elaborated on it. "Erotic" is not a biological concept. "Erotic" refers to certain emotional capacities or to social constructions elaborated on them. The erotic refers to a capacity or set of capacities for pleasurable excitement of certain sorts. The difficulty is to say what sorts. The following seems at least one such: *the susceptibility to joyful surprise in intimate discovery or disclosure by way of touching.* The relevant discoveries are dis/coveries of another; the relevant disclosures, dis/closures of oneself. Desires and fantasies may be understood as erotic when they are desires for or fantasies of such experience. Autoerotic behavior can be understood as erotic by way of the fantasies it involves.

I want to focus on the idea of touching as a central element of the erotic. Only what is particular and embodied can touch and is touchable. Erotic communication is thoroughly carnal. Although carnal, it need not be skin to skin, however. It can occur by eye contact and even by the spoken and written word. Still, it is not touching in the requisite sense unless the party touched feels the touch. I am touched, in this sense, when someone moves me, succeeds in reaching me, makes me feel something.

Although carnal, the erotic need not be sexual. Connections of sexuality with the erotic are more contingent than is ordinarily assumed. It is the political institution of sexuality that construes erotic play as a sexual invitation. Thomas Nagel's essay "Sexual Perversion," which some critics have claimed never gets around to sex, takes for granted the context of this institution of sexuality, according to which the erotic play he describes is construed as a sexual invitation.[36] By way of institutional norms erotic play has come to be associated with sexuality. What eros and sexuality have in common, apart from such norms, is a historical association with rituals in which physical touching and its attendant pleasures are central. The touching required for physiological reproduction, however, is not the same kind of touching as enters into the definition of erotic interaction. For physiological reproduction, neither party need *feel* anything. (This may be literally true with some forms of artificial insemination.) Numb eroticism, on the other hand, is a contradiction in terms (although insensitivity in eroticism is not).

The erotic makes no reference to gender. There is no reason why it should occur more frequently heterosexually than homosexually. There are, however, good historical reasons why same-sex eroticism is likely to be healthier than heterosexual eroticism. Under current sexual politics, parties to heterosexual eroticism are almost inevitably very unequal in political power. In same-sex eroticism, at least one major source of political inequality is absent. The problem is not the bare existence of a power inequality. Serious problems arise when such inequalities in a relationship actually become part of what is erotically exciting about it. When this occurs with inequalities that are due to oppressive social institutions, those damaged by such institutions may be drawn into supporting them for the sake of the pleasure derived from the relationships those institutions make possible. Where women are damaged by misogynist institutions, heterosexual eroticism contains this danger. Part of what many women find exciting about heterosexual relationships is the very power differential that has resulted from practices oppressive to women.

Similar dangers arise for same-sex intimacy when it is sexualized in a sexist context. The sexualization of same-sex intimacy consists in applying norms of the institution of sexuality to the parties to same-sex intimate relationships. Doing so risks attaching erotic excitement to damaging inequalities of power or to fantasized inequalities realizable only by way of oppressive practices.

Erotic interaction is a powerful bonding agent. A brief interchange can have one hooked for years. This is not true simply of the rituals of sex. Sexual behavior can also be a powerful bonding agent over time but not just overnight. A consequence of eroticizing sexual (reproductive) interaction in the context of oppressive sexual politics is that it sets up women for becoming locked into damaging long-term relationships. If lesbian love-making is then regarded as another kind of sexuality, there is the risk of importing the same values into lesbian love-making. Sexuality, as a phallic institution in a sexist society, is laden with associations between inequality and erotic pleasure. It may be impossible to purge sexuality of those associations without a much wider nonsexist reconstruction of society. Meanwhile, the erotic offers, at least potentially, an alternative to the conception of lesbian relationships as sexual.

One may wonder whether "eros" has a better history than "sex." In Plato's dialogues, the *Symposium* and the *Phaedrus*, eros leads to what Freud called sublimation, a turning away from the body.[37] Further, the contemporary pornography scene, notorious for its misogyny, caters to an emotional high that bears more than a family resemblance to what I understand by "erotic." If my understanding of erotic experience is correct, however, there is no special reason to associate the erotic with rejection of the body. And if pornography is just eroticized oppressive sexuality, what is wrong with it is first of all the oppressive sexuality, which eroticism only makes worse by getting participants hooked on it.

My understanding of the erotic leaves open the question whether what is discovered or disclosed in erotic experience is good or bad and also whether the discovery or disclosure is itself desirable or not, on the whole — for example, whether it is obtained by means employed with or without the consent of the parties involved, and so on. I do not claim that erotic relationships are necessarily good. My claim is, rather, that the conception of lesbian relationships as erotic avoids a certain phallo-centrism and, thereby, the popular horror of their conception as sexual. It offers, in those respects, a more coherent standpoint for the feminist enterprise of taking responsibility for intimacy.

A large part of one's intent in coming out as a lesbian is to reject the charge of perversion. The idea is not to embrace some perversions as good things, after all, but to support one's identity and relationships as, at the very least, no more perverted than other intimate relationships that already have society's blessings.[38] The conception of lesbianism as an erotic, rather than sexual, identity removes a certain conceptual basis of the charge of perversion. The health and success of erotic interaction as an emotional exchange is in no way contingent upon the sexes of the parties.

What the erotic captures about lesbian relationships is emotional intimacy, excitement, and a certain appreciation of our bodies. Lesbians should also be able to participate in reproduction as fully as anyone. Apart from the institution of sexuality, the lesbianism of a relationship implies little about the potentialities of such participation. The lesbianism of a relationship has to do, rather, with what turns us on, what excites us, what we appreciate in women. What turns us on is a source of the driving energies of our lives. Coming out as a lesbian is an important part of taking responsibility for what turns us on and thereby for what drives us. This is fundamental to taking responsibility for ourselves. It is a choice to embrace intimate attachments that we can stand behind. In a homophobic and misogynist society that is ripe for revolution, coming out as a lesbian potentially emancipates our intimate relationships from their historic ties to reproduction and phallic recreation. It thereby potentially emancipates us from important forms of our historic complicity in perpetuating the machinery of sex oppression. We may need to reject sexual identities in order to do it.

RACE CONSCIOUSNESS

People of (nonwhite) color and white people in the United States do not, in general, have the same consciousness of race, nor do the many peoples of color share the same consciousness of race. White people tend to have the privilege of not noticing things to which people of color are forced to attend regularly. William Julius Wilson has argued that race is declining in significance in the explanations of inequalities in the United States today.[1] Even if he were right about new introductions of inequalities for blacks in relation to whites, it would not follow that race was declining in significance for other U.S. peoples of color, nor for relations among them. Nor would it follow that *consciousness* of race is or should be declining in significance, because our pasts have not been undone. That people of color were becoming freed up from race consciousness at the same time that white people's consciousness and self-consciousness of race was growing sounds like a fantasy of poetic justice. For white people, justice may require an increasing consciousness of race, consciousness of a different sort from that of a racist society. This chapter is written from my perspective as a white woman raised, in a basically monocultural village of the heartland, with the privilege of not noticing a great deal. My consciousness of race over the past two decades has been increasing, changing, deepening.

Like the concepts of sexual orientation and gender, the very concept of race is controversial. Worlds are imaginable in which none of these concepts structures social relations. In 1945 Ashley Montagu argued, on the ground that behaviors cannot be meaningfully correlated with biological ancestry, that there are no races.[2] Although the language of race persists and many conceptualize racial difference through paradigms of gross morphological difference (in hair, skin, bone), the view is discredited that members of the most generally socially recognized racial groups are significantly more likely to share genes with each other than with members of other groups.[3] According to Anthony Appiah, "Every reputable biologist will agree that human genetic variability between the populations of Africa or Europe or Asia is not much greater than that within those populations."[4]

Like erotic orientation and gender, race is a highly institutionalized concept, or family of concepts.[5] Even if race, like baseball, were institutionalized throughout, in the sense that apart from social institutions there would be nothing for the concept to mark, racialized social distinctions are so deeply enmeshed in our histories that we can hardly ignore where we are located in their terrains if we wish to take responsibility for who we become as social and political beings. Social construction does not make races unreal, even if it makes them wrong and unnatural.

The challenge at the present time may be to acquire a race consciousness that can be helpful for resisting rac*ism*. But what kind of consciousness is that? What does taking responsibility for ourselves require of us in relation to how we are racialized? That, I think, depends on who we are. Many white people have needed to unlearn the arrogance of equating humanity with whiteness, whereas many people of color have reason to wonder how anyone could possibly make such a mistake. Yet there are levels of consciousness and many things of which to become conscious — many racial identifications, many aspects of race and its institutionalization, many points of view on race, and being targeted by racism is no guarantee that one will become conscious of all such nuances. I begin by sketching three points of view, each of which has seemed to me at one time or another compelling. They are what I call the internal view of W.E.B. Du Bois, the external view of Marilyn Frye, and the interactive view of Maria Lugones.

W.E.B. Du Bois, in his 1897 essay "The Conservation of Races," offers a positive outlook on race from an internal point of view, that is, from the point of view of people who have been racialized by the hostile projects of others. Although he seems in that essay prepared to recognize broad scientifically based racial classifications (black, white, yellow) — a view he later rejected — the objects of his concern even then were more specific groups defined sociohistorically rather than scientifically. In answer to his question, "What, then, is a race?" he writes:

> It is a vast family of human beings, generally of common
> blood and language, always of common history, traditions

and impulses, who are both voluntarily and involuntarily striving together for the accomplishment of certain more or less vividly conceived ideals of life.[6]

Du Bois was writing in a context in which the leading alternative among relatively progressive thinkers to revaluing black culture was an assimilation of black peoples to white. Appiah has argued that Du Bois had to have been relying on a scientific concept of race, after all, because in order to identify individuals as having a common history, it is necessary to have some criterion for identifying them first independently of that history, and what criteria are left besides those of a scientific understanding of race? Citing as analogous John Locke's problem in trying to define personal identity by way of shared memories, when the only way to identify a memory *as shared* is by having an independent criterion of identity for the person being the same person at different times, Appiah argues that "sharing a common group history cannot be a *criterion* for being members of the same group, for we would have to be able to identify the group in order to identify *its* history."[7]

Yet why can we not identify individuals as members of the same group by way of their traditions, if we understand those traditions as partly constitutive of the identities of those who share them? There may be no way to identify a merely psychological memory apart from someone who has it. But traditions — objectified memories — take on lives of their own. They become embodied in social institutions. We may be able to identify a tradition or institution independently — that is, without knowing all who participate in it — and then discover who is connected with whom (and is thus a member of the group constituted by that tradition or institution) by finding out who actually does participate in that tradition or institution. Discovering the identity of parentally transmitted traditions can offer evidence that one is intergenerationally connected with others who were practitioners of those same traditions, a matter to which I return at the end of this chapter. The questions are not thereby settled, of course, whether those connections should be recognized as imposing special responsibilities and whether the tradition or institution in question is worth supporting.

David Theo Goldberg disagrees with Appiah's view that "the only contestant for criterion of racial membership is the false belief in biological heritability," arguing that popular usage also supports cultural interpretations of race.[8] It appears that Du Bois held such a cultural interpretation.[9] If Goldberg is right that "race" is a "family resemblance" concept, we can expect to find in popular usage more than one understanding of it, represented by different paradigms (including some constructed around false beliefs). Still, there may be important truth in Appiah's claim that, "History may have made us what we are, but the choice of a slice of the past in a period before your birth as your own history is always exactly that: a choice."[10] And yet such choices may not be entirely free but may be constrained by moral and political considerations.

Taking the point of view of racialized African Americans, Du Bois argues in his 1897 essay that there are cultural potentialities that a race may need many generations to fulfill and that, given time, the fulfillment of those potentialities can make a significant contribution to humanity.[11] He might have held this to be true regardless of how negatively the concept of race originated in the unfriendly projects of others. Thus, he suggests the possibility of nonracist uses of the concept of race, that is, nonracist uses other than simply the use of "race" to acknowledge or address its racist uses by others. His plea for the conservation of races can be read as supporting the taking on of responsibility for one's race. The plausibility of his view that there is, sociohistorically, a Negro race (to use his term) whose preservation is at stake seems to me to rest on whether a case can be made out for identifying a coherent body or family of traditions as constitutive of so vast and diverse a group as he seems to have envisioned.

In contrast to Du Bois and other Pan Africanists, Marilyn Frye offers, in her essays on being white and female, a thoroughly negative picture of race, treating the concept as imposed on peoples by outsiders whose interests were to mark them for domination, set them apart as inferior, prohibit intermarriage, and so on.[12] Although racializers also become racialized, I think of this picture as giving an external view of race because of the origins of the concept on this view, the idea that "race" was applied first of all to those regarded as "other." Acknowledging that it is probably not in her power to abolish her race, Marilyn Frye's aim has been to achieve the next best thing by disaffiliating from it, that is, being disloyal to what she calls "whiteliness," where "whiteliness" is to color as gender is to sex. Seeing no positive use for the concept of race except to identify historical distinctions wrongfully introduced and institutionalized, her response is to withdraw in the only ways available. This is similar to the response I support in the previous chapter for lesbians in regard to the concept of sexual (as opposed to erotic) identity, in that it disavows responsibility for one's racial identity rather than taking on responsibility for it.

In a series of essays that address issues arising from cultural confrontations and interpenetrations, Maria Lugones's work suggests yet another dimension of the construction of race, that of interaction.[13] She stresses the interactive nature of rac*ism* in a way that suggests that the concept of *race* also develops interactively, regardless how it originates. To whatever extent race is a product of racism, as Joel Kovel has argued, the interactive character of race would seem to follow, if rac*ism* is an interactive phenomenon.[14] Her work also suggests that an *interactive solution* is required to address racism satisfactorily, that it is not enough either for beneficiaries of racism to withdraw as individuals from supporting racist practices or for targets of racism to try to put the most positive possible future construction on what has been done historically. Applied to the idea of taking responsibility, the suggestion is that we who have been differently racialized are in some sense responsible together, interactively (however different our moral roles), for who we have become and that to end racism, we will need to take responsibility together, interactively, for who *we* are going to be.

Thus, in commenting on Lorraine Bethel's poem, "What Chou Mean *We*, White Girl?" she says, "white/anglo women theorizers did not really hear an interactive demand," but "what they heard was a radical attack on the activity of white women theorizing," which "seemed to them to undermine fundamentally the possibility of any theorizing to the extent that it requires generalization."[15] This hearing of Lorraine Bethel's question, she speculates, is what has generated "the problem of difference" as conceived in contemporary white/anglo feminist theory, namely, the problem of "how to generalize without being guilty of false inclusion."[16] And this "problem of difference," she argues, is the wrong problem for those concerned about racism.

The right problem, she finds, is the more concrete one of not seeing, not noticing, the differences. Asking, "What would it be to be noticed?" she answers, speaking as a woman of color to white feminists:

> We are noticed when you realize that we are mirrors in which you can see yourselves as no other mirror shows you. . . . It is not that we are the only faithful mirrors, but I think we *are* faithful mirrors. Not that we show you as you *really* are; we just

show you as one of the people you are. What we reveal to you is that you are many — something that may in itself be frightening to you. But the self we reveal to you is also one that you are not eager to know for reasons that one may conjecture.[17]

She goes on to conjecture that a reason white people block identification with the self mirrored by people of color is that knowing that self would require "self-conscious interaction" and a different sense of responsibility. Continuing to address white feminist theorizers, she says:

Not all the selves we are make you important. Some of them are quite independent of you. Being central, being a being in the foreground, is important to your being integrated as one responsible decision maker. Your sense of responsibility and decision-making are tied to being able to say exactly who it is that did what, and that person must be one and have a will in good working order. And you are very keen on seeing yourself as a decision maker, a responsible being: It gives you substance.[18]

My preceding chapter develops a somewhat interactive interpretation of taking responsibility for one's erotic orientation, calling attention to the luck required in social receptivity for a lesbian to succeed in coming out as she wants to. The interaction in question, however, is more limited than that envisaged by Maria Lugones in that it does not really depend on inclusion of heterosexual parties but appeals only to interaction among lesbians (although heterosexuals *could* also participate). Maria Lugones appears to envisage interaction across racial boundaries, not only among people of color, but also including anglos. If there is luck in being able successfully to take responsibility for one's erotic orientation, as argued in Chapter Seven, there is even more luck in being able successfully to address racial oppression interactively as Maria Lugones envisages. For success depends not only on what many do in groups that have been able to rely on each other's support but also on what many do in groups some of which have treated others badly.

The views of race as internally, externally, and interactively constructed need not be regarded as alternatives. Each of these philosophers has had his or her purposes for stressing different aspects of race and racism. There may be ways of fitting them together as complementary elements of a comprehensive view.

If "race" has internal, external, and interactive aspects, "rac*ism*" connotes first and foremost negative external views or practices, that is, negative views of or negative practices in regard to members of another group. Like "sexism," "rac*ism*" refers to oppressive behaviors, policies, and attitudes ranging from unwitting support of insensitive practices by the well-intentioned to fanatical hatred and institutionalized murder.[19]

"Racism" appears to be a contraction of the earlier "racialism," suggesting the verb, "to racialize," which, in turn, suggests social construction.[20] Appiah has adopted the term "racialism" to refer to the belief that there are biological races, a belief that he finds not yet racist (although false).[21] This use may be confusing, for "racialist" easily suggests "racializer," and yet being race *conscious* is not racializing. It is one thing to make something a matter of race and another to acknowledge it after the fact. After five centuries of Euro-American racializing of Africans, Asians, and Native Americans, we can hardly proceed as though racial categorization were no more than a fantasy.

For Du Bois, however, race consciousness was not only about oppression. He took issue with the integrationists regarding possible sources of pride and on what there might be of value in the preservation of races for African Americans and for humanity in general. He was not thinking first of all of holding whites accountable for their oppression of blacks. He was concerned here with the development of black talent and genius.

The *American Heritage Dictionary* speculates that the word "race" may come from the Latin, *ratio,* meaning "a reckoning, account."[22] What "accounts"? What "reckonings"? Rendered by whom to whom? One possible answer is that the "reckonings" or "accounts" were rendered to conquerors regarding the conquered, that in this way histories of conquest and enslavement are embedded in the concept of race. This interpretation supports the view of race as a construction externally imposed, as in Marilyn Frye's understanding of the concept, that is, applied first to others. Another possible answer, however, is that the "reckoning" or "account" refers to one's own record of one's ancestors, handed on to one's descendants, documenting their heritage. This interpretation suggests an internal view of race, that is, a conception applied first of all to oneself. This interpretation is also compatible with a negative view, however, insofar as it may be combined with chauvinism and hostility toward outsiders.

Alternatively, one may hear, as Orlando Patterson suggests in his discussion of the "natal alienation" of slaves, a different internal conception of "race" embedded in the "deracination," uprootedness, of peoples who have been cut off from their heritages and homelands.[23] Here, "race" suggests "roots," which might be of many kinds, and is derived by way of the Old French *desraciner* from the late Latin *radicina*.[24] If deracination is a source of the contemporary concept of race, it offers us a picture of the exposure or discovery of a people's roots in the process of their destruction. This is an interesting metaphor in that roots tend to be destroyed when they are pulled up and exposed. This metaphor might also yield, however, a positive interactive understanding in that healthy roots, ordinarily invisible, are embedded in a soil or other natural environment by which they are nourished.

"Race" was sometimes used by Charlotte Perkins Gilman — Du Bois's contemporary — in her classic *Women and Economics* to refer to a people who share a lineage and a social history.[25] This might be an interesting idea conceived as applying to oneself if individual races were not defined too broadly — if they were not, say, reduced to four or five in the world. Neither she nor Du Bois does so. They usually identify races not by color but by nationality or geographic origin. When races are defined so broadly that one can list them on the fingers of one hand, intraracial differences become more significant than interracial differences, and it strains the imagination to think of such groups as sharing a social history.

Among social critics, *ethnicity* is often embraced as positive, while *race* arouses suspicion and skepticism. Yet the differences are not always clear or obvious.[26] Both suggest birthplaces and birthrights. Both races and ethnic groups may become dispersed through the homelands of others. Like "national," "ethnic" may suggest geographic origins.[27] Like "race," it suggests heritage. But "race," unlike "ethnicity," suggests the physical as well as the sociopolitical. Thus, Pierre L. van den Berghe has defined "race" as "a group that is *socially* defined but on the basis of *physical* criteria" and ethnic groups as "socially defined but on the basis of *cultural* criteria."[28] According to this distinction, what Du Bois called races in 1897 sound more like ethnic groups (although it is difficult to suppose that he really meant to put all Africans and

African Americans into one ethnic group). Because the social heritage of *race* is commonly one of oppression or privilege, it is plausible that races are products of conquest, a way of maintaining social hierarchy and of preventing intermarriages that would entail property dispersals and consequent power dispersals. Because the heritage of *ethnicity*, on the other hand, tends to include such things as language, literature, religion, cuisine, and humor, ethnicity seems more internally constructed.

In Europeanized parts of the world, "race," unlike "ethnicity," suggests color. "Ethnic" is sometimes a euphemism for "racial" where it is thought impolite (or impolitic) to refer to color (as "erotic" in "erotic art" can be a euphemism for "pornographic" where it is thought impolite or impolitic to refer directly to sex). In the United States, "ethnic" is popularly used (misused) to refer to anything not white Anglo-Saxon Protestant (WASP), as in the "ethnic" section of the library, "ethnic" restaurants, and so forth, as though WASP were not ethnic. If one accepts van den Berghe's distinction between race and ethnicity, WASP is a hybrid of race (white) and ethnicity, with ethnicity identified two ways: by linguistic origin (anglo) and by religious connection (Protestant). Thus, when "ethnic" is used to refer to groups other than WASP, it can refer either to nonwhite races or to nonanglo ethnicities. Thomas Sowell's *Ethnic America* offers chapters on Irish, Germans, Jews, Italians, Chinese, Japanese, Puerto Ricans, Mexicans, and blacks, identifying only blacks by color and including from white Protestants only Germans.[29]

"Ethnicity" suggests culture, especially folk culture, produced by people who share a history that is usually tied to a geographical territory. In the case of Jewish ethnicity, the shared history is tied to a religion or, at least, a body of texts. Either way leaves it open whether co-ethnics share biological ancestry or color identification. Ethnic groups sometimes fall within socially recognized racial groups and in other cases cut across them. If race is associated with color, ethnicity cuts across it in the case of Jewish blacks and whites but falls under it in the case of whites who may be Italian or German.

Du Bois treated Slavic as a race within which there are Russian and Hungarian ethnicities. But is "Slavic" a racial identification? or an ethnic one? Like Anglo and Semitic, Slavic names a language group, which, as a cultural phenomenon, suggests ethnicity. According to the *Oxford English Dictionary*, however, the term "slave" comes from the medieval Latin *sclavus,* which was identical with the proper name "Sclavus" applied to the Slavonic populations of central Europe who were reduced to servility (and sold by Germans, according to Milton Meltzer), and "the transferred sense is clearly evidenced in documents of the 9th century."[30] Perhaps Slavic peoples were *racialized* by the practice of slavery, even though there was no color difference between them and their captors. That is, perhaps Slavic peoples did not identify with one another as members of one group until the category of being inferiors was imposed on them by their captors, as may be also true of Africans sold as slaves by Europeans. But if so, neither of van den Burghe's categories quite seems to apply: What unites members of the group marked for slavery may be neither culture nor color (or other physical characteristics) but their *not* belonging to the group or groups of their captors and those regarded as peers by their captors (at least, those not considered for enslavement). Or, there may be only a thin cultural identification, as in speaking related languages.

The apparent asymmetry of external and internal construction between race and ethnicity is reflected in vocabulary. There is no noun "ethnicism" corresponding to "racism." Instead, there is "ethnocentrism," referring to one's (friendly) attitudes regarding one's own ethnicity and only by implication, if at all, to one's attitudes toward others. "Racism," on the other hand, refers first of all to (hostile) attitudes and practices toward other races, only by implication suggesting arrogance regarding one's own. The structures of the concepts of race and ethnicity thus seem opposite. There are, however, terms such as "ethnic prejudice" (and more specific terms, such as "anti-Semitism") and "race supremacist" for attitudes running the other direction in each case.

Maria Lugones once argued that ethnocentrism need not be racist, meaning that it need not involve a negative attitude toward others and that it need not be a bad thing. In her early essay, "Pedagogy and Racism," she offers the analogy of a mother saying that her child is "the most beautiful in the world," meaning simply that the child is the center of the mother's attention but not intending objectively the comparative value judgment that the words seem to imply. If ethnocentrism were the analogue of this, it would be, presumably, a healthy pride and joy in one's own culture. However, in "Hablando cara a cara/Speaking Face to Face" she offers a revised conception of ethnocentrism as basically arrogant, arguing that an absorption in one's own culture (like a mother's absorption in her child) is not necessarily ethnocentric (arrogant). Yet she retains the idea that ethnocentrism — although arrogant — is not necessarily racist. Ethnocentrism becomes racist, she argues, when it involves the idea of the racial state, when the culture in regard to which one is arrogant is racist.[31] So understood, "racist ethnocentrism" is not redundant but combines the orientations of racism and ethnocentrism.

Because histories and ancestries crisscross and their boundaries are arbitrary and vague, racial identifications are bound to be in a certain sense arbitrary, regardless of their motivations (which need not have been arbitrary).[32] They may be more arbitrary than ethnic identifications if one's ethnicity — enculturation — is less liable to multiplicity than one's genealogy. It may seem as though an individual's ethnicity *is* liable to serious multiplicity, in that biculturalism is common, especially among the oppressed in ethnocentrically racist societies. However, biculturalism need not involve *identifying with* or *identifying as a member of* both cultures. It may simply be a matter of facility in negotiating one's way in two cultures. People bicultural in that sense might think of themselves as " 'world'-travelers," as Maria Lugones uses that term, without identifying themselves as belonging to all of the "worlds" in which they have learned to travel well. By " 'world'-traveling" Maria Lugones understands a "willful exercise" of a certain flexibility, spontaneously acquired by members of a minority in an oppressive society, in shifting from one construction of life in which one is at home, although many others are outsiders, to other constructions of life in which some of those former outsiders are at home, or more nearly at home and in which one may figure oneself as an outsider.[33] "World"-traveling, as she presents it, develops new aspects of oneself, even new "selves." It seems not, however, to create new *ethnic identities,* perhaps because one's ethnicity has a historical element that remains unchanged by "world"-traveling and perhaps also because one may not identify with both worlds or others may refuse to acknowledge such an identification.

Neither one's race nor one's ethnicity seems reducible to one's loyalties, however. An interesting question is what significance, if any, one's self-identification has for one's racial or ethnic identity, especially if one's ancestry or one's cultural heritage is evidently recently mixed.[34]

Recall Appiah's view that "the choice of a slice of the past in a period before your birth as your own history is always exactly that: a choice."[35] To what extent can one choose a racial or ethnic identity?

As I note in Chapter Seven, John De Cecco and Michael Shively's analysis of "sexual identity" includes one's self-identification (or sense of oneself) as female or male as one of four components of one's sexual identity. If there is an analogue in the case of racial identity, perhaps it is most evident in the case of people of recently "mixed race" who choose to identify with ancestors whose heritage is not suggested to others by their physical appearance.

Identifying someone as a member of a certain race may suggest either that they do identify with a certain ancestry and history, or that the speaker thinks they should identify with it, perhaps for political reasons. From a political point of view, the latter sort of view need not be arbitrary, even if the relevant biological ancestry is evidently mixed. Even if self-identification is an element, however, it is often not decisive for the social identity one comes to have, as many Europeans of Jewish descent discovered under Hitler's Nuremberg laws and as many preoperative transsexuals find today. It is not only that others may refuse to respect one's self-identification, however. There is also the phenomenon of "passing," successfully claiming an identity that others would not acknowledge if they knew one's history or origins, or even pretending successfully to an identity that is not one's true identity at all (as in the case of John Howard Griffin, a white man who wrote in *Black Like Me* of his experiment in darkening his skin to live among blacks in the southern United States, or, to take a nonracial example, Mark Twain's novel *The Prince and the Pauper,* in which a look-alike street child and child prince trade clothes and exchange social positions).[36] Although one may be justified in claiming or in disowning a heritage, the implications for one's identity of doing so may be less clear than the implications for one's social relationships with others. If I disown my Protestant heritage, I may alienate some people, but others will not cease to identify me as WASP, and there is no alternative heritage that I am in a position to claim.

History indicates that I hail, on my father's side, from a line of Scots. Should I identify with that? I have not particularly identified with Scottish ethnicity. My love of music does not extend to bagpipes. I like plaids but for decades have not worn skirts, not even kilts. And I seem not to have inherited proverbial Scottish attitudes toward money. Yet, such choices (if that is what they are) may not be decisive for who I am. Some of my sensibilities and dispositions may be inherited through generations of parenting by Gaelic and Anglo-Saxon ancestors whether or not I have any desire to affirm or identify with their culture. My unreflective attitudes and values may also be influenced by a more palpable Presbyterianism despite my disavowal of the Shorter Catechism. Such characteristics may have enabled me throughout my life to hook into advantageous social networks and to develop assets that others value in me (and that I value in myself). If such influences are transmitted through parenting processes, and if they construct me ethnically, the connection of my ethnicity with my choices or voluntary identifications may be complex. To reject my ethnicity, it would not be enough simply to disavow it verbally, however sincerely. I would need to work first to become conscious of what my ethnicity consists in, to learn to recognize it in myself. My success in that endeavor may be helped by the "mirrors" that Maria Lugones writes about. But even if I succeed in identifying my ethnicity, the question of getting rid of it may also take on moral dimensions. By profiting in various ways, willingly or not, from ethnic privilege, I may now have acquired moral responsibilities. Being an ethnic Scot may be part of my moral luck, something to be taken into account if I am to appreciate the political meanings of my relationships and interactions with others.

Just as combatting ethnocentrism may require developing a consciousness that many of one's values, attitudes, and so forth have roots in one's ethnic heritage, antiracism may require — as it has, in my case — developing a higher order race consciousness: becoming conscious not only of such things as how one has learned to process perceptions of racial difference (in order to deny them, for example) but also of how one's whiteness has been socially constructed through social and political institutions from I.Q. tests to real estate practices.[37] Joel Kovel's distinctions among *dominative* racism ("direct, physical oppression"), *aversive* racism ("the racism of coldness and the fantasy of dirt"), and *metaracism* may be helpful here. In the case of metaracism, which is characterized by economic and technocratic means, he finds that there need be no particular psychological mediation, that is, no particularly racist attitudes or beliefs on the part of individuals.[38] At this level, racism is embodied in social and political institutions. For this reason, Kovel rejects as misleading William Julius Wilson's contention that race, by contrast with socioeconomic class, has declined in significance in the United States since the civil rights movement.[39] Kovel maintains, rather, that what has declined in significance are at most racist psychological attitudes.[40] If rac*ism* has become even further entrenched through social and political institutions, a declining consciousness of race may make more difficult the tasks of resisting and combatting racism. Acquiring a helpful consciousness of race, like acquiring an ethnic consciousness, would appear to be a complex endeavor, involving much more than the psychological introspection characteristic of white activist workshops on racism.

Race consciousness goes against the grain of my upbringing. In my corner of anglo culture terms like "color consciousness" evoke negative psychological attitudes. They suggest such thoughts as that if people are classified by readily visible physical characteristics, such as color, those characteristics will not be treated as value-neutral, and then masses of people will be instantly targetable by one another for friendship (as in elitist cliques) or hostility (as in people of color being tracked by white security guards in predominantly white department stores), independently of who they are as individuals.[41] "Racial" thinking, I was taught, blocks getting to know people as they really are. Stereotyping is not even the worst danger. Generalizing at all in terms of race about highly problematic or highly desirable characteristics (such as aggression or intelligence) is readily enlisted in the service of oppression.

Yet among those who are in fact targets of racism, instant recognition of potential friends or potential enemies is an aid to survival. Instant recognition of contexts in which racism is a potential danger can be necessary for effective resistance by anyone. Color consciousness facilitates positive contacts among the oppressed as well as oppressive contacts of dominant with subordinate. It facilitates political separatism of the oppressed as well as segregation and oppressive avoidance by the dominant.[42] The segregationist potentialities are terrifying: capture, concentration of peoples, imprisonment, enslavement. Yet these are hardly reasons to reject color consciousness in a society already racist — rather the opposite: Such dangers can hardly be combatted without it. This creates a challenge for white people in a society such as the United States: how to be race or color conscious without being racist or in other ways oppressive. As Pat Parker puts it in her poem "For the White Person Who Wants to Know How to Be My Friend":

The first thing you do is to forget that i'm Black.
Second, you must never forget that i'm Black.[43]

And yet, color consciousness on this level is focused on *the color of individuals* who stand to gain or lose in consequence of their racializations. More important is consciousness of what Kovel calls metaracism, the way color structures the social and political institutions by which individuals stand to gain or lose. It is at this level, for example, that Bernard Boxill has argued against "color blindness" in his philosophical examinations of bussing and affirmative action.[44] (Because "blindness" here connotes ignoring, we may need another term — perhaps "color obliviousness" — out of respect for the physically blind.)

One may want to ask: Must color consciousness, or race consciousness, be at best only a necessary evil? Can good purposes, other than resistance to oppression, be served by race consciousness? Du Bois seemed interested in the good for African Americans of affirming racial identity. But he also spoke of its value to humanity. His idea was that different cultural developments distinguish racial groups and that it takes many generations to produce these cultural developments. He feared that if races were not conserved — if, for example and in particular, African Americans assimilated to European Americans — valuable cultural developments would be lost. Du Bois's focus on culture may suggest a concern more with ethnicity than with race. And yet, how separable are they, if he is also right that significant cultural developments require many generations?

Du Bois, in his essay on conserving races, thinks of race as having internal aspects, which he identifies as cultural potentialities that may require generations to realize, as well as whatever external aspects may be defined by practices of others. As he may have realized in his observation that members of a race strive together "both voluntarily and involuntarily," neither the internal nor the external aspects need have been originally the object of choice on the part of those to whom they apply, although individuals may later choose to affirm or deny them.

In my liberal anglo upbringing, the reason most frequently offered for the moral irrelevance of race was that individuals have no control over their racial identity, and individuals were supposed to have control over who they really are. What was important about people, I was taught, were their individual choices. Only for one's choices could one be held morally responsible. Thus the idea of constitutive moral luck was implicitly rejected.

It often seems that one can adopt or reject many *aspects* of an ethnicity — as I do with the Scots. Perhaps for that reason, anglo liberals have tended to worry less about the importance of ethnicity than about that of race. On both biological and social constructivist conceptions, the racial identity of individuals has often been thought *totally* involuntary — except for the choice to procreate, which can affect the race of one's offspring although it does not affect one's own identity.

Marilyn Frye's essay "On Being White" partly challenges the assumption that one has no control with respect to one's race, arguing that we can at least choose where to place our loyalties.[45] This position preserves the idea that the individual, morally speaking, is basically revealed by her choices. At any rate, it does not challenge that idea. I want to question, however, the historically liberal view that who we *really are* is determined only by our choices, which has seemed to support the position that one's race is morally irrelevant. Although who I am is importantly affected — and revealed — by my choices, I do not choose everything that is important to my identity, nor even all of it that matters morally. Even my *individual* past imposes constraints on my present choices. If I have been a misogynist in the past, for example, but recognize and reject misogyny today, I cannot completely disavow that past. It does not suddenly become someone else's past. It is still mine to contend with. I am still sufficiently identical with my previous self that I might be held responsible for whatever harm my prior misogyny did to others. The extent of my identity's dependence on factors beyond my power to change is, however, even more deeply revealed by the realization that I am a relational being and that my choices alone are not decisive for all my relations. A heritage that has given me privileges or liabilities from birth, whether I affirm it or reject it, is important to who I am and to who I can become. Even whether I have a heritage to which to be loyal or disloyal is not the product of my choices.

"Heritage" is a slippery term. If we think of it as whatever led up to one's existence, then everyone has a heritage. But what makes a past *one's own* is not just causal precedence. On that score, Appiah is right. Choices matter. But the choices that matter are not always one's own. When a heritage is a cultural legacy, one can be disinherited or alienated from it. One can be robbed of one's culture. Cultures of one's ancestors may have been appropriated by others.[46] Thus, not all have the privilege of being able to claim a heritage. Nor do all of us want to claim as our heritage some of the pasts that produced us (rape and slavery, for example). Amoja Three Rivers writes: "One of the most effective and insidious aspects of racism is cultural genocide. Not only have African-Americans been cut off from our African tribal roots, but . . . we have been cut off from our Native American roots as well. Consequently most African Native Americans no longer . . . even know for certain what people they are from."[47] If race in its internal aspect refers to certain aspects of cultural heritage — as is suggested in Du Bois's usage in "The Conservation of Races" — an insidious aspect of racism is the *destruction* of races. (This is compatible, of course, with its also *con*structing races.) Thus Patterson describes the "natal alienation" of slavery as a "loss of ties of birth in both ascending and descending generations" and observes, as noted above, that it "also has the important nuance of a loss of native status, of deracination."[48] Building on Patterson's concept of natal alienation, Laurence Thomas maintains that under American slavery, by the seventh generation cultural death would be complete in that there would be no more of the memories on which participation in cultural traditions that should have been one's own depends.[49]

Race and ethnicity can come together, to some extent, in the notion of a heritage. Cultural death may be less complete than it appears if what is destroyed are the most natural means of identifying cultural developments (conscious memories, for example) but not necessarily those developments themselves. Further, in pondering the question what significance, if any, one's biological heritage has for one's social identity, perhaps we should ask, What counts as "biological"? Marilyn Frye once wrote, in thinking about gender: "Enculturation and socialization are misunderstood . . . if one pictures them as processes which apply layers of cultural gloss over a biological substratum. It is with that picture in mind that one asks whether this or that aspect of behavior is due to 'nature' or 'nurture'." She goes on to paint a bodily portrait of gender:

> Socialization molds our bodies; enculturation forms our skeletons, our musculature, our central nervous systems. By the time we are gendered adults, masculinity and femininity *are* "biological." They are structural and material features of how our bodies are. . . . They are changeable just as one would ex-

pect bodies to be — slowly, through constant practice and deliberate regimens, designed to remap and rebuild nerve and tissue.

But she also notes that now "biological" does not mean "genetically determined" or "inevitable" but rather, "of the animal."[50]

Likewise, much of what is "biological" in "race" may not be genetic and what is "cultural" in ethnicity may not have been chosen by the individuals whose ethnicity it is, nor even open to them to reject if they can identify it. For self-understanding it may be important to know our earliest unchosen caretakers and the also often unchosen social contexts of their lives, and their early caretakers and the social contexts of their lives (and so on). Such histories might be considered genealogies. Consider the following three examples of genealogies where what are of interest are the histories of parenting and cultural formation and transmission.

An issue of *Lilith* a few years ago contained an article on Indian Catholic Jews of New Mexico, descendants of sixteenth-century *conversos* (Jews forced to convert to Christianity) who fled the Inquisition in Mexico.[51] These descendants are reported to be practicing Catholics who still also practice Jewish customs privately at home without knowing what they mean or even that the customs are Jewish. Some, who by accident discovered the Jewish meanings, now speak of discovering their Jewish heritage. And what customs, one may wonder, do they likewise practice without knowing their Native American meanings? Calling the Indian Catholics of New Mexico *Jews* on the basis of such connections is an example of identifying individuals as members of a group on the basis of shared customs that are taken to be partly constitutive of the identities of those who share them. There is no independent criterion, such as Appiah has insisted we would need, for recognizing the sixteenth-century *conversos* and contemporary Indian Catholics as members of the same group. Such an identification may be controversial, but it is neither totally arbitrary nor totally a matter of choice. It seems to fit with Du Bois's 1897 idea of shared traditions as definitive of what he wanted to call a "race" in the sociohistorical sense.[52] What is critical here is not shared biological ancestry but traditions transmitted from generation to generation through parenting (child-rearing).

Enslaved Africans in the Americas were often separated from biological kin at early ages and raised by others who were enslaved from totally different regions of Africa. Such foster parents may have borne little resemblance to the children's biological kin and may not even have spoken a related language. If a common African American heritage has been developing in this country, generations of such parenting under conditions of slavery may be a more significant factor in its unification and development than the genetic impositions of white rapists who claimed to own African slaves and their descendants.

And what is the heritage of whites who were raised by black servants or slaves? Or, for that matter, of whites today in the United States, regardless who parented them? Thanks to generations of enforced interracial care-taking and many forms of cultural appropriation, the culture of most whites in the United States is probably more mixed in its genealogy than that of the Indian Catholics of New Mexico. And white folk are characteristically no more aware of the meanings of these heritages. Consider, for example, Nikki Giovanni's ruminations on a nursery song from my childhood:

> Just listen to "Rockabye Baby" and picture a Black woman singing it to a white baby. . . . They didn't know we were laughing at them, and we unfortunately were late to awaken to the fact that we can die laughing.[53]

I was rocked to sleep as a baby to this song. As a teenager, I was raised on Dick Clark's daily afternoon television show *American Bandstand,* where exclusively white teenagers danced to rock 'n' roll hits mostly written and recorded by black artists.[54] One cannot read through a list of the names of the artists and performers, many still famous today, without being struck by the irony and injustice of only white teenagers participating in programs made possible by African American talent, programs that have become part of "white nostalgia" for many of my generation. And how many generations of white children were raised on the Uncle Remus tales as appropriated and retold by Joel Chandler Harris and portrayed in the animated film *Song of the South?*[55]

To return in conclusion to the idea of lifting veils of ignorance, uncovering particular histories, such as those underlying our racial and ethnic social identities, can help us to appreciate who it is our moral luck to have become, to determine what responsibilities we now have, how we are related to one another, the meanings of the institutions in which we now participate and by which we have been formed, and what kinds of choices we now have. Approaches to justice that take our social and political identities and institutions to be transparent, in the sense of supposing that we are ordinarily conscious and in general equally conscious of who we are and of the rules defining our social practices, will probably fail to see such a need. However, becoming race conscious, in the sense of developing an awareness and appreciation of histories and practices underlying contemporary racisms, is required even to recognize issues of justice in a society such as that of the United States today. Whether such recognition should lead eventually to dismantling of constructions of race, with a consequent abandonment of the very concept, or instead, to their transformations into something more benign may be fruitfully discussable only if we confront those constructions together in their historical contingencies and specificities.

Preface

1. Friedrich Nietzsche, *On the Genealogy of Morals,* trans. Walter Kaufmann and R. J. Hollingdale (New York: Vintage, 1967).
2. Claudia Card, "On Mercy," *The Philosophical Review* 81, no. 2 (Apr. 1972): 182–207.
3. Claudia Card, "Retributive Penal Liability," in *American Philosophical Quarterly, Monograph #7: Studies in Ethics* (Oxford: Blackwell, 1973), pp. 17–35.
4. Carol Gilligan, *In a Different Voice: Psychological Theory and Women's Development* (Cambridge, Mass.: Harvard University Press, 1982).

Chapter One

1. B.A.O. Williams and Thomas Nagel, "Moral Luck," *Proceedings of the Aristotelian Society,* supp. vol. 50 (1976): 115–51. Williams's contribution is reprinted in his *Moral Luck: Philosophical Papers, 1973–1980* (Cambridge: Cambridge University Press, 1981), pp. 20–39, and Thomas Nagel's in his *Mortal Questions* (Cambridge: Cambridge University Press, 1979), pp. 24–38.
2. Martha Nussbaum, *The Fragility of Goodness: Luck and Ethics in Greek Tragedy and Philosophy* (Cambridge: Cambridge University Press, 1986). Margaret Urban Coyne (now Walker), "Moral Luck?" *The Journal of Value Inquiry* 19 (1985): 319–25, and Margaret Urban Walker, "The Virtues of Impure Agency," *Metaphilosophy* 22, nos. 1–2 (Jan.–Apr. 1991): 14–27, the latter reprinted in *Moral Luck,* ed. Daniel Statman (Albany: State University of New York Press, 1993).
3. Many of these essays are collected in *Moral Luck,* ed. Statman.
4. *The Nicomachean Ethics of Aristotle,* trans. Sir David Ross (London: Oxford University Press, 1925), p. 17.
5. *The Moral Law: Kant's Groundwork of the Metaphysic of Morals,* trans. H. J. Paton (London: Hutchison, 1948), pp. 74–113.
6. See, for example, my review essay, "Oppression and Resistance: Frye's Politics of Reality," *Hypatia* 1, no. 1 (Apr. 1986): 149–66.
7. Marilyn Frye, *The Politics of Reality: Essays in Feminist Theory* (Trumansburg, N.Y.: Crossing Press, 1983), pp. 1–16.
8. Iris Marion Young, "Throwing Like a Girl: A Phenomenology of Feminine Bodily Comportment, Motility, and Spatiality," in *Throwing Like a Girl and Other Essays in Feminist Philosophy and Social Theory* (Bloomington: Indiana University Press, 1990), pp. 141–59.
9. What happens to female self-respect in oppressively sexist environments is discussed in detail by Robin Dillon in "Self-Respect: Emotional, Moral, Political," presented to the Oberlin Colloquium in Philosophy, Apr. 23, 1995.

10. Iris Marion Young, *Justice and the Politics of Difference* (Princeton, N.J.: Princeton University Press, 1990), pp. 39–65.

11. Laurence Mordekhai Thomas, *Vessels of Evil: American Slavery and the Holocaust* (Philadelphia: Temple University Press, 1993).

12. On "total institutions," see Erving Goffman, *Asylums: Essays on the Social Situation of Mental Patients and Other Inmates* (Garden City, N.Y.: Anchor Books, 1961).

13. Simon Wiesenthal, *The Sunflower,* trans. H. A. Pichler, with a Symposium (contributions in German, trans. H. A. Pichler) (New York: Schocken Books, 1969).

14. The first three issues appeared as special issues of *Women's Studies International Forum,* vol. 6, no. 6 (1983), vol. 7, no. 5 (1984), and vol. 8, no. 3 (1985). Most of these essays are reprinted in Azizah Y. Al-Hibri and Margaret A. Simons, eds., *Hypatia Reborn: Essays in Feminist Philosophy* (Bloomington: Indiana University Press, 1990).

15. Carol Gilligan, *In a Different Voice: Psychological Theory and Women's Development* (Cambridge, Mass.: Harvard University Press, 1982), and many subsequent essays. In "Hearing the Difference: Theorizing Connection," *Hypatia* 10, no. 2 (spring 1995): 120–27, she distinguishes between a feminine and a feminist voice.

16. See, for example, Michelle Moody-Adams, "Gender and the Complexity of Moral Voices," in *Feminist Ethics,* ed. Claudia Card (Lawrence: University Press of Kansas, 1991), pp. 195–212.

17. Judith Lewis Herman, *Trauma and Recovery* (New York: Basic Books, 1992).

18. Theodor Reik, *Listening with the Third Ear* (New York: Farrar, Straus & Co., 1948), p. 155.

19. Nel Noddings, *Caring: A Feminine Approach to Ethics and Moral Education* (Berkeley: University of California Press, 1984).

20. Nel Noddings, *Women and Evil* (Berkeley: University of California Press, 1989).

21. Susan Griffin first used the term "protection racket" to describe chivalry as a practice dependent on rape in her classic essay, "Rape: The All-American Crime," first published in *Ramparts* magazine, Sept. 1971, 26–35, reprinted in *Feminism and Philosophy,* ed. Mary Vetterling-Braggin, Frederick A. Elliston, and Jane English (Totowa, N.J.: Littlefield, Adams & Co., 1977), pp. 313–32 (see p. 320 on the protection racket).

22. Claudia Card, *Lesbian Choices* (New York: Columbia University Press, 1995), esp. chaps. 2 and 3.

23. See, for example, Bernard Boxill, *Blacks and Social Justice* (Totowa, N.J.: Rowman and Allanheld, 1984).

24. Currently edited by Leonard Harris, Philosophy Department, Purdue University, West Lafayette, IN 47907.

25. See, for example, David Theo Goldberg, ed., *Anatomy of Racism* (Minneapolis: University of Minnesota Press, 1990), and David Theo Goldberg, *Racist Culture: Philosophy and the Politics of Meaning* (Oxford: Blackwell, 1993).

26. In addition to Thomas, *Vessels of Evil,* see, for example, Howard McGary and Bill E. Lawson, *Between Slavery and Freedom* (Bloomington: Indiana University Press, 1992).

27. See, for example, Alison Jaggar, *Feminist Politics and Human Nature* (Totowa, N.J.: Rowman and Allanheld, 1983).

28. Frye, *Politics of Reality* and *Willful Virgin: Essays in Feminism, 1976–1992* (Freedom, Calif.: Crossing Press, 1992). Sarah Lucia Hoagland, *Lesbian Ethics: Toward New Value* (Palo Alto, Calif.: Institute of Lesbian Studies, 1988).

29. See, for example, Judith Butler, *Gender Trouble: Feminism and the Subversion of Identity* (New York: Routledge, 1990), and my review in *Canadian Philosophical Reviews* 10, no. 9 (Sept. 1990): 356–59.

30. For scholarly examination of this and related concepts, see Julia Penelope, *Speaking Freely: Unlearning the Lies of the Fathers' Tongues* (New York: Pergamon, 1990).

31. For a discussion of these issues, see Shane Phelan, *Getting Specific: Postmodern Lesbian Politics* (Minneapolis: University of Minnesota Press, 1994).

32. The same thing is even truer of derogatory ethnic terms. See Irving Lewis Allen, *Unkind Words: Ethnic Labeling from Redskin to Wasp* (New York: Bergin and Garvey, 1990).

33. Joyce Trebilcot, *Dyke Ideas: Process, Politics, Daily Life* (Albany: State University of New York Press, 1994).

34. See, also, my introductory essay, "The Feistiness of Feminism" in *Feminist Ethics*, esp. pp. 20–21.

35. For Plato's *Apology*, see Edith Hamilton and Huntington Cairnes, eds., *The Collected Dialogues of Plato* (New York: Bollingen, 1961), pp. 3–26.

36. Consider, for example, Socrates' derogatory references to his wife, Xanthippe, and to women generally when he talks about emotional display in the *Apology*.

37. Ruth Ginzberg, "Philosophy Is Not a Luxury," in *Feminist Ethics*, ed. Card, pp. 126–45.

38. For a fuller discussion, see Card, "The Feistiness of Feminism," esp. pp. 21–22.

39. On the breakdown of these oppositions in a cybernetic age, see Donna J. Harraway, "A Cyborg Manifesto: Science, Technology, and Socialist Feminism in the Late Twentieth Century," in *Simians, Cyborgs, and Women: The Reinvention of Nature* (New York: Routledge, 1991), pp. 149–81.

40. Classics of ecofeminism include Susan Griffin, *Woman and Nature: The Roaring Inside Her* (New York: Harper & Row, 1978), and Mary Daly, *Gyn/Ecology: The Metaethics of Radical Feminism* (Boston: Beacon, 1978). See also Andree Collard, *The Rape of the Wild: Man's Violence Against Animals and the Earth* (Bloomington: Indiana University Press, 1988), and Karen J. Warren, ed., *Ecological Feminism* (New York: Routledge, 1994). On social ecology, see Murray Bookchin, *Toward an Ecological Society* (Montreal: Black Rose, 1980), and *Remaking Society: Pathways to a Green Future* (Boston: South End, 1990).

41. Some philosophers, such as Friedrich Nietzsche in *Beyond Good and Evil*, seem to view "good and bad" as *not* a dichotomy but a continuum and to prefer it, for that reason, to the dichotomy of "right and wrong." But that view is too simple. Although there are degrees of goodness and badness, and we speak of the less good as "worse than" and of the less bad as "better than," it does not follow that the less good (what is worse than) is bad or that the less bad (what is better than) is good.

42. Marcus G. Singer, *Generalization in Ethics* (New York: Knopf, 1961). John Rawls, *A Theory of Justice* (Cambridge: Harvard University Press, 1971).

43. See Rawls's Dewey Lectures, *Journal of Philosophy* 77, no. 9 (Sept. 1980): 515–72; "Justice as Fairness: Political Not Metaphysical," *Philosophy and Public Affairs* 14, no. 3 (summer 1985): 223–51; and *Political Liberalism* (New York: Columbia University Press, 1993).

44. Rawls, *A Theory of Justice*, pp. 4–5, 453–62; *Political Liberalism*, pp. 35–40.

45. Rawls, *A Theory of Justice*, p. 315. My Ph.D. dissertation, "Retributive Justice in Legal Punishment" (Harvard University, 1969), constructed a principle of punishment from behind a thick Rawlsian veil of ignorance, but when asked to illustrate its implications, I was at a loss.

46. Rawls, "The Law of Peoples," in *On Human Rights: The Oxford Amnesty Lectures, 1993*, ed. Stephen Shute and Susan Hurley (New York: Basic Books, 1993), pp. 41–82, esp. pp. 71–77.

47. See Laurence Thomas, "Liberalism and the Holocaust: An Essay on Trust and the Black-Jewish Relationship," in *Echoes from the Holocaust: Philosophical Reflections on a Dark Time*, ed. Alan Rosenberg and Gerald E. Myers (Philadelphia: Temple University Press, 1988), pp. 105–17, for discussion of the contrast between the relative states of black and Jewish histories in this regard.

Chapter Two

1. B.A.O. Williams and Thomas Nagel, "Moral Luck," *Proceedings of the Aristotelian Society*, supp. vol. 50 (1976): 115–51.

2. Bernard Williams, "Moral Luck," in *Moral Luck: Philosophical Papers, 1973–1980* (Cambridge: Cambridge University Press, 1981), p. 38.

3. Thomas Nagel, *The View from Nowhere* (New York: Oxford University Press, 1986), p. 123.

4. Martha C. Nussbaum, *The Fragility of Goodness: Luck and Ethics in Greek Tragedy and Philosophy* (Cambridge: Cambridge University Press, 1986).

5. Williams, *Moral Luck*, pp. 22–30. Count Leo Tolstoy, *Anna Karenina*, trans. Constance Garnett (New York: Modern Library, 1950). Thomas Nagel, "Moral Luck," *Mortal Questions* (Cambridge: Cambridge, 1979), p. 26.

6. Bernard Williams, "The Idea of Equality," in *Philosophy, Politics, and Society*, 2d ser. (Oxford: Blackwell, 1962), pp. 110–31.

7. John Dewey, "Philosophies of Freedom," in *On Experience, Nature, and Freedom*, ed. Richard J. Bernstein (Indianapolis: Bobbs-Merrill, 1960), pp. 261–87. *The Nicomachean Ethics of Aristotle*, trans. Sir David Ross (London: Oxford University Press, 1925), pp. 28–29. Friedrich Nietzsche, *On the Genealogy of Morals*, trans. Walter Kaufmann and R. J. Hollingdale (New York: Vintage, 1967), pp. 57–62. Nietzsche, who apparently believed in the inheritability of acquired characteristics, presented a naturalistic account of how a sense of responsibility might have been developed in the human species.

8. Herbert Fingarette, *On Responsibility* (New York: Basic Books, 1967), p. 6.

9. Arnold A. Kaufman, "Responsibility, Moral and Legal" in *Encyclopedia of Philosophy*, ed. Paul Edwards, 8 vols. (New York: Collier Macmillan, 1967), 7:183–88.

10. Joyce Trebilcot, "Taking Responsibility for Sexuality," in *Dyke Ideas: Process,*

Politics, Daily Life (Albany: State University of New York Press, 1994), pp. 97–109. Nussbaum, *Fragility of Goodness*, pp. 1–21.

11. Williams, *Moral Luck*, pp. 33–34. John Rawls, *A Theory of Justice* (Cambridge, Mass.: Harvard University Press, 1971), pp. 407–16.

12. Nagel, *View from Nowhere*, p. 127.

13. P.F. Strawson, "Freedom and Resentment," in *Freedom and Resentment and Other Essays* (London: Methuen & Co., 1974), pp. 1–25. Thanks to Jonathan Bennett for calling to my attention the relevance of this essay.

14. Carol Gilligan, *In a Different Voice: Psychological Theory and Women's Development* (Cambridge, Mass.: Harvard University Press, 1982).

15. Thomas Hill, Jr., "The Importance of Autonomy," in *Women and Moral Theory*, ed. Eva Feder Kittay and Diana T. Meyers (Totowa, N.J.: Rowman and Littlefield, 1987), pp. 129–37.

16. Hill, "Importance of Autonomy," pp. 132–33.

17. Lynn McFall, "Integrity," *Ethics* 98, no. 1 (Oct. 1987): 5–19.

18. Immanuel Kant, *Fundamental Principles of the Metaphysic of Morals*, trans. Thomas K. Abbott (Indianapolis: Bobbs-Merrill, 1949), p. 12. Margaret Urban Coyne (now Walker), "Moral Luck?" *The Journal of Value Inquiry* 19 (1985):319–25.

19. Kant, *The Doctrine of Virtue: Pt. II of The Metaphysic of Morals*, trans. Mary J. Gregor (New York: Harper & Row, 1964), p. 28.

20. *Kant's Critique of Practical Reason and Other Works on the Theory of Ethics*, trans. Thomas K. Abbott, 6th ed. (London: Longmans, Green & Co., 1909), app. 1, pp. 361–66.

21. Jean-Paul Sartre, "The Wall," in *Intimacy*, trans. Lloyd Alexander (New York: Berkeley Medallion, 1960), pp. 59–80.

22. Edith Wharton, *Ethan Frome* (New York: Charles Scribner's Sons, 1911).

23. See, for example, essays by Norvin Richards, Henning Jensen, Michael J. Zimmerman, and Judith Andre in *Moral Luck*, ed. Daniel Statman (Albany: State University of New York Press, 1993).

24. Henning Jensen, "Morality and Luck," in *Moral Luck*, ed. Statman, pp. 131–40.

25. Coyne (Walker), "Moral Luck?" pp. 322–23.

26. *The Nichomachean Ethics of Aristotle*, pp. 19–23.

27. Kant, *Anthropology from a Pragmatic Point of View*, trans. Mary J. Gregor (The Hague: Nijhoff, 1974), pp. 151–93, and *Observations on the Feeling of the Beautiful and Sublime*, trans. John T. Goldthwait (Berkeley: University of California Press, 1960), pp. 76–116.

28. Nagel, *View from Nowhere*, p. 123.

29. Coyne (Walker), "Moral Luck?" p. 319.

30. Coyne (Walker), "Moral Luck?" pp. 321–22. She also agrees with Williams that the ahistorical, noumenal Kantian self has to go but proposes modifications of the democratic-egalitarian picture to which it gives rise that may survive, maintaining that "even if the burdens morality assigns are not equal" "nonetheless we are all *equally* judgeable in the *same* deep way in light of such burdens as have fallen to us" (p. 323).

31. Nel Noddings, *Caring: A Feminine Approach to Ethics and Moral Education* (Berkeley: University of California Press, 1984), p. 6.

32. It is jarring to have examples constructed to have us sympathizing with the bad luck of the lorry driver or concentration camp officer, when their victims were so much unluckier. The intention, however, is not to excuse; it is to maintain that the luck of the driver and of the officer is *moral* rather than excusing.

33. See, for example, the work of Alice Miller: *The Drama of the Gifted Child: The Search for the True Self,* trans. Ruth Ward (New York: Basic Books, 1981); *For Your Own Good: Hidden Cruelty in Child-Rearing and the Roots of Violence,* trans. Hildegarde Hannum and Hunter Hannum (New York: Farrar, Straus, Giroux, 1983); and *Thou Shalt Not Be Aware: Society's Betrayal of the Child,* trans. Hildegarde Hannum and Hunter Hannum (New York: New American Library, 1984).

34. Euripides, "Hecuba," trans. E. P. Coleridge, *The Complete Greek Drama,* ed. Whitney J. Oates and Eugene O'Neill, Jr., 2 vols. (New York: Random House, 1938), 1:807–41.

35. "Survivor" is also a problematic term insofar as it suggests that those who did not survive might have survived had they tried harder.

36. For skepticism regarding the validity of recovered memories, see Elizabeth Loftus, *The Myth of Repressed Memory: False Memories and Allegations of Sexual Abuse* (New York: St. Martin's Press, 1994). For defense of many such memories, see Lenore Terr, *Unchained Memories: True Stories of Traumatic Memories, Lost and Found* (New York: Basic Books, 1994).

37. *Diagnostic and Statistical Manual of Mental Disorders,* 3rd ed., rev. (Washington, D.C.: American Psychiatric Association, 1987), p. 271.

38. *Diagnostic and Statistical Manual of Mental Disorders,* 4th ed. (Washington, D.C.: American Psychiatric Association, 1994), p. 485.

39. An example of a male diagnosed with multiple personality disorder is the campus rapist, Billy Milligan, allegedly raped in childhood repeatedly by his stepfather. See Daniel Keyes, *The Minds of Billy Milligan* (New York: Random House, 1981). Multobiographies of women with histories of childhood sexual abuse are documented by Flora Rheta Schreiber in *Sybil* (New York: Warner, 1974), by the Troops for Truddi Chase in *When Rabbit Howls* (New York: Dutton, 1987), and by Kathy Evert in *When You're Ready: A Woman's Healing, from Childhood Physical and Sexual Abuse by Her Mother* (Walnut Creek, Calif.: Launch Press, 1987).

40. Ian Hacking, *Rewriting the Soul: Multiple Personality and the Sciences of Memory* (Princeton, N.J.: Princeton University Press, 1995).

41. Stephen E. Braude, *First Person Plural: Multiple Personality and the Philosophy of Mind* (London: Routledge, 1991).

42. Schreiber, *Sybil.* The therapist was Dr. Cornelia B. Wilbur.

43. The Troops for Truddi Chase, *When Rabbit Howls.* The therapist and apparent scribe was Robert A. Philips, Jr., to whom the book is also dedicated.

Chapter Three

1. Carol Gilligan, *In a Different Voice: Psychological Theory and Women's Development* (Cambridge: Harvard University Press, 1982). Also important are Carol Gilligan, Janie Victoria Ward, and Jill McLean Taylor, with Betty Bardige, *Mapping the Moral*

Domain: A Contribution of Women's Thinking to Psychological Theory and Education (Cambridge: Harvard Graduate School of Education, 1988); Carol Gilligan, Nona P. Lyons, and Trudy J. Hanmer, eds., *Making Connections: The Relational Worlds of Adolescent Girls at Emma Willard School*; and Gilligan's essays "Moral Orientation and Moral Development," in *Women and Moral Theory*, ed. Eva Feder Kittay and Diana T. Meyers (Totowa, N.J.: Rowman and Littlefield, 1987), and "Hearing the Difference: Theorizing Connection," *Hypatia* 10, no. 2 (summer 1995): 120–27.

2. Gilligan, *In a Different Voice*, p. 2.

3. Gilligan, "Moral Orientation and Moral Development," p. 25.

4. For another tradition in moral theory, see Annette Baier, "Hume, the Women's Moral Theorist?" in *Moral Prejudices: Essays on Ethics* (Cambridge: Harvard University Press, 1994), pp. 51–75; and see Joan Tronto on the eighteenth-century Scottish Enlightenment tradition in *Moral Boundaries: A Political Argument for an Ethic of Care* (New York: Routledge, 1993), pp. 25–59.

5. Sandra Harding, "The Curious Coincidence of Feminine and African Moralities: Challenges for Feminist Theory," in *Women and Moral Theory*, ed. Kittay and Meyers, pp. 296–315.

6. Tronto, *Moral Boundaries*, p. 82.

7. Gilligan, *In a Different Voice*, p. 100.

8. Gilligan, "Moral Orientation and Moral Development," pp. 22–23.

9. For an extended critique of the "gestalt view," see Owen Flanagan and Kathryn Jackson, "Justice, Care, and Gender: The Kohlberg-Gilligan Debate Revisited," *Ethics* 97, no. 3 (Apr. 1987): 622–37.

10. Marilyn Friedman, "Beyond Caring: The De-moralization of Gender" in *Science, Morality, and Feminist Theory*, ed. Marsha Hanen and Kai Nielson (Calgary: University of Calgary Press, 1987).

11. Lawrence Kohlberg, *The Philosophy of Moral Development: Moral Stages and the Idea of Justice* (San Francisco: Harper & Row, 1981); John Rawls, *A Theory of Justice* (Cambridge: Harvard University Press, 1971).

12. Baier, *Moral Prejudices*; Virginia Held, *Feminist Morality: Transforming Culture, Society, and Politics* (Chicago: University of Chicago Press, 1993); Sarah Lucia Hoagland, *Lesbian Ethics: Toward New Value* (Palo Alto, Calif.: Institute of Lesbian Studies, 1988); Tronto, *Moral Boundaries*.

13. See Adrienne Rich, "Women and Honor: Notes on Lying," in *On Lies, Secrets, and Silence: Selected Prose, 1966–1978* (New York: Norton, 1979), pp. 185–94.

14. Charlotte Perkins Gilman, *Women and Economics: A Study of the Economic Relation Between Men and Women as a Factor in Social Evolution*, ed. Carl N. Degler (1898; reprint, New York: Harper & Row, Torchbooks, 1966).

15. *The Nicomachean Ethics of Aristotle*, trans. Sir David Ross (London: Oxford, 1925), p. 193.

16. *Nicomachean Ethics of Aristotle*, p. 207.

17. *Nicomachean Ethics of Aristotle*, p. vi.

18. Sigmund Freud, "Some Psychological Consequences of the Anatomical Distinction between the Sexes," in *The Collected Papers*, ed. James Strachey, 5 vols. (London: Hogarth, 1950), 5:186–97.

19. Gilligan, *In a Different Voice*, p. 18.

20. Arthur Schopenhauer, *On the Basis of Morality,* trans. E.F.J. Payne (1841; reprint, Indianapolis: Bobbs-Merrill, 1965), p. 151. The Royal Danish Society did not award this essay a prize even though it was the only entry in the contest.

21. Immanuel Kant, *Observations on the Feeling of the Beautiful and Sublime* (hereafter, *OBS*), trans. John T. Goldthwait (Berkeley: University of California Press, 1960), p. 81.

22. Arthur Schopenhauer, "On Women," in *Parerga and Paralipomena,* trans. E.F.J. Payne, 2 vols. (Oxford: Clarendon Press, 1974), 1:619.

23. Kant, *OBS,* p. 81.

24. Kant, *OBS,* p. 61.

25. On dispositions to animality and to personality, see Immanuel Kant, *Religion Within the Limits of Reason Alone,* trans. T. M. Greene and H. H. Hudson (New York: Harper, 1960), p. 21. They also sound like what he called "pathological love" by contrast with "practical love"; see *The Moral Law: Kant's Groundwork of the Metaphysic of Morals,* trans. H. J. Paton (London: Hutchinson, 1948), p. 67. For more on Kant's theory of moral character and his views on women's characters, see Jean Rumsey, "The Development of Character in Kantian Theory," *Journal of the History of Philosophy* 27, no. 2 (Apr. 1989): 247–65, and "Agency, Human Nature, and Character in Kantian Theory," *Journal of Value Inquiry* 24 (1990): 109–21.

26. Kant, *Groundwork,* p. 102.

27. Immanuel Kant, *Critique of Judgment,* trans. J. H. Bernard (New York: Hafner, 1951), pp. 37–45.

28. Immanuel Kant, *Anthropology from a Pragmatic Point of View,* trans. Mary J. Gregor (The Hague: Martinus Nijhoff, 1974), pp. 166–73.

29. Schopenhauer, *On the Basis of Morality,* pp. 120–67.

30. Barbara Herman argues in "On the Value of Acting from the Motive of Duty," *The Philosophical Review* 90, no. 3 (July 1981): 359–82, that Kant can acknowledge the virtue of agents who act from sympathy, provided they have the general scruple of subjecting their maxims to the test of duty. Marcia Baron argues in "The Alleged Moral Repugnance of Acting from Duty," *The Journal of Philosophy* 81, no. 4 (Apr. 1984): 197–220, that a Kantian understanding of the motive of duty can be stretched to include the motive of sympathy if one has cultivated the sympathy from the motive of duty. Neither of these views attributes moral value to sympathy itself.

31. Gilligan, *In a Different Voice,* p. 44.

32. Kant, *OBS,* p. 74.

33. Kant, *Groundwork,* p. 88.

34. Held, *Feminist Morality,* p. 71.

35. Friedrich Nietzsche, *On the Genealogy of Morals,* trans. Walter Kaufmann and R. J. Hollingdale (New York: Vintage, 1967).

36. Alice S. Rossi, ed., *Essays on Sex Equality: John Stuart Mill and Harriet Taylor Mill* (Chicago: University of Chicago Press, 1970).

37. Mary Wollstonecraft, *A Vindication of the Rights of Woman* (Harmondsworth: Penguin, 1982).

38. Gilligan, *In a Different Voice,* pp. 43–45.

39. Gilligan, Ward, Taylor, with Bardige, *Mapping the Moral Domain*, p. 9.
40. Adrienne Rich, "Compulsory Heterosexuality and Lesbian Existence," *Signs* 5, no. 4 (summer 1980): 631–60.
41. Gilligan, *In a Different Voice*, pp. 39–45; cf. Gilligan, Ward, Taylor, with Bardige, *Mapping the Moral Domain*, pp. 245–62.
42. For a groundbreaking study, see Menachem Amir, *Patterns in Forcible Rape* (Chicago: University of Chicago Press, 1971), which is discussed in Chapter 5.
43. Rawls, *A Theory of Justice*, pp. 60–74.
44. Notable contributions include Elizabeth Telfer, "Friendship," *Proceedings of the Aristotelian Society* 71 (1970–71): 221–41; Michael Stocker, "The Schizophrenia of Modern Ethical Theories," *Journal of Philosophy* 73, no. 14 (Aug. 12, 1976): 453–66; Lawrence Blum, *Friendship, Altruism, and Morality* (London: Routledge & Kegan Paul, 1980); Janice G. Raymond, *A Passion for Friends: Toward a Philosophy of Female Affection* (Boston: Beacon, 1986); and Marilyn Friedman, *What Are Friends For? Feminist Perspectives on Personal Relationships and Moral Theory* (Ithaca, N.Y.: Cornell University Press, 1993).
45. Baier, *Moral Prejudices*, pp. 95–129.
46. Rawls, *A Theory of Justice*; see p. 3 on justice as the first virtue; on the original position and the veil of ignorance, see pp. 118–92.
47. Rawls, *A Theory of Justice*, p. 7.
48. Susan Moller Okin, "*Political Liberalism*, Justice, and Gender," *Ethics* 105, no. 1 (Oct. 1994): 23–43 and *Justice, Gender, and the Family* (New York: Basic Books, 1989), pp. 89–109.
49. Rawls has not, to my knowledge, admitted to any such ambivalence. In *Political Liberalism* he says, "I believe . . . that the alleged difficulties in discussing problems of gender and the family can be overcome" and "I do assume that in some form the family is just" (p. xxix).
50. Both of these points have been noted by Okin in relation to the family. Okin, *Justice, Gender, and the Family*, pp. 89–109.
51. Rawls, *A Theory of Justice*, p. 7.
52. Rawls, *A Theory of Justice*, p. 544. Rawls tended to use "self-respect" and "self-esteem" interchangeably in *A Theory of Justice*. Differences between these concepts have been pointed out by Laurence Thomas and others (see Thomas, "Self-Respect: Theory and Practice," in *Philosophy Born of Struggle: Afro-American Philosophy from 1917*, ed. Leonard Harris [Dubuque, Iowa: Kendall/Hunt, 1983], pp. 174–89). Here I follow Rawls in ignoring those differences, on the assumption that in children some very basic sorts of self-esteem are probably important to the development of self-respect.
53. Robin Dillon gives a detailed account of the undermining of self-respect in "Self-Respect: Emotional, Moral, Political," presented to the Oberlin Colloquium in Philosophy, Apr. 23, 1995.
54. Kant, *Groundwork*, chap. 2; *The Doctrine of Virtue: Pt. II of The Metaphysic of Morals*, trans. Mary J. Gregor (New York: Harper & Row, 1964), pp. 7–28.
55. Jung Chang, *Wild Swans: Three Daughters of China* (New York: Simon & Schuster, 1991).

Chapter Four

1. Nel Noddings, *Caring: A Feminine Approach to Ethics and Moral Education* (Berkeley: University of California Press, 1984), and *Women and Evil* (Berkeley: University of California Press, 1989). Sarah Lucia Hoagland, *Lesbian Ethics: Toward New Value* (Palo Alto, Calif.: Institute of Lesbian Studies, 1988), and "Some Thoughts About Caring," in *Feminist Ethics,* ed. Claudia Card (Lawrence: University Press of Kansas, 1991), pp. 246–63.

2. In Claudia Card, *Lesbian Choices* (New York: Columbia University Press, 1995).

3. John Rawls, *A Theory of Justice* (Cambridge, Mass.: Harvard University Press, 1971), *Political Liberalism* (New York: Columbia University Press, 1993), and "The Law of Peoples," in *On Human Rights: The Amnesty Lectures, 1993,* ed. Stephen Shute and Susan Hurley (New York: Basic Books, 1993), pp. 41–82.

4. Not all who support care ethics reject the importance of justice. For example, Virginia Held and Joan Tronto both insist on the importance of justice and question its detachability from care. See Held, *Feminist Morality: Transforming Culture, Society, and Politics* (Chicago: University of Chicago Press, 1993), and Tronto, *Moral Boundaries: A Political Argument for an Ethic of Care* (New York: Routledge, 1993). In her response to commentators on *Caring,* Noddings also says "my critics may be right that a concept of justice is needed" but adds that "a great deal of work must be done on exactly what it contributes" (*Hypatia* 5, no. 1 [spring 1990]: 122.

5. Laurence Mordekhai Thomas, *Vessels of Evil: American Slavery and the Holocaust* (Philadelphia: Temple University Press, 1993).

6. For this reason Julia Penelope objects to the term "sexual abuse" when it is applied to the domestic rape of children (as though there were a proper sexual use of children). See Penelope, *Call Me Lesbian: Lesbian Lives, Lesbian Theory* (Freedom, Calif.: Crossing Press, 1992).

7. Virginia Held's feminist morality is also pluralistic, although hers is a pluralism of *contexts,* according to which some contexts call for one kind of ethical focus and others call for another. She leaves unanswered, however, the question how we are to determine which context calls for which kind of focus. See her *Feminist Morality,* p. 218; *Rights and Goods* (New York: Free Press, 1983), pp. 21–39; "Feminism and Moral Theory," in *Women and Moral Theory,* ed. Eva Feder Kittay and Diana T. Meyers (Totowa, N.J.: Rowman and Littlefield, 1987), pp. 111–28.

8. Held, *Feminist Morality,* pp. 70–75.

9. Noddings, *Caring,* pp. 6, 102.

10. Susan Moller Okin, *Justice, Gender, and the Family* (New York: Basic Books, 1989), pp. 89–109.

11. In *A Theory of Justice* Rawls also treats parent-child relationships as the place where the foundations are laid for the development of a sense of justice (pp. 462–67). This aspect of the theory is not discussed in *Political Liberalism.*

12. Rawls, *A Theory of Justice,* pp. 462–96.

13. Also worth mentioning in this regard are Susan Sherwin, *No Longer Patient: Feminist Ethics and Health Care* (Philadelphia: Temple University Press, 1992), pp. 99–240; Tronto, *Moral Boundaries,* pp. 101–80; and Annette Baier's work on the concept

of trust in *Moral Prejudices: Essays on Ethics* (Cambridge, Mass.: Harvard University Press, 1994), pp. 95–202.

14. Noddings, *Caring*, p. 9.

15. Noddings, *Caring*, pp. 9–26.

16. Hoagland, *Lesbian Ethics*, p. 127.

17. Similarly, Tronto defines care as having the three elements of engagement, reaching out, and leading to "some type of action" (*Moral Boundaries*, pp. 102–3). In contrast to Noddings, Tronto's care ethic emphasizes the action aspect of caring.

18. Noddings, *Women and Evil*, p. 184.

19. Tronto distinguishes "taking care of," as a kind of administrative taking of responsibility, from "care giving" (*Moral Boundaries*, pp. 106–7). I tend to use "care taking" and "care giving" to refer to activities all of which she might regard as "care giving."

20. Seyla Benhabib, *Situating the Self: Gender, Community, and Postmodernism in Contemporary Ethics* (New York: Routledge, 1992).

21. Noddings, *Women and Evil*, p. 172.

22. Noddings, *Women and Evil*, p. 121.

23. Noddings, *Women and Evil*, p. 91.

24. Noddings agreed with this point during discussion at a symposium on her book *Caring* at the American Philosophical Association Central Division conference in Cincinnati, Apr. 28, 1988. The symposium was published in *Hypatia* 5, no. 1 (spring 1990): 101–26.

25. Noddings, *Caring*, pp. 46–48.

26. Noddings, *Caring*, p. 47.

27. Noddings, *Caring*, p. 47.

28. Noddings's understanding of encounter appears to be face-to-face, not the sort exemplified by addressing a crowd; her teaching examples do not readily suggest university lecturing.

29. Noddings, *Caring*, p. 54.

30. See Marcus G. Singer, *Generalization in Ethics* (New York: Knopf, 1961), p. 15. See, also, Singer, "The Golden Rule," *Philosophy* 38, no. 146 (Oct. 1963): 293–314, or "Golden Rule," in *Encyclopedia of Philosophy*, ed. Paul Edwards, 8 vols. (New York: Collier Macmillan, 1967), 3:365–67.

31. Noddings says a pregnant woman can "confer sacredness" on an embryo if she loves the biological father to whom it is connected (*Caring*, pp. 87–89).

32. Noddings, *Caring*, p. 28.

33. Noddings, *Caring*, p. 175.

34. See Robert Jay Lifton, *The Nazi Doctors: Medical Killing and the Psychology of Genocide* (New York: Basic Books, 1986).

35. Noddings, *Caring*, p. 2.

36. I owe this point to Victoria Davion's critique of Sara Ruddick's "Maternal Thinking" and "Preservative Love and Military Destruction" (both in *Mothering: Essays in Feminist Theory*, ed. Joyce Trebilcot [Totowa, N.J.: Rowman and Allanheld, 1984], pp. 213–62) in "Pacifism and Care," *Hypatia* 5, no. 1 (spring 1990): 90–100.

37. Nina Simone, "Mississippi goddam" (1964), Philips 812 378–1 (1983), side 1, band 2.

38. Michele Moody-Adams also develops this idea in "Gender and the Complexity of Moral Voices," in *Feminist Ethics*, ed. Card, pp. 213–32.

39. "Domestic Abusers Keep Cops on Run," *The Capital Times*, June 26, 1995, p. A1.

40. Lenore E. Walker, *The Battered Woman* (New York: Harper & Row, 1979), pp. 55–70.

41. Noddings, *Caring*, pp. 113–20. See Faith McNulty, *The Burning Bed* (New York: Bantam, 1981), on Francine Hughes of Michigan, acquitted of murder although, after years of abuse and unsuccessful attempts to use the law, she doused her former husband with gasoline and incinerated him as he slept.

42. Bernard Williams, *Problems of the Self: Philosophical Papers, 1956–1972* (Cambridge: Cambridge University Press, 1973), p. 179.

43. See Noddings, *Caring*, pp. 109–10, for the case of siding, despite her racism, with Aunt Phoebe (for years of personal kindness) against those fighting for racial justice and p. 55 for the case of whether to inform on one's mobster neighbor, although we are not told who wants to know what, nor how one learned of the mobster involvements, which makes the case unclear.

44. See Marilyn Frye, "In and Out of Harm's Way: Arrogance and Love," in *The Politics of Reality: Essays in Feminist Theory* (Trumansburg, N.Y.: Crossing Press, 1983), pp. 52–83, for discussion of learning through abuse to anticipate others' needs.

45. Max Scheler, *The Nature of Sympathy*, trans. Peter Heath (Hamden, Conn.: Archon Books, 1970), p. 5.

46. Rawls, *A Theory of Justice*, pp. 62, 92.

47. Rawls, *Political Liberalism*, p. 106; on the moral powers, p. 81.

48. Rawls, *A Theory of Justice*, p. 92.

49. Iris Marion Young, *Justice and the Politics of Difference* (Princeton, N.J.: Princeton University Press, 1990), pp. 39–65.

50. Noddings, personal correspondance, Sept. 19, 1994.

51. Here I follow Harry Frankfurt, "Freedom of the Will and the Concept of a Person," in *The Importance of What We Care About: Philosophical Essays* (New York: Cambridge University Press, 1988), pp. 11–25, in distinguishing between higher- and lower-order psychological states.

52. Perhaps Noddings means to acknowledge the positive value of guilt in her remarks on guilt in relationships (*Caring*, pp. 37–40).

53. Young, *Justice and the Politics of Difference*, pp. 15–38.

54. The quotation is from Rawls, *A Theory of Justice*, p. 3.

55. Rawls, *Political Liberalism*, p. 5.

56. Rawls, *Political Liberalism*, pp. 181–82.

Chapter Five

1. Bat-Ami Bar On, "Why Terrorism Is Morally Problematic," in *Feminist Ethics*, ed. Claudia Card (Lawrence: University Press of Kansas, 1991), pp. 107–25.

2. For a historical survey of martial rape, see Susan Brownmiller, *Against Our Will: Men, Women, and Rape* (New York: Simon & Schuster, 1975), pp. 31–113, and for a more recent study, see *Mass Rape: The War Against Women in Bosnia-Herzogovina*, ed. Alexandra Stiglmayer (Lincoln: University of Nebraska Press, 1994).

3. Peggy Reeves Sanday, *Fraternity Gang Rape: Sex, Brotherhood, and Privilege on Campus* (New York: New York University Press, 1990).

4. Judith Lewis Herman, *Trauma and Recovery* (New York: Basic Books, 1992).

5. See Jean Genet, *Our Lady of the Flowers*, trans. Bernard Frechtman (New York: Grove, 1963).

6. See Rose Giallombardo, *Society of Women: A Study of a Women's Prison* (New York: Wiley, 1966), chap. 9.

7. Harriet Baber, "How Bad Is Rape?" *Hypatia* 2, no. 2 (summer 1987): 125–38.

8. Representative of current literature that so understands terrorism are Walter Laqueur, *The Age of Terrorism*, rev. and expanded (Boston: Little, Brown, 1987); Benjamin Netanyahu, ed., *Terrorism: How the West Can Win* (New York: Farrar, Straus, Giroux, 1986); and Gayle Rivers, *The War Against the Terrorists: How to Win It* (New York: Stein & Day, 1986).

9. For silence-breaking philosophical inquiries into what is wrong with rape, see the four essays in the "Rape" section of *Feminism and Philosophy*, ed. Mary Vetterling-Braggin, Frederick A. Elliston, and Jane English (Totowa, N.J.: Littlefield, Adams, 1977), by Susan Griffin, Pamela Foa, Carolyn Shafer and Marilyn Frye, and Susan Rae Peterson, pp. 313–71. See, also, the bibliography at the end of that section, pp. 372–76.

10. Susan Griffin, "Rape: The All-American Crime" in *Feminism and Philosophy*, ed. Vetterling-Braggin, Elliston, and English, pp. 313–32. It also appears as the first chapter of Susan Griffin, *Rape: The Power of Consciousness* (New York: Harper & Row, 1979).

11. Barbara Mehrhof and Pamela Kearon, "Rape: An Act of Terror" in *Radical Feminism*, ed. Anne Koedt, Ellen Levine, and Anite Rapone (New York: Quadrangle, 1973), pp. 228–33.

12. For Rawls's definition of "practice" or "institution" see his *A Theory of Justice* (Cambridge, Mass.: Harvard University Press, 1971), p. 55.

13. Kate Millett, *Sexual Politics* (New York: Random House, 1970).

14. Philosophical essays of the late 1950s and early 1960s discuss this ambiguity of "punishment." See H. B. Acton, ed., *The Philosophy of Punishment* (London: Macmillan, 1969).

15. For development of this point regarding punishment, see H.L.A. Hart, "Prolegomenon to the Principles of Punishing," *Punishment and Responsibility: Essays in the Philosophy of Law* (New York: Oxford University Press, 1968). Hart distinguishes between "general justifying aims" of punishment and justifications offered by rules for particular moves within the practice.

16. See J. D. Mabbott, "Punishment," *Mind*, n.s. 48, no. 190 (Apr. 1939), pp. 152–67, reprinted in *Philosophy of Punishment*, ed. Acton.

17. See Rawls, *A Theory of Justice*, pp. 241, 314, 575, for sketches of such an understanding.

18. Mehrhof and Kearon, "Rape: An Act of Terror," p. 232.

19. Jonathan Glover, "State Terrorism," in *Violence, Terrorism, and Justice,* ed. R. G. Frey and Christopher W. Morris (New York: Cambridge University Press, 1991), p. 256. Emma Goldman develops the same position in "The Psychology of Political Violence" and "Anarchism: What It Really Stands For," both in *Anarchism and Other Essays* (New York: Dover, 1969), pp. 79–108 and 47–67.

20. Annette Baier, "Violent Demonstrations" in *Violence, Terrorism, and Justice,* ed. Frey and Morris, p. 33.

21. See, for example, Marilyn Frye's discussion of pimps' seasoning of new prostitutes, "In and Out of Harm's Way: Arrogance and Love," in *The Politics of Reality: Essays in Feminist Theory* (Trumansburg, N.Y.: Crossing Press, 1983), pp. 61–66, and accounts in Kathleen Barry, *Female Sexual Slavery* (Englewood Cliffs, N.J.: Prentice Hall, 1979), including the terrorizing of Patty Hearst, pp. 118–36.

22. On the two targets, see Onora O'Neill, "Which Are the Offers You Can't Refuse?" in *Violence, Terrorism, and Justice,* ed. Frey and Morris, pp. 170–95.

23. On rape and lynching, see Ida B. Wells-Barnett, *On Lynchings* (New York: Arno Press, 1969), which reprints pamphlets from her antilynching campaigns of the 1890s and the turn of the century.

24. Griffin, "Rape: The All-American Crime," p. 320.

25. Susan Rae Peterson, "Coercion and Rape: The State as a Male Protection Racket," in *Feminism and Philosophy,* ed. Vetterling-Braggin, Elliston, and English, pp. 360–71.

26. The idea is not, of course, that rape meets Rawlsian principles of justice but only that it fits Rawls's understanding of the concept of a practice, as indicated above.

27. *Hegel's Philosophy of Right,* trans. T. M. Knox (London: Oxford University Press, 1942), pp. 69–74, pars. 99–104, and "Additions," pp. 246–47.

28. See Frye, *Politics of Reality,* pp. 95–109, on access as a face of power.

29. Menachem Amir, *Patterns in Forcible Rape* (Chicago: University of Chicago Press, 1971).

30. Amir, *Patterns,* p. 143.

31. Amir, *Patterns,* p. 314.

32. Amir seems to move in that direction in the theoretical discussion at the end of *Patterns.*

33. George Orwell, *Nineteen Eighty-Four* (New York: Harcourt, Brace, 1949).

34. See Susan Estrich, *Real Rape* (Cambridge, Mass.: Harvard University Press, 1987), on "simple rape" as nearly impossible to establish in court as *real rape.* "Simple rape" contrasts in law with "aggravated rape," which is rape aggravated by such conditions as the assailant's being a stranger to the victim or using a weapon.

35. Lily Tomlin says she actually saw a man walk up to four women in a bar and ask, "What are you doing here sitting all alone?" See *Lily Tomlin: On Stage* (New York: Arista Records, 1977), Act I (side 1, end of band 4).

36. This rule is discussed by Shafer and Frye, "Rape and Respect," in *Feminism and Philosophy,* ed. Vetterling-Braggin, Elliston, and English, p. 335.

37. I owe this analogy to Frye, *Politics of Reality,* pp. 4–5.

38. For practical strategies that have worked, see Pauline Bart and Patricia H. O'Brien, *Stopping Rape: Successful Survival Strategies* (New York: Pergamon, 1985),

and Denise Caignon and Gail Groves, eds., *Her Wits About Her: Self-Defense Success Stories by Women* (New York: Harper & Row, 1987).

39. Feminist self-defense classes often do include consciousness-raising about rape in a way that does address its institutionalization at the level of women's awareness.

40. I viewed the film more than fifteen years ago but have been unable to find documentation on it. Critics soon pointed out that all the imprisoned rapists interviewed on the film appeared to be black (one white rapist's face was in shadow), thereby contributing unintentionally to a racist stereotype. The film seems to have disappeared from circulation shortly thereafter.

41. Interestingly, the King Arthur film *First Knight* (1995) portrays Sir Lancelot as refusing to rape Queen-to-be Guinevere, although it is also clear that he sees this refusal as his to bestow.

42. J. S. Mill, *On Liberty*, in *The Philosophy of John Stuart Mill: Ethical, Political and Religious*, ed. Marshall Cohen (New York: Modern Library, 1961), pp. 196–97. (*On Liberty* was originally published in 1859.)

43. J. S. Mill, *The Subjection of Women*, in *Essays on Sex Equality: John Stuart Mill and Harriet Taylor Mill*, ed. Alice S. Rossi (Chicago: University of Chicago Press, 1970). (*Subjection of Women* was first published in 1869.) See esp. chaps. 1 and 3 (Rossi, *Essays*, pp. 125–56, 118–215).

44. Mill, *On Liberty*, pp. 252–54.

45. Mill, *On Liberty*, p. 253.

46. Bar On, "Why Terrorism Is Morally Problematic," pp. 111–12; Leo Lowenthal, "Terror's Atomization of Man," *Commentary* 1, no. 3 (Jan. 1946): 1–8; Frye, *The Politics of Reality*, pp. 52–83; Barry, *Female Sexual Slavery*, pp. 45–136.

47. Bar On, "Why Terrorism Is Morally Problematic," pp. 116–22. She is, however, neither unconcerned with justice nor interested in substituting empathy for justice. Her view is that "both empathy and justice have to be accorded a serious place in moral thinking" (p. 121).

48. According to Paul Harvey, *Oxford Companion to Classical Literature* (New York: Oxford University Press, 1984), p. 320, the instrument's inventor, Perillus, became its first victim.

49. Bar On, "Why Terrorism Is Morally Problematic," pp. 116–22. She also points out that terrorism has a significant impact on the children of those terrorized, citing the fact that children of Holocaust survivors have Holocaust nightmares. Presumably, it also has an impact on the children of terrorizers.

Chapter Six

1. The most extended philosophical treatment of the topic is Terrance McConnell, *Gratitude* (Philadelphia: Temple University Press, 1993), which usefully discusses nearly everything philosophers have had to say about it.

2. Friedrich Nietzsche, *On the Genealogy of Morals*, trans. Walter Kaufmann and R. J. Hollingdale (New York: Vintage, 1967), pp. 62–65.

3. Marcel Mauss, *The Gift: Forms and Functions of Exchange in Archaic Societies*, trans. Ian Cunnison (New York: Norton, 1967).

4. Immanuel Kant, *The Moral Law: Kant's Groundwork of the Metaphysic of Morals*, trans. H. J. Paton (London: Hutchinson, 1948), pp. 90–91.

5. In his general introduction to *The Metaphysic of Morals*, Kant holds that obligations cannot conflict with one another although the grounds of obligations can conflict, which leaves us to determine what the obligation really is. See *The Doctrine of Virtue: Pt. II of the Metaphysic of Morals*, trans. Mary J. Gregor (New York: Harper & Row, 1964), p. 23.

6. For a discussion of this point about supererogation, see Joel Feinberg, "Supererogation and Rules," in *Doing and Deserving: Essays in the Theory of Responsibility* (Princeton, N.J.: Princeton, 1970), pp. 3–24.

7. G.E.M. Anscombe, "Modern Moral Philosophy," *Philosophy* 33, no. 124 (Jan. 1958): 1–19.

8. John Rawls, "Justice as Fairness," *The Philosophical Review* 67, no. 2 (Apr. 1958): 164–94.

9. See Kant, *Doctrine of Virtue*, pp. 115–46; Henry Sidgwick, *The Methods of Ethics*, 7th ed. (Chicago: University of Chicago Press, 1907), pp. 259–63, 430–39; and W. D. Ross, *The Right and the Good* (Oxford: Clarendon Press, 1930), p. 27.

10. Michael Stocker discusses a similar problem about friendship and contemporary ethical theory in "The Schizophrenia of Modern Ethical Theories," *The Journal of Philosophy* 73, no. 14 (Aug. 12, 1976): 453–66.

11. Fred Berger, "Gratitude," *Ethics* 85, no. 4 (July 1975): 298–309.

12. A. Cohen, *Everyman's Talmud* (New York: E. P. Dutton, 1932), p. 224.

13. For a summary of passages on various kinds of charity, see Cohen, *Everyman's Talmud*, pp. 219–26. Loving acts are distinguished as superior to alms-giving (*Sukkah* 49b), the former (*Gemiluth Hasadim*), including hospitality, visits to the sick, taking charge of orphans, and providing an outfit and dowry for a poor bride; the latter (*Zedakah*, "righteousness"), donations for the poor. Practice of the latter is said to be "mere righteousness." And regarding the former, "highest of all is benevolence performed to the dead, since it must be done from pure motives" (p. 226).

14. Kant, *Doctrine of Virtue*, p. 123. Cf. Immanuel Kant, *Lectures on Ethics*, trans. Louis Infield (New York: Harper & Row, 1963), pp. 118–19.

15. Kant, *Lectures*, pp. 118–19.

16. Kant, *Doctrine of Virtue*, p. 124.

17. Kant, *Doctrine of Virtue*, pp. 115–31.

18. Kant, *Lectures*, p. 118.

19. Kant, *Doctrine of Virtue*, p. 123. Cf. Aristotle's discussion of "unequal friendships," in *The Nicomachean Ethics of Aristotle*, trans. Sir David Ross (London: Oxford University Press, 1925), pp. 203–4.

20. Kant, *Doctrine of Virtue*, p. 140.

21. Nietzsche, *Genealogy*, pp. 93–94.

22. *Nicomachean Ethics of Aristotle*, p. 92.

23. Ralph Waldo Emerson, "Gifts," *Essays, Second Series*, in *The Complete Writings of Ralph Waldo Emerson*, 2 vols. (New York: Wm. H. Wise, 1929), 1:287.

24. Ruth Benedict, *Patterns of Culture* (New York: Mentor, 1946), pp. 160–205.

25. Kant, *Doctrine of Virtue*, p. 123.

26. Kant, *Doctrine of Virtue*, p. 123.

27. Thomas Hobbes, *De Cive; or, The Citizen,* ed. Sterling P. Lamprecht (New York: Appleton-Century-Crofts, 1949), p. 47.

28. Hobbes, *Leviathan; or, The Matter, Forme and Power of a Commonwealth, Ecclesiasticall and Civil,* ed. Michael Oakeshott (Oxford: Blackwell, 1955), p. 99.

29. H.L.A. Hart, "Are There Any Natural Rights?" *Philosophical Review* 64, no. 2 (Apr. 1955): 185.

30. Rawls, "Justice as Fairness," pp. 179–81. In *A Theory of Justice* (Cambridge, Mass.: Harvard University Press; 1971), Rawls renames the principle underlying the "duty of fair play" (now called the *obligation* rather than the *duty* of fair play) as the "principle of fairness" and holds this principle to be the source of all *obligations.* He also distinguishes between obligations as voluntarily incurred and "natural duties," defined only by ostension, which apply without regard to our voluntary choices (*Theory,* pp. 108–17). In *Political Liberalism* (New York: Columbia University Press, 1992), he abandons the idea of presenting a comprehensive moral theory and restricts his ambitions to presenting a conception of justice that might represent an overlapping consensus of many different, more comprehensive philosophies.

31. Rawls, "Justice as Fairness," p. 181, including footnote. Berger agreed on the ground that compliance with the duty of fair play does not require benevolence (Berger, "Gratitude," p. 301). In informal practices, this is not so clear.

32. On differences among the concepts of deserts, rights, and claims, see Joel Feinberg, "Justice and Personal Deserts," in his *Doing and Deserving,* pp. 55–94.

33. Kant, *Doctrine of Virtue,* pp. 7–28.

34. Hart, "Are There Any Natural Rights?" p. 183.

35. Hart, "Are There Any Natural Rights?" p. 181.

36. Carol Gilligan, *In a Different Voice: Psychological Theory and Women's Development* (Cambridge, Mass.: Harvard University Press, 1982).

37. Emerson, "Gifts," 1:286–87.

38. See, for example, "Legal and Moral Obligation" in *Essays in Moral Philosophy,* ed. A. I. Melden (Seattle: University of Washington Press, 1958), pp. 3–39.

39. Richard Brandt, "The Concepts of Duty and Obligation," *Mind* 73, no. 291 (July 1964): 373–93.

40. For an example, see Hart on the U.S. President's responsibility to execute the law of the land, in "Legal and Moral Obligation," p. 99.

41. "Of Friendship," *Essays or Counsels Civil and Moral: 1597–1625* in *Selected Writings of Francis Bacon,* ed. Hugh G. Dick (New York: Modern Library, 1955), p. 75.

42. Judith Martin, *Miss Manners' Guide to Excruciatingly Correct Behavior* (New York: Warner Books, 1983), p. 6.

43. Max Scheler, *The Nature of Sympathy,* trans. Peter Heath (Hamden, Conn.: Shoestring Press, 1970), p. 164.

44. For a perceptive discussion of generosity that brings out why, see Lester Hunt, "Generosity," *The American Philosophical Quarterly* 12, no. 3 (July 1975): 235–44.

45. A classic discussion is *The Nicomachean Ethics of Aristotle,* pp. 79–85.

46. On these and other issues regarding trust, see Annette Baier, *Moral Prejudices: Essays on Ethics* (Cambridge, Mass.: Harvard University Press, 1994), pp. 95–202.

47. Emerson, "Gifts," 1:286.

Chapter Seven

1. For a review of recent books on this question, see Richard Horton, "Is Homo-sexuality Inherited?" *New York Review of Books* 42, no. 12 (July 13, 1995): 36–41. Two double issues of the *Journal of Homosexuality* (vol. 28, nos. 1–4 [1995], "Sex, Cells, and Same-Sex Desire: The Biology of Sexual Preference") are devoted to this topic.

2. For evidence, however, that social oppression of overt same-sex eroticism has not been universal, see John Boswell, *Same-Sex Unions in Premodern Europe* (New York: Villard, 1994); Serena Nanda, *Neither Man nor Woman: The Hijras of India* (Belmont, Calif.: Wadsworth, 1990); and Walter L. Williams, *The Spirit and the Flesh: Sexual Diversity in American Indian Culture* (Boston: Beacon Press, 1986).

3. See, for example, Jonathan Katz, *Gay American History: Lesbians and Gay Men in the U.S.A.* (New York: Thomas E. Crowell, 1976), pp. 209–79, on lesbians who passed as men.

4. George Chauncey, *Gay New York: Gender, Urban Culture, and the Making of the Gay Male World, 1890–1940* (New York: Basic Books, 1994), p. 7.

5. Nel Noddings, *Caring: A Feminine Approach to Ethics and Moral Education* (Berkeley: University of California Press, 1984), p. 6.

6. Carol Gilligan, *In a Different Voice: Psychological Theory and Women's Development* (Cambridge, Mass.: Harvard University Press, 1982), and Noddings, *Caring.*

7. Joyce Trebilcot, *Dyke Ideas: Process, Politics, Daily Life* (Albany: State University of New York Press, 1994), pp. 98–99.

8. Joan Didion, "Self-Respect," in *Slouching Toward Bethlehem* (Middlesex, England: Penguin, 1974), p. 123.

9. This is something like the distinction that John Rawls argues clarifies the justification of punishment in "Two Concepts of Rules," *The Philosophical Review* 64, no. 1 (Jan. 1955): 3–32.

10. Trebilcot, *Dyke Ideas,* pp. 104–8.

11. Marcus G. Singer, for example, argues in *Generalization in Ethics* (New York: Knopf, 1961) that if the consequences of everyone's failing to do x would be disastrous, then it would be wrong for anyone to fail to do x, provided that the referent of x is not too narrowly or too broadly specified.

12. For philosophical discussions that tend to ignore this ambiguity, see papers by male contributors in Alan Soble, ed., *Philosophy of Sex* (Totowa, N.J.: Littlefield, Adams, 1980), pt. 1.

13. Kate Millett, *Sexual Politics* (Garden City, N.Y.: Doubleday, 1970).

14. John P. De Cecco and Michael G. Shively, "From Sexual Identity to Sexual Relationships: A Contextual Shift," in *Origins of Sexuality and Homosexuality,* ed. John P. De Cecco and Michael G. Shively (New York: Harrington Park, 1985), pp. 1–16.

15. Janice G. Raymond, *The Transsexual Empire: The Making of the She-Male* (Boston: Beacon, 1979).

16. Jeffrey Weeks, *Coming Out: Homosexual Politics in Britain, from the Nineteenth Century to the Present* (London: Quartet, 1977), p. 3.

17. Michel Foucault, *The History of Sexuality,* trans. Robert Hurley (New York: Random House, 1978), p. 43.

18. Foucault, *History of Sexuality*, p. 43.

19. Thomas Szasz, *The Manufacture of Madness* (New York: Harper & Row, 1970).

20. Trebilcot, *Dyke Ideas*, pp. 100–101.

21. See, for example, Noretta Koertge, ed., *Philosophy and Homosexuality* (New York: Harrington Park, 1985). The same was true of turn-of-the-century homosexual rights activists. See James D. Steakley, *The Homosexual Emancipation Movement in Germany* (New York: Arno, 1975).

22. On the origins of "gay," see John Boswell, *Christianity, Social Tolerance, and Homosexuality: Gay People in Western Europe from the Beginning of the Christian Era to the Fourteenth Century* (Chicago: University of Chicago Press, 1980), p. 43 n 6.

23. See, for example, Kath Weston, *Families We Choose: Lesbians, Gays, Kinship* (New York: Columbia University Press, 1991), and Phyllis Burke, *Family Values: Two Moms and Their Son* (New York: Random House, 1993).

24. I discuss this issue at greater length in *Lesbian Choices* (New York: Columbia University Press, 1995), pp. 11–57.

25. Edwin Schur, *Labeling Deviant Behavior: Its Sociological Implications* (New York: Harper & Row, 1971), p. 11.

26. Friedrich Nietzsche, *On the Genealogy of Morals*, trans. Walter Kaufmann and R. J. Hollingdale (New York: Vintage, 1967), pp. 79–80.

27. Nietzsche, "Appendix: Seventy-Five Aphorisms from Five Volumes," in *Genealogy*, p. 180.

28. Nietzsche, *Genealogy*, p. 80.

29. See Alan Goldman, "Plain Sex," in *Philosophy of Sex*, ed. Soble, pp. 119–38.

30. For development of this idea using other arguments, see Marilyn Frye, "Lesbian 'Sex'," in *Willful Virgin: Essays in Feminism, 1976–1992* (Freedom, Calif.: Crossing Press, 1992), pp. 109–19.

31. For more on the nature and consequences of clidoridectomy, see Mary Daly, *Gyn/Ecology: The Metaethics of Radical Feminism* (Boston: Beacon, 1978), pp. 153–77, and Alice Walker and Pratibha Parmar, *Warrior Marks: Female Genital Mutilation and the Sexual Blinding of Women* (New York: Harcourt, Brace, 1993).

32. On the physiology of the clitoris, see William H. Masters and Virginia E. Johnson, *Human Sexual Response* (Boston: Little, Brown, 1966), pp. 45–67.

33. Sigmund Freud, *Three Essays on the Theory of Sexuality*, trans. James Strachey (New York: Avon, 1965), pp. 66–106.

34. This was the view of Arthur Schopenhauer, Freud's philosophical predecessor on sexuality, in "The Metaphysics of Sexual Love" and its Appendix on pederasty in *The World as Will and Representation*, trans. E.F.J. Payne, 2 vols. (New York: Dover, 1966), 2:538–67. Cf. 1:326–31.

35. *The Nicomachean Ethics of Aristotle*, trans. Sir David Ross (Oxford: Clarendon Press; 1925), pp. 72–74.

36. Thomas Nagel, "Sexual Perversion," in *Philosophy of Sex*, ed. Soble, pp. 76–88.

37. For Plato's *Symposium* and *Phaedrus*, see *Plato: The Collected Dialogues*, ed. Edith Hamilton and Huntington Cairns (New York: Pantheon, 1961), pp. 527–74, 476–525.

38. Nagel suggests that perverted sex might be better as sex than unperverted sex ("Sexual Perversion," p. 88), meaning, perhaps, that it may be more fun.

Chapter Eight

1. William Julius Wilson, *The Declining Significance of Race: Blacks and Changing American Institutions,* 2d ed. (Chicago: University of Chicago Press, 1980).

2. M. F. Ashley Montagu, "On the Phrase 'Ethnic Group' in Anthropology," *Psychiatry* 8, no. 1 (Feb. 1945): 27–33, reprinted as " 'Ethnic Group' and 'Race,' " in Ashley Montagu, *Race, Science, and Humanity* (New York: Van Nostrand, 1963), pp. 61–71. See, also, Ashley Montagu, *Man's Most Dangerous Myth: The Fallacy of Race* (Cleveland: Meridian, 1964).

3. On responses to scientific racism by African Americans (including W.E.B. Du Bois, whose views I take up in this chapter) and Jews, see Nancy Leys Stepan and Sander L. Gilman, "Appropriating the Idioms of Science: The Rejection of Scientific Racism," in *The Bounds of Race: Perspectives on Hegemony and Resistance,* ed. Dominick LaCapra (Ithaca, N.Y.: Cornell University Press, 1991), pp. 72–103.

4. Kwame Anthony Appiah, *In My Father's House: Africa in the Philosophy of Culture* (New York: Oxford University Press, 1992), p. 35.

5. On the ethnicity, class, and nation paradigms of race, see Michael Omi and Howard Winant, *Racial Formation in the United States from the 1960s to the 1980s* (New York: Routledge & Kegan Paul, 1986), pp. 9–54, and David Theo Goldberg, *Racist Culture: Philosophy and the Politics of Meaning* (Oxford: Blackwell, 1993), pp. 61–89.

6. W.E.B. Du Bois, "The Conservation of Races," *W.E.B. Du Bois Speaks: Speeches and Addresses, 1890–1919,* ed. Philip S. Foner, 2 vols. (New York: Pathfinder, 1970), 1:75–76. Lucius Outlaw first called my attention to this essay at a conference on racism and sexism at Georgia State University in 1991.

7. Appiah, *In My Father's House,* pp. 28–46.

8. Goldberg, *Racist Culture,* pp. 70–74. Tommy Lott also argues that Du Bois's intention was to offer a revisionist sociohistorical conception of race to resolve the dilemma of African American double consciousness. See Lott, "Du Bois on the Invention of Race," *The Philosophical Forum* 24, nos. 1–3 (fall-spring 1992–93): 166.

9. In 1897 Du Bois thought "the final word of science" was that "we have at least two, perhaps three, great families of human beings — the whites and Negroes, possibly the yellow race"; in the sense of "race" that he thought was supported by historical usage, he said, however, "we find upon the world's stage today eight distinctly differentiated races," namely, "the Slavs of Eastern Europe, the Teutons of middle Europe, the English of Great Britain and America, the Romance nations of Southern and Western Europe, the Negroes of Africa and America, the Semitic people of Western Asia and Northern Africa, the Hindoos of Central Asia and the Mongolians of Eastern Asia" (Du Bois, "Conservation of Races," pp. 76–77).

10. Appiah, *In My Father's House,* p. 32.

11. Du Bois, "Conservation of Races," pp. 73–85.

12. Marilyn Frye, *The Politics of Reality: Essays in Feminist Theory* (Trumansburg, N.Y.: Crossing Press, 1983), pp. 110–27, and *Willful Virgin: Essays in Feminism, 1976–1992* (Freedom, Calif.: Crossing Press, 1992), pp. 147–69.

13. The earliest of these essays by Maria Lugones, "Pedagogy and Racism," was presented in Minneapolis at a conference of the Midwest Society of Women in Philosophy in 1984 and printed in the Carleton College campus periodical *Breaking*

Ground 6 (spring 1984): 38–43. It was later revised and expanded as "Hablando cara a cara/Speaking Face to Face: An Exploration of Ethnocentric Racism," in *Making Face, Making Soul: Haciendo Caras,* ed. Gloria Anzaldua (San Francisco: Aunt Lute, 1990), pp. 46–54. See, also, Maria Lugones, "Playfulness, 'World'-Travelling, and Loving Perception," *Hypatia* 2, no. 2 (summer 1987): 3–10, and 'Hispaneando y lesbiando: On Sarah Hoagland's *Lesbian Ethics,*" *Hypatia* 5, no. 3 (fall 1990): 138–46. This material is developed further in her forthcoming book, *Peregrinajes/Pilgrimmages* (Albany: State University of New York Press).

14. Joel Kovel, *White Racism: A Psychohistory* (New York: Columbia University Press, 1984), p. xlv.

15. Maria Lugones, "On the Logic of Pluralist Feminism," in *Feminist Ethics,* ed. Claudia Card (Lawrence: University Press of Kansas, 1991), pp. 39–40. Lorraine Bethel, "What Chou Mean *We,* White Girl? or, The Cullud Lesbian Feminist Declaration of Independence (Dedicated to the Proposition that All Women Are Not Equal, I.E., Identical/ly Oppressed)" The Black Women's Issue: *Conditions: Five* 2, no. 2 (autumn 1979): 86–92.

16. Lugones, "On the Logic of Pluralist Feminism," pp. 40–41.

17. Lugones, "On the Logic of Pluralist Feminism," pp. 41–42.

18. Lugones, "On the Logic of Pluralist Feminism," p. 42.

19. For examples of the latter, see Amoja Three Rivers, *Cultural Etiquette: A Guide for the Well-Intentioned* (1990); distributed by Market Wimmin, Box 28, Indian Valley, VA 24105.

20. Marcus G. Singer, "Some Thoughts on *Race* and *Racism,*" *Philosophia* (Philosophical Quarterly of Israel) 8, nos. 2–3 (Nov. 1978): 153–83, first called my attention to this history.

21. Appiah, *In My Father's House,* pp. 13–14. Outlaw agrees that "race thinking" need not be socially divisive and finds it an error to think "that 'race thinking' must be completely eliminated on the way to an emancipated society," "Toward a Critical Theory of Race," in *Anatomy of Racism,* ed. David Theo Goldberg (Minneapolis: University of Minnesota Press, 1990), p. 78.

22. *The American Heritage Dictionary of the English Language,* New College Edition, 1969, s.v., "race."

23. Orlando Patterson, *Slavery and Social Death: A Comparative Study* (Cambridge: Harvard University Press, 1982), p. 7.

24. *American Heritage Dictionary,* s.v., "deracinate."

25. Charlotte Perkins Gilman, *Women and Economics: A Study of the Economic Relation Between Men and Women as a Factor in Social Evolution,* ed. Carl N. Degler (1898; reprint, New York: Harper & Row, Torchbooks, 1966). Sometimes she uses "race" to refer to the human species and at other times for more specific human groups. Her views about people of color were often insensitive. See "A Suggestion on the Negro Problem" in *Charlotte Perkins Gilman: A Nonfiction Reader,* ed. Larry Ceplair (New York: Columbia University Press, 1991), pp. 176–83, and her novel *Herland* in *Herland and Selected Stories by Charlotte Perkins Gilman,* ed. Barbara H. Solomon (New York: Signet, 1992), pp. 1–146.

26. Goldberg presents "ethnorace" as one of the masks of race, *Racist Culture,* pp. 74–78.

27. See, also, Goldberg, *Racist Culture*, pp. 78–80, on "race as nation."

28. Pierre L. van den Berghe, *Race and Racism: A Comparative Perspective*, 2d ed. (New York: Wiley, 1967, 1978), pp. 9–10.

29. Thomas Sowell, *Ethnic America: A History* (New York: Basic Books, 1981).

30. *The Compact Edition of the Oxford English Dictionary*, s.v., "slave." Milton Meltzer, *Slavery: A World History*, updated edition (New York: Da Capo Press, 1993), p. 3.

31. On the racial state, see Omi and Winant, *Racial Formation*, pp. 57–69.

32. As Goldberg argues in *Racist Culture*, it is misleading to regard racism as simply arbitrary discrimination insofar as that suggests irrationality, because racisms have had definite rationales in the purposes for which they have been instituted and maintained.

33. Lugones, "Playfulness, 'World'-Travelling, and Loving Perception," p. 3.

34. For a critique of the concept of race from the perspectives of mixed race, see Naomi Zack, *Race and Mixed Race* (Philadelphia: Temple University Press, 1993). See, also, Naomi Zack, ed., *American Mixed Race: The Culture of Microdiversity* (Lanham, Md.: Rowman and Littlefield, 1995).

35. Appiah, *In My Father's House*, p. 32.

36. John Howard Griffin, *Black Like Me* (Boston: Houghton Mifflin, 1960). Mark Twain, *The Prince and the Pauper* (Toronto: J. Ross Robertson, 1882).

37. For detailed examination of how whiteness has been constructed in the United States, see Ruth Frankenberg, *White Women, Race Matters: The Social Construction of Whiteness* (Minneapolis: University of Minnesota Press, 1993).

38. Kovel, *White Racism*, p. xi.

39. Wilson, *Declining Significance of Race*.

40. Kovel, *White Racism*, p. xv.

41. For another example of invidious color identification, see Cornel West's account of how long it took him to hail a taxi on the corner of 60th Street and Park Avenue in Manhattan in the 1990s, in *Race Matters* (Boston: Beacon, 1993), p. x.

42. I here follow Malcolm X and Marilyn Frye in using "separatism" to refer to the voluntary separation from an oppressor by the oppressed in the interests of the oppressed and "segregation" to refer to separations from the oppressed imposed by an oppressor, in the interests of the oppressor. See Malcolm X, with the assistance of Alex Haley, *The Autobiography of Malcolm X* (New York: Grove, 1964), p. 246, and Frye, *Politics of Reality*, p. 96.

43. Pat Parker, *Movement in Black* (Oakland, Calif.: Diana Press, 1978), p. 68.

44. Bernard R. Boxill, *Blacks and Social Justice* (Totowa, N.J.: Rowman and Allanheld, 1984), pp. 9–18, 73–172.

45. Frye, *Politics of Reality*, pp. 110–27.

46. Regarding cultural death and cultural appropriation, see Laurence Mordekhai Thomas, *Vessels of Evil: American Slavery and the Holocaust* (Philadelphia: Temple University Press, 1993), on the "natal alienation" of descendants of enslaved Africans in the Americas.

47. Three Rivers, *Cultural Etiquette*, p. 8.

48. Patterson, *Slavery and Social Death*, p. 7.

49. Thomas, *Vessels of Evil*, pp. 150–52.

50. Frye, *Politics of Reality*, pp. 35–37.

51. Maria Steiglitz, "New Mexico's Secret Jews," *Lilith* 16, no. 1 (winter 1991): 8–12. On contemporary descendants of *conversos* (a.k.a. *marranos,* which means "pigs" in Spanish and is derogatory) in New Mexico, see also La Escondida, "Journal Toward Wholeness: Reflections of a Lesbian Rabbi," in *Twice Blessed: On Being Lesbian, Gay, and Jewish,* ed. Christie Balka and Andy Rose (Boston: Beacon, 1989), pp. 218–27.

52. See Raphael Patai and Jennifer Patai, *The Myth of the Jewish Race,* rev. ed. (Detroit: Wayne State University Press, 1989), for analysis, discussion, and refutation of views that there is a Jewish race (or that there are Jewish races) in the scientific (genetic) sense. For contemporary views on Jewish identity, see David Theo Goldberg and Michael Krausz, eds., *Jewish Identity* (Philadelphia: Temple University Press, 1993).

53. Nikki Giovanni, *Gemini: An Extended Autobiographical Statement on My First Twenty-Five Years of Being a Black Poet* (New York: Penguin, 1971), p. 97.

54. A special Dick Clark selection of these pieces from 1954 to 1961 has been issued on Compact Disks as "The Rock 'N' Roll Era" (Time-Life Music, Warner Special Products, 1987, 1988, and 1992), OPCD 2533, 2535, 2536, 2538, 2541, 2543, and 2544.

55. See Alice Walker's discussion of Joel Chandler Harris and the Uncle Remus stories in *Living by the Word* (New York: Harcourt, Brace, Jovanovich, 1988), pp. 25–32.